261.8
CAM

Y0-BKQ-188
BT738 .C34 C.1 STACKS 1970

BT　　　**Campbell, Thomas C.**
738　　　The fragmented layman
C34

+BT738 .C34

THE
FRAGMENTED
LAYMAN

STUDIES IN RELIGION AND SOCIETY EDITED BY W. WIDICK SCHROEDER AND GIBSON WINTER

OTHER VOLUMES IN THE "STUDIES IN RELIGION AND SOCIETY" SERIES:

W. WIDICK SCHROEDER AND VICTOR OBENHAUS, *RELIGION IN AMERICAN CULTURE,* NEW YORK: THE FREE PRESS, 1964

JOHN FISH, GORDON NELSON, WALTER STUHR AND LAWRENCE WITMER, *THE EDGE OF THE GHETTO,* NEW YORK: SEABURY PRESS, 1968

VICTOR OBENHAUS, *AND SEE THE PEOPLE,* CHICAGO: CHICAGO THEOLOGICAL SEMINARY, 1968

GIBSON WINTER, *RELIGIOUS IDENTITY,* NEW YORK: MACMILLAN, 1969

THE FRAGMENTED LAYMAN

AN EMPIRICAL STUDY OF LAY ATTITUDES

BY THOMAS C. CAMPBELL AND YOSHIO FUKUYAMA

PILGRIM PRESS
PHILADELPHIA   BOSTON

SBN 8298-0182-0
Library of Congress Catalog Card Number 79-125960

Copyright © 1970 United Church Press
Philadelphia, Pennsylvania

To Donna and Toshiko

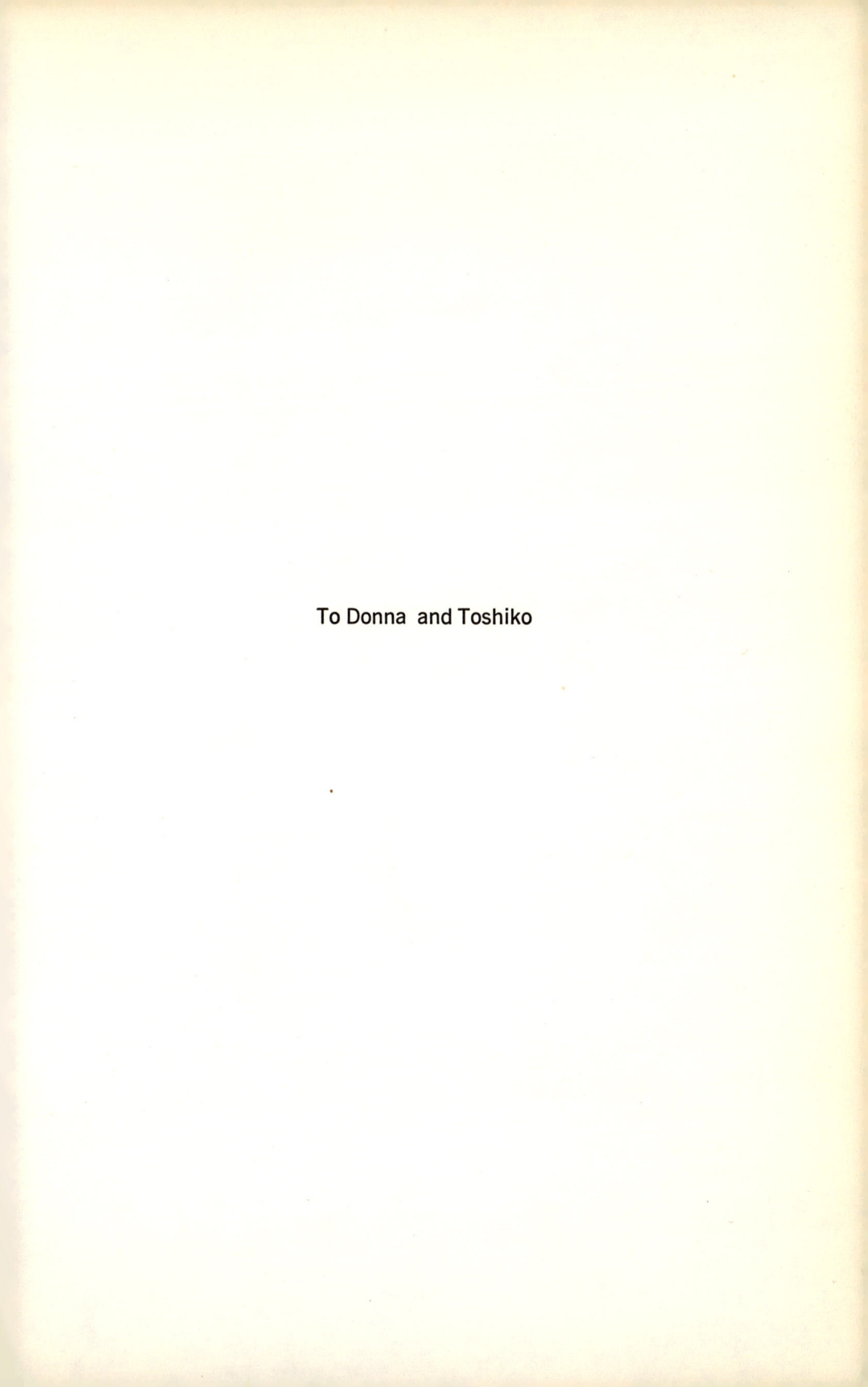

Introduction by W. Widick Schroeder and Gibson Winter xi
Preface xiii
Research Indices xv
Part 1   Introduction 1
    Chapter 1   The Layman Faces Church and World 1
    Chapter 2   The Survey Design 23
    Chapter 3   Description of the Survey Population 40
Part 2   The Sociology of Church Participation 55
    Chapter 4   The Layman Faces the Church 55
    Chapter 5   A Typology of Church Participation 65
    Chapter 6   Some Factors Affecting Church Participation 75
Part 3   Church Participation Related to Social Issues 107
    Chapter 7   The Layman Faces the World 107
    Chapter 8   Church Participation and Public Policy 128
    Chapter 9   Church Participation and the Racial Crisis .. 151
    Chapter 10 The Means of Social Change 169
Part 4   Conclusion 179
    Chapter 11 Contributions to the Sociology of Religion .. 179
    Chapter 12 Reflections on the Church in
                Contemporary Society 202
Appendix   The Questionnaire 226
Notes 243

Research Indices

The following designations and labels will be used frequently in the text. For ease of identification and reference while reading, they are listed at this point.

Independent Indices:
    ISEC = Index of Socio-Economic Class
    IROI = Index of Relative Organizational Involvement

Church Participation Indices:
    IOI = Index of Organizational Involvement
    IRK = Index of Religious Knowledge
    IDO = Index of Devotional Orientation
    IBO = Index of Belief Orientation

Consequential Indices:
    IFA = Index on Federal Activity
    ISA = Index of Social Acceptance
    ICR = Index of Civil Rights
    IIC = Index of Individual Conscience
    ICSR = Index of Collective Social Responsibility

Introduction

The Fragmented Layman continues and advances the social scientific investigation of lay attitudes and types of church membership in contemporary American religious institutions which social scientists have undertaken in the last two decades.

Yoshio Fukuyama has long been interested in types of church membership, and he has pursued this issue in some of his previous research. (See "The Major Dimensions of Church Membership," *Review of Religious Research*, Vol. 2, No. 4, Spring 1961, pp. 154-61. Thomas Campbell became interested in this problem in context of his interest in lay attitudes and practices during the time that he and Professor Fukuyama were both serving on the staff of the United Church Board for Homeland Ministries. This volume is an outgrowth of their collaborative research on lay attitudes in the United Church of Christ initiated at that time.

Charles Y. Glock first proposed the delineation of four or five distinguishable styles of church membership a decade or so ago. In collaboration with students and colleagues at the Survey Research Center of the University of California at Berkeley, Professor Glock has continued to develop his interest in styles of church membership. *Religion and Society in Tension* (co-authored with Rodney Stark, Chicago: Rand McNally and Company, 1965) and *To Comfort and To Challenge* (co-authored with Benjamin B. Ringer and Earl R. Babbie, Berkeley and Los Angeles: University of California Press, 1967), utilize these notions extensively. N. J. Demerath III employs them in his study, *Social Class in American Protestantism* (Chicago: Rand McNally, 1965). Mr. Campbell and Mr. Fukuyama relate to and draw upon these investigations in this study.

Several scholarly works appearing in the past decade have focused on lay attitudes, and *The Fragmented Layman* utilizes and refines some aspects of these studies. *The Religious Factor* (Gerhard Lenski, New York: Doubleday, 1961) and *Religion in American Culture* (W. Widick Schroeder and Victor Obenhaus, New York: The Free Press, 1964) both raised issues which stimulated the authors' interests in lay attitudes.

Because this study is based on responses from over 8,000 members of a single denomination, it employs controls and introduces refinements in analysis not possible in the earlier research just cited. Professors Campbell and Fukuyama have employed a method of elaboration, a research style very fashionable in the social sciences today, and they have adhered to the methodological canons of this approach in their analysis of the data.

At the same time, they are vitally concerned with the substantive aspects of their findings, for they are both churchmen who want the resources of the Judeo-Christian tradition to contribute positively to our lives together. The findings of the study offer some hope to others with similar commitments, for they show that persons with high degrees of religious commitment tend to entertain values and to make decisions more consonant with the Judeo-Christian tradition than persons with low degrees of religious commitment.

We are pleased to offer this study to persons in both the social scientific and religious communities, for it helps us understand some of the complexity of a salient aspect of man's life. *The Fragmented Layman* is the initial volume in the "Studies in Religion and Society" series published by Pilgrim Press in collaboration with the Center for the Scientific Study of Religion. Under an agreement with Pilgrim Press, future volumes in the "Studies in Religion and Society" series will be published by them. These studies are conducted by persons who have had some relation with the Center for the Scientific Study of Religion, a non-profit, interfaith research facility used primarily by faculty and graduate students of several theological schools in Chicago.

W. Widick Schroeder
Gibson Winter

Preface

To engage in study related to the field of the sociology of religion is to be caught in the midst of a number of perplexing alternatives. Is one most concerned about the larger questions of the relation between organized religions and their surrounding cultures or is one more concerned about specific religious bodies and their internal organization? Is one going to spend one's energies in seeking to develop a coherent theory about the relations between religion and culture or is one going to engage in empirical research recognizing theoretical limitations? Does the intellectual commitment of the student fall toward the academic discipline so that "religion" is the subcategory of general sociology where one chooses to devote time, or is his intellectual commitment more toward the religion under study and "sociological analysis" is the subtype knowledge one employs to gain insight? Such alternatives demand at least tentative choices even if, as the present authors believe to be the case, there are finally no clear-cut distinctions to be drawn between the alternatives to which allusion has been made. The choices made end up being somewhere along a continuum between extremes and few men indeed find themselves to be "ideal" representatives of one alternative or the other.

The authors find themselves in this study to be more concerned with one very specific denomination, though at many points reference will be made to possible generalizability of the findings to religion and culture in the American scene. They have devoted their energies in this case to the task of adding empirical data to the knowledge about sociology of religion, and yet they will set their findings within a theoretical framework as they proceed with the presentation of the findings. Both authors have training in academic sociology and are seminary graduates, and they are very self-conscious about choices with respect to the third set of alternatives. This study is primarily a study in the sociology of religion and should be judged according to the criteria of that discipline as an academic discipline. However, the authors also believe that such "knowledge" has import for those concerned about institutional churches, and they have written the concluding chapter as an essay giving their reflections on how the findings of the study have implications for the life of the churches.

In the presentation of the findings, detailed analysis and tables are presented throughout the study. This detailed presentation is intended to make it possible for persons with research interests to follow out the full results of the study, even when the findings do not directly relate to the overall theses of the book. Too often in a study, the authors tend to leave out details that are not essential for their thesis but which may have important implications for other researchers in the field. We have tried not to leave out such material. However, this means that some readers may want to follow out the general argument of the book without spending time on the detailed findings. For these readers the authors suggest a careful reading of chapters 1 and 2, the introductions and summaries of chapters 3 through 10, and finally, all of chapters 11 and 12.

The basic funds for the study were provided by the Board for Homeland Ministries of the United Church of Christ. Supplemental funds for computer analysis have been made available by the Divinity School of Yale University and the Yale Computer Center as well as by the Central Research Fund of the Pennsylvania State University. To all of these sources we are most grateful. Over the years that this study has been under way a number of persons in the United Church of Christ, United Theological Seminary of the Twin Cities, and Yale University have been involved. Their number is too long to list and it is possible only to mention a few of them. Special thanks are due to Serge Hummon and Shirley Greene for seeing the value of such analysis and for helping to secure the funds and support necessary and to Toshiko Fukuyama who patiently and accurately punched the data on more than 35,000 I.B.M. cards and prepared the original tabulations for the study. Phebe Haugen, Janet Schupbach, Kathy Turner, and Alberta Wells were all the kind of research assistants one is delighted to have in such an undertaking as this, and Zoe Churms deserves special mention for her cheerful and careful preparation of the manuscript. The authors are deeply indebted to W. Widick Schroeder and Gibson Winter for their reading of the manuscript and helpful suggestions.

A final word of thanks is certainly due to the American Association of Theological Schools under whose Faculty Fellowship Program a grant was made to one of the authors so that he could spend sufficient time in connection with his university's sabbatical program to complete the analysis and writing of this study.

This preface would not be complete without mention of the time lapse between the data-gathering process and the final publication, an issue not unrelated to appreciation for funds received. This project was conceived in 1963 as research related to some programatic questions within the United Church of Christ (see chapter 2). At that time, both authors were related to work of the Board for Homeland Ministries of the United Church of Christ in professional capacities, and they suggested that the programatic questions could be answered while at the same time much wider questions of the relation between church and culture could be addressed and the responses to the survey research analyzed from a quite different point of view, without substantially increasing the cost of the study. There were no objections voiced to this procedure. Therefore, a number of questions were introduced into the questionnaire which fit the larger concerns of the authors but were only tangentially related to the programatic concerns of the Board. The questionnaires were sent out and returned in 1964.

Interim reports were given to various agencies of the Board, and were internally published and distributed by the Board in 1966. These reports contributed to discussion within the Board concerning some changes which were made with respect to functional responsibilities and divisions of labor.

During these years both authors changed professional positions and also learned how overly optimistic they had been to suggest that the "cost" of a "larger study" is "not substantially greater" than that involved in a more limited study. The cost in both time and money has been far greater than either of them imagined. It is only now, during the academic year 1968-69 that additional funds and a sabbatical for one of the authors have made possible the completion of the full intent of the original design. In the intervening years several important studies related to similar concerns have been published (two of which also had problems of "timing," one being six years between data gathering and publication and the other having a time "lapse" of fifteen years). These studies and their findings have been incorporated into the present volume at relevant places, and they have significantly contributed to some additional forms of analysis which were not envisioned in the original design but which could be introduced without great difficulty. They have enriched the present study greatly, and we are grateful for this somewhat "invisible" community of scholars.

Though a great deal has happened to both the institutional churches and the social order in four and a half years, the authors are of the opinion that patterns of participation in social institutions do not vary so rapidly that the conclusions of this study have been invalidated. Where the content of certain questions is clearly "time bound," reference will be made to the special circumstances behind the questions, but our chief concern is with the implications of the general patterns made manifest by the data. In many ways the issues addressed in this study are more crucial today than they were when this study was only a last agenda item under "New Business" at a committee meeting.

Thomas C. Campbell
Yoshio Fukuyama

THE FRAGMENTED LAYMAN

Part 1–Introduction

Chapter 1–The Layman Faces Church and World

The Problem

Participants in most American religious organizations are similar to Americans who participate in other voluntary associations in that they remain in relation to the dominant social order while they differentiate themselves to some extent from that social order through the decision to participate in a particular religious body. Even when, as is presently the case, the majority of Americans claim membership in churches or synagogues,[1] *all* Americans do not claim such membership. While less than 4 percent of the American population claims to have *no* religious "preference,"[2] the churches claim to have only about 64 percent of the population as "members," and yet a figure near 30 percent of the population is probably a generous one for regular church "attendance." Thus even numerically it makes a great deal of difference how participation in religious organizations is defined when one is discussing the matter of how much differentiation there is between the church "participant" and the general social order. As men with religious "preference" one would expect very little differentiation, and as "attenders" one might expect more differentiation. However, even this last assertion is open to some question. Exactly why one might "expect" differentiation (and what kind of differentiation) will be discussed below.

This study concerns itself with a group of church "participants" in one particular American Protestant denomination. They had in some way acted so that their names were on a mailing list of a local congregation of that denomination. We can safely assume that they had a religious "preference," but they were not necessarily "members" or "attenders." Such ambiguity of definition with respect to "participants" is intended since the study is primarily interested in assessing whether or not one finds any meaningful distinctions which can be drawn between a variety of "styles" of church participation. The authors believe that there are a variety of ways in which men participate in religious organizations and they have undertaken to investigate empirically some of those ways of participation. They are interested both in the causes and consequences of the various "styles" of participation.

Many apparent contradictions in the literature of the sociology of religion can be clarified by careful attention to the kinds of participation in religious organizations which various authors are addressing. Illustrations of such apparent contradictions can be found in both historic and contemporary writings. Historically, Durkheim's thesis that religious practice and symbols were simply a reflection of the values of a culture expressed in general terms[3] seems to contradict Weber's thesis that a particular religious pattern, namely Calvinism, influences in an important way the values of a culture, namely the "spirit" of Capitalism.[4] Though there are many important differences between Durkheim and Weber which are not our concern at the moment, this apparent contradiction can be clarified by pointing to the very different kinds of "participation" they were addressing. Durkheim gained his insights by examining religious "participation" in a relatively homogeneous culture in which one did *not* choose to be part of the religious "organization" but rather participated in the religion by simply being part of the culture. Weber on the other hand was dealing with a more heterogeneous culture in which *all* men were *not* Calvinists and hence at least some differentiation between culture and religion was possible and some influence of the religion upon the culture at least theoretically plausible. Weber remained "agnostic" concerning the "source" of the religious ideas, but was arguing for a relative autonomy of religion from cultural values. The situation Weber was addressing was one in which men were making some form of conscious choice with respect to participation in religious organizations while in Durkheim's case religious participation had a more "natural" character to it. Before pointing to an illustration in modern literature where the variety of forms of participation helps to clarify seemingly contradictory theses, it is well to point out that Weber, while arguing for a relative autonomy of religion from its surrounding culture, was still very conscious of the ways in which there is a cultural conditioning of religion. He pointed to the tendency for men in a particular social status to emphasize certain aspects of religion while more or less ignoring others. Upper status men will often have concern for certain rational, ethical aspects of religion while men in lower social strata will give more emphasis to particular salvation doctrines.[5] The point here is that Weber is dealing with both large-scale effects of "autonomous" religion upon culture, often in an unconscious or unintended way, as well as with the ways in which culture exerts a conditioning effect upon various forms of church participation.

Turning to a more recent illustration of seeming contradiction, Will Herberg has argued that religion in America, in all three of its major groupings is little more than an expression of "The American Way of Life" and its underlying value structure.[6] In a very important sense Herberg stands closer to Durkheim than to Weber, for he emphasizes the elements of homogeneity between majority religion and its surrounding culture. In his last chapter, Herberg makes an appeal for a more differentiated religion which stands against the culture. Contrary to Herberg, Gerhard Lenski sought to show that there are varieties of consequences for behavior and attitudes in the American culture which correlate highly with participation in the major religious traditions of this country.[7] He was of the opinion that his data gathered by survey research methods, supported his thesis that "the religious factor" was as important as the class factor in explaining American behavior and attitudes in a variety of areas. Though his critics have challenged his argument on the grounds that the differences he found between groupings of White Protestants, Negro Protestants, Catholics and Jews can be explained on the basis of some measure of "ethnicity" in the respective groups,[8] Lenski was sensitive to the diversity of forms of participation and used four measures for this diversity, each of which correlated in significant ways with differing social behavior and attitudes. Those oriented toward "doctrinal orthodoxy" were different from those oriented toward "devotionalism," and his "communal" participants were different from the "associational" participants. Thus one can legitimately argue Lenski's kinship with the Weberian tradition of granting certain autonomous character to religion while at the same time recognizing important ways in which social forces condition religious behavior.

It is important to note that even this brief survey relating to the varieties of church participation has produced two major issues and not one. The first issue is related to the relative homogeneity or diversity of cultures and their religious organizations, while the second is related to the relative autonomy (or lack of it) of religion in relation to its culture. These issues are hardly the same, though they may well be interrelated. Durkheim seems to deny religion any "autonomy" while Weber seeks to prove that religion has autonomy and therefore is a source for social change.[9] Yet Durkheim was dealing with relatively homogeneous cultures while Weber had interests in a relatively differentiated culture. It may well be a truism to say that to the extent a culture is homogeneous, the religion associated with it can be expected to be related closely to the cultural value structure, and to the extent a culture is heterogeneous, one will expect heterogeneous religious expressions. However, this truism appears to be often ignored by writers, and even when it is observed, it still does not address the issue of whether or not religion has any "autonomy" in relation to any culture either of a homogeneous or differentiated type. Assuming contemporary differentiated American culture, two different but related questions need to be asked. These are *the* basic questions of the study. The first is, under the conditions of differentiation, is there any significant diversity of forms of church participation *other than* the diversity that reflects closely the forms of cultural diversity? The second is, can one discern any conscious or unconscious consequences of the diversity of forms of church participation that are not "explained" by the cultural diversity underlying it? Herberg concentrates upon the common aspects of a differentiated culture, sees common elements within the differing major religious subdivisions, then examines some of the differences within the culture and relates the religious subdivisions to these differences, and concludes that contemporary American religion is simply the "American Way of Life" with both its commonalities and its differences. He answers *both* of our questions negatively. He "believes" in the autonomy of religion, as his last chapter shows, but he finds no evidence of it. Lenski on the other hand is not clear in his answer to the first question, for he puts his problem in a slightly different form, but he clearly gives an affirmative answer to the second question. Durkheim would be expected to answer "no" to both questions, and Weber would probably answer both questions affirmatively though one is more certain of his answer to the second than the first question.

Because the two questions are both different as well as related, it should be possible to get any combination of affirmations and denials of the two questions. However, though one could deny the first and affirm the second, it seems very unlikely that one would affirm the first and deny the second. Empirical data is needed to help answer the questions. The authors would further state that given the theoretical and empirical bias of contemporary sociology, the burden of proof lies with those who would affirm either or both questions. Lenski's case, for example, is severely weakened by the "ethnic" critique, and the argument surrounding Weber's thesis is difficult to resolve given the problems of research design and the marshalling of evidence for or against great historical "movements."

There must be common elements that tend to hold a social order in some degree of stability, making it possible to talk about a common culture and common values. Yet in a modern, differentiated culture characterized by numerous subgroupings and related voluntary associations, most men live a life of fragmental loyalties. They are in particular groupings defined by age, sex, occupation, family, type and place of residence, political opinions, class, and status. Furthermore, men in these groupings do not participate in them in the same way. How much and in what way men "give" themselves to each of the subgroupings, probably will differentiate them from each other in significant ways, granted the force of social conditioning. In this study we are concerned with men who participate in a particular religious organization in a variety of ways and especially with the diversity of participation that is not explained by the underlying cultural diversity. In summary, this is a study of fragmental church participation, its patterning in terms of factors affecting it, and in terms of consequences.

Previous Analysis of the Problem

The case for the socially conditioned character of American religious institutions has been made often and convincingly. For example, it has been shown by countless studies that denominations in America can be arranged in a continuum from those which draw primarily from the upper classes to those which draw from the lower classes.[10] Both the theoretical work of Durkheim and Weber would lead one to suppose that such "selective" appeal would be associated with the self-interest of the dominant group of parishioners and thus would lead to emphasis in the teaching of a particular denomination on those aspects of the faith which are consistent with that group's self-interest. H. Richard Niebuhr, writing in 1929, perhaps more than any other one figure surveyed the American denominational scene, and pointed out both the social origins of the various denominational groupings as well as their transition over periods of time. He related the origins and the transitions to socially conditioning factors such as immigrant status, class interest, racial divisions, and sectionalism.[11] The case is so convincing that even reading the volume four decades later, there are very few places where one would want to challenge the author's thesis. The book continues to have a peculiarly contemporary "ring" to it. More recently, Schroeder and Obenhaus sought to examine the contemporary viability of denominational divisions.[12] Their study of one county area in Midwestern America led them to conclude that class and intellectual ability correlated much more highly with theological understanding and participation patterns than do denominational divisions. Thus their case is still one which emphasizes social conditioning of church participation.

The list of replicative studies could be extended to a very impressive number and the authors wish to be very clear at the outset that they have no intention or desire to deny such an impressive amount of research data. Indeed, at many points throughout this study references will be made to the operation of social conditioning on church participation. However, particularly given the position which Weber and his followers would want to maintain concerning the relatively "autonomous" character of religion, we want to consider whether social conditioning as an exclusive focus of attention does not tend to paint the scene of religion in America with an oversimplified "one-directional" emphasis. Even granting social conditioning as a thesis, one should be interested in carrying the thesis to its logical conclusion. That is, if social situation tends to affect social attitudes, then once a person decides to participate in a religious group (for socially conditioned reasons), his participation becomes a "new" form of social conditioning and should affect his social attitudes in a way in which those who have not participated in religious groups have not been affected. To make such a statement does not commit one to any theory of the "autonomy" of religion. It may just be another form of social conditioning. It could very well simply reinforce those attitudes that were associated with the social situation that brought about participation in the first place. Indeed, that would be the most logical expectation of the social conditioning thesis. On the other hand, if the effect of church participation were in a direction different from the direction predicted on the basis of social factors that "caused" the participation, then one would be on firmer ground for arguing that religion was a relatively "autonomous" factor.

A number of essays have been published which utilize the findings regarding social conditioning as a basis for a critique of the church from a variety of theological perspectives. Most of them plead that the church has become "irrelevant" in that it does not influence either its members or the larger culture in any way that is different from the influence of the social situation of its constituency. Gibson Winter has written in this way about the "suburban captivity" of the church,[13] and Peter Berger argued that the churches were simply assemblies that made ineffective "noise."[14] Such essays assume that religion could have "autonomy" and "ought" to be influencing culture in a certain way. It could be argued that such writings assume that the influence should be "against" the mainstream of the culture. We believe that such an assumption *is* behind Berger's work but it is not necessarily true of men like Winter.

These men could argue, as Winter does more clearly in a later volume,[15] that the church "should" support values which are present in the culture but it will be selective in choosing to support some cultural values while ignoring (or fighting) others. Some strains of this argument come under what is currently called a "secular theology." Taking such a culturally "supportive" view still commits one to a position that religion has some autonomy in order to be able to select which values it intends to support. Are men like Winter seeking to find new "functions" for religion in a society which has both sociologically conditioned religious behavior and at the same time taken over such traditional religious "functions" as education and social welfare? Does a position supporting relative religious "autonomy" necessarily emerge because of one's theological biases?

Talcott Parsons implies a "yes" answer to the first question and a "no" to the second in an essay he wrote in 1958.[16] Here, from a theoretical stance firmly rooted in sociology rather than theology, he argues a thesis that religion is relatively autonomous but that its functional position in the culture is becoming more closely differentiated. Religion deals with the "meaning" men attach to their actions. It does not perform educational or social welfare functions which it may well have performed at different points in history or in different cultures. Parsons would of course expect that the religious groups would be highly supportive of various values present in the total culture, because of his theory of a functioning social "system." He would further grant that conflicts or "strains" might be present within the larger system due to the operation of subsystems or other factors. He argues in another context that such a functioning of religion might be productive of social change in a "gradual cumulative" way.[17]

There is an inherent problem in all such essays. Given certain assumptions derived from either sociological theory or theological presuppositions, the arguments have validity, but their appeal to empirical data is not the result of research design. Rather it is taken selectively from empirical work done by the authors themselves or by others. It is important to ground empirical research in theory and to develop theory from empirical research, but the empirical support for any of the essays noted is marginal at best. It is even difficult to know how seriously Winter or Parsons, for example, are interested in empirical verification. Winter uses the substantial data on the social conditioning of religion in his critique of religious groups. But what empirical basis does he have to believe that any type of religious group (either the present types he criticizes or the new types he proposes) will have sufficient autonomy to be able to select from among extant cultural values those values which they wish to support in the "New Creation"? Will change in organizational form "create" such antonomy? What empirical reason does he have for so hoping? Parsons is even more difficult to relate to empirical data. Evidence of religious support of cultural values would be support for the religious function of "meaning," while tensions between religious groups and cultural values could be interpreted as strain between the factors of a social system coming to a new kind of equilibrium. Such essays are clearly related to the issues underlying the present study in a theoretical way, but they do not add a great deal to the solution of the questions of the study. In Part 4 of the study we will need to return to the theoretical implications of the findings which will be presented.

In very recent years some authors have become interested in a rigorously empirical way in this question of whether or not it is at all possible to talk of the *"religious"* conditioning of participants in religious organizations. Lenski[18] made a notable effort along these lines. He was not denying social conditioning; he simply wanted to test whether one could find any connection between social attitudes and religious participation that was other than what could be explained by position in the class hierarchy. As was mentioned earlier, the belief that he had found such a "religious factor" in the four major religious subgroupings has been seriously challenged. He was accused of having found only the factor of "ethnicity" and not a "religious factor." Lenski's sample size and research design prevent him from answering the critique.

However, Lenski did introduce into the research community some important operational concepts, including the distinctions between two sets of types of religious participation. "Associational" and "communal" were types of "socio-religious group membership," while "doctrinal orthodoxy" and "devotionalism" were types of "religious orientation." Again, primarily for reasons of sample size, he did not follow up the social attitude "consequences" of these four types of participation to the extent that he could argue the case for religious "autonomy." However, he did follow them up well enough to cause one to believe that he had uncovered some very important distinctions which other authors were ignoring. For example, he found that "communal membership" was associated with tension *between* religious subgroups (Protestant, Catholic and Jew) while "associational" membership was not.[19] Likewise he found that "doctrinal orthodoxy" and "devotionalism" seemed to transcend the more typical subgroupings of Catholic and Protestant. Thus one had more in common with an "orthodox" Catholic, if one were an "orthodox" Protestant, than one had in common with "devotional" Protestants.[20] Moreover, an "orthodox orientation" tended to be associated with a "compartmentalized" view of life, separation of the sacred and the secular, while the "devotionally oriented" man tended to have a more "unitary" view of life.

At this point it is important to reemphasize the commonalities between Lenski's work and a "Weberian" stance on the relative "autonomy" of religion. Lenski did not expect to find "conscious" connections between group membership or religious orientation and the "secular" issues under question. As with the Weberian thesis that the Protestant Ethic was related to the Spirit of Capitalism, unconsciously, so Lenski was testing most often for *unconscious* connections. Schroeder and Obenhaus[21] showed without much question that there is little or no conscious connection between one's religious subgroup and one's social attitudes, whether or not the religious subgroup has sought to teach some particular social attitude. It should be emphasized, however, that there is an important difference between the work of Lenski and that of Schroeder and Obenhaus. Lenski never used denomination as a type of religious subgrouping while Schroeder and Obenhaus used denomination as their primary type of religious subgrouping. Furthermore Schroeder and Obenhaus pointed to the fact that in all of the denominations there was at least a "small nucleus of persons of superior intellectual ability,"[22] and they argued that it was this group "which was able to deal with cognitive structures most adequately."[23] By this they meant that it was this group which was able to make some connection between their church participation and their social attitudes. Thus from both Lenski and Schroeder and Obenhaus, one has some support for pursuing the issues of differential types of church participation. And, from each work one has some reason *not* to define the differential types along two traditional lines: (1) Catholic, Protestant and Jew, or (2) denominational labels.

Using categories other than traditional denominational labels or Catholic, Protestant and Jew to evaluate religious participation has intrigued other authors. Glock and Stark developed a system of utilizing five dimensions of religiosity.[24] They spoke of experiential, ritualistic, ideological, intellectual, and consequential. In various writings they have used these five, or some close approximation of them. We shall have reason at several points in this study to refer to their findings, but at this point it is sufficient to say that the work of Glock and Stark has been instructive and stimulating for the present authors.[25] The work of Glock and Stark has been better at the level of suggesting possible differentiations of types of church participation than at the level of research into the social consequences of the types of participation.[26] Thus far, when they have addressed the issues of the consequences of church participation, it has been to stress the tendency for the consequences as well as the participation itself to be socially conditioned. One has every reason to expect that their future work will follow this pattern given the summary chapter in one of their key volumes.[27] On the basis of their work to date, Glock and Stark's answers to the two questions posed near the end of the previous section above would be clearly negative ones.

It is important to note that Glock and Stark defined one of their categories of religious orientation as the "consequential" orientation while in commenting upon their work we refer to the "consequences" of religious participation. This confusion needs to be clarified. For Glock and Stark the "consequential" dimension of religiosity is identified with the notion of "good works" and "in the language of Christian belief, the consequential dimension deals with man's relation to man rather than with man's relation to God."[28] They grant that it is different in kind from the other four dimensions, but just how they propose to operationalize the definition they have given to it remains unclear. When in a later volume they again list five types of dimensions, they have changed the nomenclature to "belief, practice, knowledge, experience, and consequences."[29] The "consequences" dimension is defined in the later work in a way which is almost word for word a repeat of the definition given to the earlier "consequential" definition. We are again told that it "differs from the other four,"[30] but we are also told that "we shall not take up the study of religious consequences in this volume."[31] The analysis will be left for the later unpublished work which was mentioned in an earlier footnote.[32] Thus we are still not sure exactly what is meant by the term in any operational way. We believe that "consequences" not only "differs" from other types of religious participation but is so different that though it would be possible to operationalize it as Demerath does, it is most helpful for our present purposes to talk about the "consequences" of the other forms of church participation and not to regard "consequences" as a type of church participation.

Demerath, a student of Glock's, has been drawn to the study of the relation between social class and denominationalism.[33] His study, however, deviates from previous work by being a study of a single denomination which places it in a significant relation to the present study. He acknowledges the findings of class dominance in various denominations, but by studying one denomination near the center of the class spectrum, he examines how class plays a part in *intra*denominational analysis rather than interdenominational analysis. He points out that people of high and low classes are present in most denominations and their class positions are highly correlated with selective orientation toward religion even *within the same* denomination. This selective orientation (and selective participation) makes for a certain degree of tension within denominations which Demerath sees as difficult to sustain on the short run (sometimes leading to actual organizational division). However he feels it is productive in the long run since each group prevents the other from leading the denomination in question too far to the right or left of its true position. The lower class "sectarian" members left alone would cause the denomination to lose touch with the realities of the contemporary world, while the higher class "church-like" members would lead the church into total secularism if unencumbered by the "sectarians."

This brief summary of one of Demerath's key points illustrates how he has modified the traditional point of denominational affinity for certain classes by utilizing the familiar church-sect dichotomy applied to a single denomination. In defending his case, Demerath makes use of several of the "types" of church participation mentioned earlier. His "church" type of member is closely related to Lenski's "associational" member, and his "sectarian" reflects much of Lenski's "communal" member.[34] He self-consciously uses the work of Glock and Stark as a background and utilizes their "ritualistic" and "ideological" categories, ignoring their "experiential" category due to a lack of questions by which to measure it. Demerath's study adds weight to the validity of making distinctions on other than a denominational basis between types or styles of religious participation, but his study does not really address the questions asked at the end of the above section except by implication. One could, without doing Demerath's work any great injustice, argue that his answers would tend to be negative on the basis of his findings, but they were not intended to answer those questions. His findings are very useful in terms of understanding the internal operation of American denominations, but one would have little difficulty fitting his findings into what we have called earlier a "Durkheimian" thesis rather than a "Weberian" thesis. That is, he gives no support for the question of the relative autonomy of religion in relation to its culture or subculture.

As previously mentioned, Demerath does use a "consequential" category in a way which he derives from Glock's definition, but he also differs from the use of the term in the present study. Again clarification is required. Demerath measures the "consequential" category in terms of whether or not the respondent claims that he has received aid and reward from his church participation.[35] However, he also used the respondent's attitudes on ministerial participation in secular affairs as a "consequential" matter. Thus he is faithful to Glock's definition by including in the category items which imply that the respondent is oriented to the church in believing that the church should be related to worldly affairs (in this case through the minister) and in believing that the church has in fact affected the participant (in this case a subjective opinion).

We would certainly grant that it is quite possible to identify a type of church participation as being that expressed by persons who desire their church to be involved in the world and then to go on to identify those social factors that seem to be "causally" related to such a view of the church. However, unless the research design is such that this "type" (along with others) is related to other social issues *while the socially causal variables are held constant,* we will still not be able to know anything about whether religion is or is not a relatively "autonomous" factor or even if it is a "new" socially conditioning factor for those who participate in churches in any of the ways one wishes to discuss. Demerath does not treat *any* of his religious dimension variables as "intervening" variables in the way just described. Thus rather than confuse the issue we are seeking to address, we have chosen not to speak of a "consequential" type of church participation or to seek to measure such a type. We have reserved the term "consequences" for those issues which we treat as being the possible "results" of the various types of church participation.[36] Furthermore we are more interested in "unconscious" results than we are in "conscious" results, therefore under "consequential" variables we have not included any questions which ask for the respondent's subjective opinion on whether or not he thinks the church has helped him.

Glock collaborated with two other authors in a study of a single denomination (the Episcopal Church) utilizing some of the previously mentioned types of religiosity.[37] In this study the three men were self-consciously addressing the contemporary debate about the role of the church in society. Is the church meant to comfort the afflicted or afflict the comfortable? Should the church stress its priestly role and bring comfort, or stress its prophetic role and bring challenge? Because they were utilizing data which had been gathered for another purpose, they were not able to use all of their categories due to a lack of questions relating to some of the types. Thus they confined themselves to the "ritualistic," "intellectual," and "consequential." They also introduced a new type referred to as "organizational" which was measured by whether one participates exclusively in church organizations or is active also in "outside" organizations.[38] Their use of "consequential" religiosity in this volume is closer to the use of the idea which shall be made in the present study. Indeed, they call the second part of their study "The Consequences of Church Involvement."

The findings of the Glock, Ringer, and Babbie study added some important knowledge concerning church participation, but their study also raised some serious questions that need to be addressed. One important new dimension that they added to the knowledge of church participation emerged from the form of analysis they used in assessing the priestly or comforting role of the church. Instead of judging the "comforting role" of the church by the use of gross statistics measuring social class membership differentials (a process which shows in countless studies that the church draws disproportionately from the more privileged segments of the culture and thus can be quite fairly criticized for being the "country club at prayer") they first used three church participation variables to develop a composite index of involvement.[39] Through the use of the composite index they showed that the greatest participation is not found in the middle class nuclear family (a finding which gross statistics will support) but rather is to be found among the lower status persons, the aged, youth, women and those without nuclear family relationships (divorced, widowed, childless, etc.). Indeed they showed the value which a "predisposition index" will have on predicting church involvement. Such an index is made up of characteristics of age, sex, family and social status, etc. Thus, though the church may be disproportionately drawing from the culture in terms of attracting people who do not seem to need much "comforting," namely successful stable middle class persons, their closer analysis reveals that when the church does attract those "in need" they participate in more intense ways than do the people of more "normal" circumstances in life. Glock, et al., thus argue that the church is in fact performing a legitimate "comforting" function for those who are "dispossessed" by the culture in one way or another.

It must be remembered at this point that the researchers were examining a denomination which most studies show to have a relatively "upper class" constituency thus giving their findings added importance. This is a denomination which most would call a "churchly" type, supporting the values of the dominant culture. One would expect a "composite index of involvement" to show greater participation among the "dispossessed" if one were studying a lower class "sectarian" denomination, but to find that it is the case in the Episcopal denomination reveals the importance of utilizing a variety of participation variables rather than simply assuming that membership statistics for example are a sufficient measure of participation.

The study then went on to examine the "consequences" of involvement. Were church participants "challenged" by the prophetic role of the church? They examined the relation of their composite index to a variety of issues, such as involvement of the clergy in secular affairs, subjective attitudes of parishioners on a number of secular issues where the church had expressed official positions, etc. Church involvement was *not* correlated with these issues except in the most modest and moderate way. They concluded that the church was *not* challenging its participants. They went on to make a number of suggestions for improving this situation, an issue to which we shall return in chapter 12.

Given these important findings, some serious questions are raised by the Episcopal study. First, given the importance which the authors want to attach to a variety of types of church participation, one finds it curious that the types they used get combined into a *composite* index. In most of the volume they have never used the separate types of participation for analysis. They justify the decision to use the composite index by showing the high correlation between the separate types of participation. In a few cases they actually attempt separate analysis claiming that they all showed the same tendencies of correlation.[40] The question is then, why use a series of types at all? Alternately, one must ask whether the questions they used to measure the various types were adequate to get at the differentials present within the various types. We shall return to this issue in chapter 4.

The second question is related to the first, namely by measuring church participation with a composite index, would one really expect to find that the group which is most "comforted" (in need of comfort too, according to the argument) would also be the one most challenged? Based on the findings of Demerath mentioned earlier, one would expect that different "types" of people have different "types" of participation in the same denomination. Thus the denomination performs different functions for *different* people and not different functions for the *same* people. If one's theoretical position assumes social causation for church participation, then one's simplest logical expectation will be that different people will be comforted by the church from those who are challenged by the church. To assume that once people who have socially caused reasons for needing comfort are in fact comforted by the church they will then turn and become critical of the culture which produced their discomfort, is an intricate matter. It either involves one in a much more complex social causation argument,[41] or it is evidence that one has abandoned the social causation argument in favor of a more limited social "conditioning" argument, therein granting some autonomy to religious participation.

The value of the Glock, Ringer, and Babbie study for the present study is that it showed the presence of a group in a "comfortable" denomination which needed comforting and indicated that group's high participation in the denomination using different types of church participation. But it, like all of the other studies left the question of the relative autonomy of religion unanswered. Once again, it seems quite clear that Glock and his associates would read their findings as pointing to a negative answer to the two questions posed in the earlier section. However we believe that though their research design *could* have shown that religion had a kind of relative autonomy, it is highly unlikely that it *would* have shown this, since the only way it could have done so would have been for those who were "escaping" from the culture to have been the same ones who would turn about and "attack" the culture. Such radical change may be expected by some churchmen, but it is hardly expected by most sociologists, even those standing in the "Weberian" tradition. A different design from the one they used is still needed.

This look at previous research indicates that while there is a significant and growing body of knowledge with respect to differential church participation, there remain some very significant issues and

15

questions to be analyzed. We have considerable evidence to show that the various "types" or "styles" of church participation are highly correlated with certain social factors. Church participation is certainly socially conditioned in some predictable ways. These relatively established patterns will be useful in developing a theoretical framework for our study. However, the issue of the "consequences" of the various styles of church participation has been examined in an unsatisfactory way. The designs of the studies have made it impossible to deal with the question of the relative autonomy of religion in any conclusive way. Either there have been too few cases in the study to permit utilizing all of the types of participation as "intervening" variables between social factors and social consequences, or else the design has made no careful effort at using the church participation variables as "intervening variables." In the latter case the church participation variables themselves have usually been treated as the "consequences" of social factors rather than as the causes of other "consequences." We are now in a position to turn to the hypotheses of this study.

The Hypotheses of the Study

The purpose of this study is to examine the religious orientations and social attitudes of participants in a denomination that has been shown to draw its members predominantly from the middle and upper middle classes of American culture. The majority of the members of the United Church of Christ come from the Congregational Christian Churches which united with the Evangelical and Reformed Church to form a new denomination in 1957. The Congregational churches have been consistently placed among the three most "upper class" churches in several studies.[42] The presence of more "middle class" members from the Evangelical and Reformed Church in the sample provides certain interesting variables for later analysis. This then is a study of a denomination which will be expected on the basis of previous research to conform in a variety of ways to the dominant values and ideals of America.

A thesis which is commonly held among sociologists of religion, and for which there is a good deal of empirical support, contends that religions have their "genesis" among the lower classes and then as the participants in the religious group achieve a higher social class standing the religion becomes ever more "secularized" until finally the distinctive character of the religion is lost.[43] This is referred to as the movement from "sect" to "church." The concept of "denomination" presents some difficulties for such a thesis, but usually one who holds the thesis simply refers to "denominations" as a transitional type somewhere between the two extremes making it possible to talk of "sectlike" denominations and "churchlike" denominations. To those holding such a thesis, we have chosen to study a particularly "churchlike" denomination which will be expected to be highly conformed to the culture with little visible remaining "religious" elements.

The above thesis is not without its critics within sociological circles. Wilson, for example, argues that only certain "types" of sects follow the above pattern.[44] He further argues that denominations are not a "middle case" but are rather "a distinctive pattern of religious adherence appropriate to modern industrial society."[45] However, the thrust of his whole volume in which this argument appears is that religions in a "secular" society have become highly "secularized" in a variety of ways and he too would expect that the denomination chosen for examination in this study would manifest "cultural" values rather than distinctively "religious" ones.

Sociological students of religion and society have often been drawn to the study of "sectarian" religion, perhaps because it is felt that this is a "better" or "clearer" case of "religion." However we, like some of the sociologists mentioned previously, prefer to examine the more "complex" and "ambiguous" case of religion in depth.

Given the work which has been done in the field, it would be most accurate to say that this study has only one major hypothesis (the third hypothesis given below). However, before proceeding to that hypothesis, it has been necessary to examine whether or not our data is following the patterns that have previously been shown in other studies. If our data should not follow those patterns, then either one would want to challenge the already "proven" theses, or one would want to argue that the data under consideration is for some reason "unrepresentative" or a "special case." And so for purposes of examining how well our data from one denomination is fitting into the growing body of empirical findings, we have chosen to say that we have three operating hypotheses, the first two of which are relatively well-established and in wide use in the sociology of religion.

The first hypothesis is related to the work done on the social conditioning of both social attitudes and religion. We state it as: *Differences in an individual's social situation result in different modes of religious orientation and social outlook.* From the point of view of this hypothesis, no value judgments can be made concerning what is "more" religious or "less" religious. It simply hypothesizes different "types" of religion and different "types" of social attitudes. If it is shown that the upper classes relate to the church in terms of the value structure and "needs" appropriate to their social position, then to support the hypothesis one must simply show the socially conditioned character of the values and "needs" and the related religious expressions of them.

Since prior work has been done on this hypothesis, it is possible to develop a subhypothesis from it, namely: Privileged social groups will choose religious orientations which reflect the dominant values of the American culture and groups experiencing some form of social deprivation will choose religious orientations which compensate in some way for the social deprivations.

The second hypothesis is also related to the work reviewed above: *Participation in religious organizations is a phenomenon which can be meaningfully described along at least four dimensions: organizational, religious knowledge, belief and devotional orientations.*[46] Relatively specific meanings will be given to each of these dimensions later. In some cases we will be very close in meaning to definitions worked out by others, while in other cases we will be defining the same or similar terms in new ways.

Again, since prior work has been done on this hypothesis, it is possible to develop a subhypothesis combining the first and second hypotheses: Privileged social groups will choose organizational[47] and religious knowledge[48] orientations to religion, while socially deprived groups will choose belief and devotional orientations.[49] Organizational activity is very much a part of dominant American culture and education (knowledge) is very much valued. Traditional religious beliefs and devotional life may give some "compensation" to the deprived in a "secular" society which questions the value of either the beliefs or the devotional life.

The third and most important hypothesis is concerned with relating the religious orientation of the church participant to a variety of issues present in the contemporary social order. We wish to know whether or not church participation is connected in any significant way with one's participation in the world. We pose the hypothesis as follows: *Different church participation orientations have different consequences for behavior and attitudes on social issues.* Interpretation of this third hypothesis must be handled with a great deal of care. At one level, this hypothesis can be interpreted as supportive of a "social causation" theory of behavior and attitudes. That is, participation in religious organizations is socially "caused," the participation becomes a "new" social condition, and behavior and attitudes result both from the original social "causal" factors as well as from the "new" social condition. This point has been made earlier when it was pointed out that one does not need to argue for any "autonomy" for religion in order to argue in favor of a "religious factor." According to the line of reasoning being taken, "the religious factor" can be merely a socially caused type of further social conditioning. However, should religious participation tend to influence social attitudes in a way which is contradictory to (or in a different "direction" from) the way in which the "original" social factors were influencing attitudes, then one has a more difficult case to handle from a purely "social causation" point of view. Either there are some "hidden" or unexamined factors which will help to explain this apparent contradiction, or else one must abandon the "social causation" thesis in favor of some form of *relative* "autonomy" being granted to religion. Hence, we need to be very careful to examine exactly *how* religion "affects" social attitudes (if it does at all). And we will want to examine the "direction" of the "religious" influence in terms of whether or not it was consistent with the influence of the "original" social conditioning factors. If discrepancy is found, then it is crucial to note whether there might be "hidden" factors or whether any consistent theory exists which can deal with the discrepancy. This last statement makes it imperative that we clarify how we intend to interrelate theory and empirical data in this study.

No person can deal with *any* empirical data without *some* theoretical assumptions. No "hypothesis" exists which is not informed at least in some measure by certain presuppositions about the nature of reality. Empirical research is, of course, meant to support or correct whatever theoretical assumptions one is seeking to use. Our operating principle is that theoretical assumptions should be kept at the most minimal or self-evident level possible until the data demands a further amplification of the theory. And accordingly, our effort in the presentation of the data is to be parsimonious with respect to theoretical material. It should be noted that we consider a pure "social causation" theory of attitudes to be a more "minimal" or more "self-evident" theory within the field of the sociology of religion than is a theory involving some form of relative "autonomy" being granted to religion. To use the terms and historic figures introduced at the beginning of this chapter, we consider a "Durkheimian" analysis to be more "self-evident" from the point of view of sociology for explaining religion and culture than is a "Weberian" type of analysis. Thus, though we have interests in both types of material, we will always test *first* whether or not a simpler "social causation" theory explains the material before we elaborate on the theory by the introduction of concepts of "social conditioning" and "relative autonomy." It is our belief that a variety of "reasonable" theories exist to "explain" empirical findings, and we are attempting as far as we can to present the empirical findings in an "uninterpreted" manner. We are well aware that a variety of types of critics will disagree with our final conclusions from the study, but we want to at least present the data in as complete and "uninterpreted" way as we can so that people from a variety of theoretical perspectives can use the data within their own "system."

We are aware that we have appeared to be using "religion" and "religious orientations" quite interchangeably. We are of course aware that there is a great difference between the two terms from many perspectives. However, based on what has been said in the above paragraph, there is no "need" to differentiate the two *from a sociological point of view* until findings with respect to religious behavior (which we *operationally* define as being what men do through religious organizations in terms of religious orientations) show that some factor appears to be operating which is not fully explained on the basis of "social" factors. If this happens, *then and only then* is it necessary for *sociology* to begin to incorporate some distinctions between "religion" and "religious orientations" into its theory.[50] This is precisely what Max Weber did, using his own historical comparisons method, and why even when he felt he had shown the relative autonomy of religion he remained, qua-sociologist, agnostic with respect to what the "source" of "religion" might be. In this study there is no need to differentiate "religion" and forms of religious orientation until the research findings make such a distinction necessary.

The sensitive reader will already have deduced that the authors are more drawn to Weber than they are to Durkheim in terms of their own constructive theory. Otherwise, given the overwhelming body of data already extant in the literature which appears to be supportive of a "social causation" point of view, we would not have persisted in pointing to logical and empirical difficulties in the material which raise questions about the adequacy of the "social causation" theory.

Consistent with the principle of parsimonious use of theory, the hypotheses and subhypotheses given above have been stated in such a way that they have demanded only the most minimal theoretical support. As they stand, they could be used for a variety of theoretical amplifications. Thus with this overview of the problem, previous attempts to deal with the problem, and the statement of the resultant hypotheses with their minimal supportive theory, only one task remains before proceeding. That task is to spell out the way in which the material will be presented.

The Organization of the Study

From what has been given above, the organization of the study is relatively self-evident. The remainder of Part 1 will be devoted to the details of the research design (chapter 2) and a reporting of the characteristics of the population which responded to the questionnaire (chapter 3). Part 2 will explore the validity of the first two hypotheses. Here the concentration will be upon defining and operationalizing the types or styles of religious orientation (forms of church participation) described in the second hypothesis (chapter 5), and then the interest will shift to seeking the most meaningful factors which seem to be related to these forms of church participation in order to test the first hypothesis (chapter 6).

Part 3 will examine the third and most crucial hypothesis through the search for relationships between church participation and attitudes on a variety of social issues. When relationships are found, the research design calls for holding the "causal" social variables constant while the "forms of church participation" are related to the social attitudes. It is then in Part 3 that the total research design comes to its fruition. The social factors will be treated as "independent" variables, the forms of church participation will be treated as "intervening" variables, and the attitudes on social issues will be treated as "consequential" variables.

Finally, in Part 4 conclusions from the findings will be drawn in two different ways, first with a view to "theory" and then with a view to "practice." Chapter 11 will be an effort to examine the findings within a particular theoretical framework. Since the first three parts of the study have self-consciously avoided all but the most necessary theoretical discussion, it is appropriate in the last part of the study to amplify on theoretical issues in order to explain the findings in a more adequately coherent way.

Chapter 12 will explore the practical implications of the research for the life of contemporary American churches. Such a chapter could be written as a further development of the study done exclusively from a sociological perspective. Self-conscious attempts would be made to avoid value judgments whenever possible. It would then be a chapter in "applied sociology." However, though it is certainly appropriate to do a chapter in this way, we have chosen to take a slightly different approach to the chapter. Though we respect attempts to work in areas of applied sociology without employing "value judgment," we believe that such attempts rarely prove to be very fruitful. There may be some very fundamental reason[51] why such concluding chapters are so often either sterile or else end up employing value judgments without acknowledgment, but whatever the reasons, a different approach has been employed here. We employ, quite self-consciously, values associated with certain theological traditions. The last chapter is employing these theological judgments *as well* as the data from the study proper.[52] As a volume in sociology of religion, the study ends with chapter 11 and chapter 12 is clearly an exploration in "practical theology."

Chapter 2–The Survey Design

Introduction

Our review of previous research has shown the basis for many of the issues present in this study as well as weaknesses in the previous work which have made this study necessary. What has not been done is to deal with the inherent strengths and weaknesses of working in the field of the sociology of religion through the methodology of survey research. Certain issues related to that topic are essential in order to put the findings of the study into proper perspective.

Data for one's research must be gathered either from previous work by others, or else a data-gathering process must be initiated when previous data is not suitable for one's purpose.[1] For this study it was necessary to gather new data, and the design would call for a large number of cases to be used in the analysis. The first issue faced by the researchers was the use of a "mail" survey versus a "personal interview" survey. One must begin to address this issue by looking first at the questions and major hypotheses which underlie the study. The concerns of this study are related primarily to unconscious consequences of a variety of types of religious orientation which are themselves largely unconscious. The unconscious ranges of social behavior pose special problems for the sociologist. To what end is he trying to study the unconscious "consequences" of unconscious "religious orientation"? Some answers to this question would move the study very close to psychology rather than sociology, or at least involve the researcher in the "middle discipline" of social psychology. We would argue that if the purpose of the study is to understand the "personal internal dynamics" of the social factor, then one is certainly involved in psychological analysis and intensive personal interviews would take on added importance. On the other hand, if one's purpose is simply to establish patterns of social behavior without a great deal of concern for "why" the *individual* actors may choose to so act, there is less importance attached to intensive personal interviews. Certainly the present study is concerned for "why" the patterns of *social* behavior are present (theory will be developed for that purpose), and certainly there are many overlapping concerns between psychological analysis and sociological analysis, but in early stages of seeking to understand social patterns of behavior the "richness" and "depth" of the individual respondent's replies to questions are not as crucial.

However, the above clarification of purpose in this study does not eliminate the advantages of personal interviews. Such interviews permit the respondent to expand on his answers to questions, as well as allow the interviewer to probe responses and clarify questions. Furthermore, the personal interviewer is able for a variety of reasons to have a much smaller percentage of nonrespondents than is usually the case with mailed questionnaires. Were large resources of time and money available for research on questions such as those undertaken in this study, there seems to be little question but that a large number of personal interviews would be preferable to mailed questionnaires.

Since the funds available for such research are severely limited one has to choose between a relatively small number of personal interviews and a much larger number of mailed questionnaires.[2] Since the purposes of the study call for holding a number of the social factor variables constant while examining how the church participation variables are related to them, it was obvious that a large number of cases was necessary to insure that such a procedure would not yield "empty cells" or cells with a very small number of responses in them.[3] Given the resources available, the use of mailed questionnaires was the only option open for this study.

Having decided on mailed questionnaires, the next important problem is the type of questions to be used. Again, since a wide range of types of questions was needed in order to satisfy the purposes of the study, it was obvious that the questionnaire would be fairly long. Research on social methodology has shown that longer questionnaires must depend almost exclusively on multiple-choice answers in order that respondents should not tire of the questionnaire before it is completed. Precoded responses of course have the advantage of reducing error and bias in the eventual process of card-punching. Multiple-choice and precoded responses have the disadvantage of "forcing" the respondent into choices which do not reveal either his own "real" opinion or permit "shadings" of opinion. Giving the respondent scaled options (strongly agree, agree, disagree, strongly disagree, etc.) helps the latter disadvantage but does not address the former.

The qualitative significance of multiple-choice survey research data in the sociology of religion depends on the sophistication (both sociological and theological) with which questions are asked. For example, the classical question used by opinion research polls, "Do you believe in God?" usually elicits an affirmative response by 95 percent of the American people. It is for precisely this reason that such questions tell us almost nothing about religion because they fail to discriminate sufficiently for analytical purposes. A more productive way to deal with the same question is to give the respondent a choice between alternative conceptions about God (based, for example, on a theologically conceived typology of doctrines of God), and to ask the degree to which the respondent agrees or disagrees with each conception. In the present study efforts at enriching the depth of response by such methods have been employed wherever possible.

It is inevitable in sociological research in areas relating to religion that some critics will argue that "religion" is not subject to analysis through giving people choices on a set of statements about religious issues. Such persons will argue that religion is not a matter of "words on paper" but is a much "deeper" or "more profound" issue. Of course there is much to be said for such a viewpoint, and the present study by no means claims to "exhaust" the "meaning" of religion. Research of the present type is meant only to deal with certain attitudes about religion which people hold and certain ways in which people appear to orient themselves toward religious institutions. Such findings may point to "deeper" issues in religion, and they may even be suitable measures of those deeper issues for certain purposes. The problem of measurement is not unique to religion, even though religion as a subject matter does affect the degree of precision which can be attained.

In other words, just as the teacher uses test scores to classify his students in terms of academic achievement, or the medical doctor uses a checklist to assess the general health of his patient, so the sociologist uses "indicators" to describe various dimensions of religious participation. The sociologist is under no illusion that his "indicators" (and/or the wording of his questions) are identical with the "real" religious dimensions, any more than any teacher believes that a 98 on a test is identical with "real" knowledge, or the physician believes that 98.6° on an oral thermometer is identical with "real" health. All such indicators are simply useful measures to differentiate between types of religious orientation or degrees of academic prowess or grades of illness.

It is common, and indeed obviously rational, to use questions in sociological research which have a kind of "face" validity in terms of being related to the dimension of religion under question. One uses common or traditional statements of religious belief to measure degrees of belief, etc. However, there is no reason in principle why, if a question does in fact differentiate between respondents in statistically significant ways, it should be eliminated from the survey because it does not deal with some subtlety or issue which the researcher or critic wishes it had. This problem of the "adequacy" of questions is particularly a matter for discussion in religious research because both theologians and sociologists have interests in the research, and the issue is particularly obvious in questions relating to religious belief. Do questions couched in traditional religious language "really" measure contemporary religious belief? The sociologist can only say that such questions do differentiate in statistically significant ways among respondents in this study (and in others) and how one *interprets* such differentiation is the more important question.[4] To this issue we will return both in chapter 5 and in Part 4. It is enough at this point to say that the sociologist uses "operational" definitions and not "ontological" definitions.

By the use of indicators as a unit of measurement and combining several indicators, the researcher can develop an "index" which is capable of differentiating the survey population along a continuum which ranges from those who regard all of the statements under consideration to be "completely true" to those who regard none of the statements to be true. For descriptive purposes, if the statements under question were "belief" questions, the various positions could be labeled from "Conservative" to "Liberal," thus providing categories which give some empirical measure of the "belief" dimension of religiousness. The use of such combined indices has the added advantage that errors of wording on a particular question are not as serious as if the question alone were used without the "balancing" influence of the other questions. Again it should be stressed that there will need to be some rational, or *prima facie* reason, why a particular question is included in any particular index.

From one point of view, it seems utterly presumptuous to assume that an individual's religion (by which we mean his most ultimate concern) can be communicated in any way to a social scientist by means of a questionnaire or an interview session. As scientists, everything we do is contingent upon the wording of our questions and answers, the meanings we impute to them, and the consequent process of abstraction by which the analysis is carried out. The subjectivity and the theological assumptions (however unintentional) of the investigator are as much a part of the investigative and analytical process as is the attempt to employ the objective methods of the social sciences. Let it be admitted that the sociologist is not detached from the particularism of his own religious commitment or from the cultural values of his social group. Values and value systems impinge on the scientist at every step of the way: values determine what is problematical, what is important, and thereby help him to choose the subject for his investigation. Values have a great deal to do with how he designs his research, what questions he asks, and how he classifies and interprets his data. What is important is to make explicit these value assumptions that inform his activities and to minimize their distorting effect on the research process.

The authors are also well aware of one other problem related to the methodology they have chosen. This is the nonrespondent problem. In most mail surveys the majority of those selected for the mailing do not respond. Though the response rate for this study is rather high by comparison with similar studies (just under 40 percent), the problem is not one to be minimized. The issue in any sampling is the universe to which one is seeking to generalize. That being the case, a common procedure is to do some form of follow-up interviewing of the nonrespondents to see just how they are different from those who responded. They are obviously different in one sense since they did not respond and the others did. This is rarely a matter of chance. Therefore, are those things which caused them not to respond in any way significantly related to the issues under examination. Such follow-up interviews are a costly and time-consuming process, but an essential one in some circumstances where knowing the differences is crucial for purposes of generalizability of the findings. In this study, though second letters were sent, no follow-up interviews were done. Aside from the fact that there were no funds to do such interviews, there was an important justification for such a decision. Our prime interest in this study is *not* to take the findings and generalize the gross statistics to the universe of participants in United Church of Christ congregations.

We will of course from time to time point out the distribution of responses on various questions, but that is *not* for the purpose of inferring that such a distribution would hold for the total population of participants in this denomination. Instead, our purpose is to do an intensive analysis of those persons' attitudes and responses *who did respond*. We are primarily interested in whether or not one can find indications *among those respondents* that the various religious orientations they had did act as "intervening variables" between independent social factors and "consequential" social attitudes. The problem of non-respondents is not nearly so great for an "internal analysis" of the type we are doing as it would be if one were interested in generalizing to larger populations than the survey group itself. Since a number of other related studies have been done, however, it will be possible at several points to compare certain types of data and proportions of response in the present study with previous work and thus have some clues as to whether or not one has some justification for generalizing the findings beyond the universe of the respondents themselves.

Another way to address this issue would be to point out that we are interested in studying those *who do* participate in the churches of this denomination in various ways. The covering letter sent with the questionnaire[5] identified the study as being supported by the denomination, identified it as a denominational evaluation process, and pointed out that the minister of the local church in question was cooperating with the study and was willing to answer questions about it. (Protection of anonymity was promised for the respondents.) It is reasonable to assume that such a procedure would tend to eliminate those with hostility toward the church and would bias the sample in favor of those who were in fact identified with the church in their own minds and would want to "help" the church. This is precisely the bias we wanted. For this is a study of those who participate in churches, not a study of those who are alienated by the church or who are on the very "fringes" of church life. Thus if there is a bias in our respondents it would seem logical to assume that it is the bias of being "good churchmen," namely those participants who are moved for a variety of reasons to respond to appeals by the church. This point will be kept in mind when interpretive statements are made about the findings of the study. Generalizations from the study will have to be of a very special kind consistent with the bias built into the research methodology itself.

A final introductory word is in order with respect to the denomination used in this study. For reasons which were explored in more detail in the previous chapter, the authors were satisfied that the United Church of Christ provided a particularly important denomination to examine when studying the effects of religious participation in contemporary American culture. A denomination consistently found to draw its constituents from the higher social class levels of the culture is an important one to study, for it is here that a number of theorists and researchers have found religious orientations to be least discernible from dominant cultural orientations.

The Sample

1. Introduction

As was mentioned in the preface, this study originated out of a concern within the Board for Homeland Ministries of the United Church of Christ about the reasonableness of continuing to administer certain of its functions relating to "church extension" through separate "urban" and "town and country" departments. Was such a division of responsibility meaningful in terms of any measurable criteria, or did such a division simply reflect needs of a different social situation from that faced by the denomination in the 1960's?

After discussion, it was agreed that this issue could be addressed through a study designed with larger concerns in mind. The Board agreed that priority of design should be given to more fundamental issues of the functioning of religion in a secularized society, and that out of such a study knowledge could still result for the particular problem of internal organization,[6] particularly since many students of contemporary church-culture issues argue that "urbanization" is a significant dimension of life which churches do not take seriously enough.

Before describing the sampling plan adopted (which has more "purposive" characteristics than "random" characteristics about it) it is necessary to explain a few of the historical factors which went into the formation of the United Church of Christ. It is a union of the Congregational Christian Churches and the Evangelical and Reformed Church. This union was formalized in 1957. The two denominations were of somewhat different backgrounds. The Congregational "wing" stems historically from the early "founding Pilgrim fathers" who settled in New England during the earliest years of American history. The Evangelical and Reformed Church finds its history in a later period of Germanic immigration to this country. For historical reasons, neither of the two previous denominations was truly "national" in the distribution of its members. However, in the new denomination there was some "balancing" of memberships so that the United Church of Christ is more "national" in distribution of members than were either of the previous denominations. However, the South would be a notable area where neither of the previous denominations was particularly well represented, and thus in that area the UCC membership would be much weaker in proportion to the total population than it would be in New England (historic place of Congregational "strength") or in Pennsylvania (historically stronger in the Evangelical and Reformed tradition).

Finally, knowing that a large sample was going to be needed to provide the number of cases needed for analysis, and knowing the severe limitations on funds available for research, it was obvious from the outset that certain pragmatic concerns of availability of personnel to help with the study needed to be balanced against the ideal of a "random" sample. It should be pointed out in this connection that a purely "random" sample of church participants in a particular denomination is very difficult if not impossible to achieve. Knowing the difficulties involved in sampling church participants, and knowing that a great deal of staff time would be necessary to even approach randomness,[7] it was recognized early that staff availability would need to be considered in the sampling plan chosen.

Given all of these factors, it was decided that part of the sample would be drawn from an area which had a predominance of "town and country" churches (churches in communities of less than 10,000 population), and part of our sample would be drawn from churches in Standard Metropolitan Statistical Areas (urban areas defined by the U.S. Bureau of the Census as being those counties with an urban center of over 50,000 population). Furthermore, given the historical factors, it was decided that both "halves"[8] of the sample should be drawn from areas where there would be a significant number of churches from both "branches" of the denomination.

2. The Town and Country Sample

Only one area of the country had a predominance of churches in communities of under 10,000 population, had a significant number of churches from both of the two previous denominations, and had a staff person able to assist in the data-gathering process. That was the Great Plains area.

Technically speaking, the ten states which the "Great Plains" include is a region more extensive than that used for this study.[9] This region takes up about one-fifth of the land area of the United States, extending 1,600 miles from the Canadian border on the north to the Mexican border on the south. At its widest point, this region includes Montana and most of North Dakota, and at the southern end, the eastern portions of Colorado and New Mexico.

For the purpose of this study, six of these states (the "northern" tier) were selected: North Dakota, South Dakota, Nebraska, Montana, Wyoming, and Colorado. A seventh state, not technically a part of the Great Plains, Minnesota, was also included in the study.[10] By definition then, when we speak of "The Great Plains" in this study we are referring to those seven states.

In 1962 there were 706 local congregations of the United Church of Christ in this region, 81 percent being Congregational Christian in background and 19 percent being formerly Evangelical and Reformed churches. These congregations reported a combined membership of 158,016 at that time.

Having decided on an area, the sample was to be drawn in such a way as to respond to the then existing "town and country" distinctions present in the United Church of Christ as well as representing the differences (real or imaginary) in churches due to the size of the congregation. At the time of the study there were persons claiming that the size of the church should be a basis for differentiating the "services and mission" tasks of the denomination to its congregations rather than the traditional distinctions of size of city. Presumably large churches would need less "aid" than small ones. With these two variables in mind, all of the churches were grouped into "cells." Three categories of size of city were used: (a) up to 10,000 (which was the figure used within the denomination for defining a "town and country" community), (b) 10,000 to 49,999, and (c) 50,000 and over (the figure used by the denomination to define an "urban" area). For the variable on size of church, four categories were used: (a) up to 100 members, (b) 100 to 300 members, (c) 300 to 1,000, (d) 1,000 members and over.[11] Needless to say, some of the cells formed by the use of such variables were vacant or nearly so for either or both of the Congregational Christian and Evangelical and Reformed churches.

With the churches then identified by cell, the total number of members could be calculated for each cell, and a decision made in terms of how large a percentage of the membership in each cell would need to be in the sample in order to equalize as far as possible the number of questionnaires to be sent for each cell.[12] Enough churches were then selected at random from within each cell so that when questionnaires were sent to a 25 percent random sample of their mailing list, the proper number of questionnaires would be sent out. The percentage of response for each cell varied from a low of 18 percent to a high of 52 percent, with an overall response rate of nearly 40 percent. The total number of questionnaires sent was 9,589 and the total number returned was 3,818. Of those returned, 30 percent were from churches formerly identified as Evangelical and Reformed. Seventy-five congregations in the Great Plains states were sampled as part of the study.

3. The Urban Sample

At the time of the study, of the Standard Metropolitan Statistical Areas, twelve had field workers in the denomination who would be able to assist with the data-gathering process and also tended to have adequate representation of churches from both the Congregational and Evangelical and Reformed traditions. These S.M.S.A.'s were as follows:

Boston
Buffalo
Chicago
Cincinnati
Columbus
Detroit
Hartford
Kansas City
Los Angeles
Louisville
San Francisco—Oakland
St. Louis

These S.M.S.A.'s had a total of about 870 congregations of the United Church of Christ with approximately 43,000 members. A 10 percent sample of churches and a 25 percent sample of members would have yielded approximately 87 churches and 10,750 respondents.

Each denominational worker in the twelve S.M.S.A.'s was sent a letter explaining the purpose of the study and what participation in the study would require of him. For one reason or another, four of these men were unable to participate (Boston, Buffalo, Kansas City, and Los Angeles), and the staff member in Ohio (who was responsible for Columbus and Cincinnati) decided to work in Cincinnati rather than attempt to gather data in Columbus as well. The cities which are therefore included in the study are: Chicago, Cincinnati, Detroit, Hartford, Louisville, San Francisco and St. Louis.[13]

Once the areas were determined, the research office identified all congregations located in the seven S.M.S.A.'s and assigned a number to each congregation. Using the Rand Corporation's *A Million Random Digits,* a 25 percent sample of congregations was drawn from each area.

Each field worker was then sent a list of the churches in his area selected by this process and asked to contact the minister of each church to solicit his cooperation in the survey. Cooperation meant not only the minister's personal support of the project but the official approval of the congregation's governing board or council and making available to the researcher the most current mailing list used by his congregation. Details of the survey procedure were explained, as well as the assurance that the data to be gathered would be kept confidential and used for research purposes only.

Several adjustments had to be made in some of the cities due to the inability of some of the churches to participate in the survey. Additional churches were selected at random in such cases.

The field workers then prepared a covering letter addressed to each prospective respondent, explaining the purpose of the survey and including a business reply envelope addressed to the research office in New York City to which the questionnaire was to be returned. These letters were sent to every fourth name on the mailing list.

In order to follow up on nonrespondents to the first request, the first letter contained a postcard addressed to the field worker at his local address and the respondent was asked to sign this card and mail it at the same time his questionnaire was mailed to the national office. All those who did not return postcards were sent a second letter and questionnaire approximately two weeks after the first mailing.

When tabulations were begun with the metropolitan area sample, there were 3,444 usable questionnaires from 67 congregations. This sample was distributed as follows:[14]

Metropolitan Area	Number of Churches	Number of Respondents
Chicago	25	1,204
Cincinnati	7	315
Detroit	7	189
Hartford	3	229
Louisville	2	132
St. Louis	13	705
San Francisco	10	670
Totals	67	3,444

The procedure for mailings was the same in both of these two major subsamples. Following the second mailing, the overall response rate was 39.7 percent.[15]

4. Additional Samples

After preliminary tabulations were made of the data, it was discovered that nonwhite parishioners were underrepresented in the study because of the sampling techniques which had been used. Nonwhite participants in the United Church of Christ (as in most so-called "white" denominations) tend to be concentrated in a relatively small number of churches which in contemporary language would be called "Black Congregations." Since the parishioners' attitudes on civil rights were an important aspect of our survey design, a special subsample of predominantly Negro churches was drawn and their ministers contacted and the usual procedure followed. All of these Negro churches were located in northern cities. From this sample of seven churches we obtained 176 usable responses.

Preliminary analysis also revealed that certain special characteristics of church participants related to education were likely to be significant in the study. Therefore a sample was drawn from one very large church whose "social situation" is adjacent to one of the major state universities of the country. This church draws heavily from university-related people, and a special study of this church was taken for comparative purposes; 1,111 respondents in the total study came from this church. At appropriate points in the study, reference will be made to this special subsample.[16]

One can summarize the total sample as being a purposive one drawn with special reference to four types of "social situation": size of city of residence, size of church congregation, racial characteristics, and "university setting." A summary table of the distribution of respondents is found in Table 2-A.

The Questionnaire

1. Introduction

Having decided on a large sample using multiple-choice questions for the reasons discussed above, a questionnaire was designed having three basic types of questions: (1) those dealing with the basic demographic and social factors common to survey research in sociology (these are factors which are treated in the design as "independent"

TABLE 2-A: The Distribution of Respondents by Subsample

Subsample	No. of Respondents	No. of Churches
1. "Town and Country" Sample	3,818	75
a. from villages of 0–9999 population	(1433)	(40)
b. from towns of 10,000–49,999 population	(1059)	(18)
c. from cities of 50,000 or more population	(1326)	(17)
2. "Urban" Sample	3,444	67
a. Chicago	(1204)	(25)
b. Cincinnati	(315)	(7)
c. Detroit	(189)	(7)
d. Hartford	(229)	(3)
e. Louisville	(132)	(2)
f. St. Louis	(705)	(13)
g. San Francisco	(670)	(10)
3. "Nonwhite" Sample	176	7
4. "University Church" Sample	1,111	1
Totals	8,549	150

variables), (2) those dealing with one's attitudes about and toward church participation (referred to throughout the study as "church participation" or "intervening"[17] variables), and (3) those dealing with attitudes on a variety of social issues, the concentration being upon attitudes concerning the racial crisis in our nation (referred to as the "consequential" variables). A total of 54 questions was asked (not necessarily in the order of the three types above) and all responses were precoded for later data processing. At many points in the questionnaire the use of scaled responses reflecting different degrees of acceptance of ideas and practices was employed. The full questionnaire itself is found in the Appendix together with the marginal tabulation of responses.

2. The Independent Variables

It is obvious for most of the independent variables that church participation does not affect them. For the most part they are "givens" which are assumed to have influence upon social attitudes and patterns

of behavior, including church participation. A list of the major "independent" variables included in the questionnaire is:
1. Age
2. Sex
3. Marital Status
4. Educational Achievement
5. Socio-economic Class (income and occupation)[18]
6. Size of City Residence
7. Race

A number of variables will be treated in the study as belonging to this class of "independent" variables, though they do not fall in such a class as obviously as do these seven. They are categorized for the purpose of this study as "independent" because they are being tested to determine whether or not one finds them meaningfully related to the church participation variables. One could of course also relate them to the seven variables for other purposes and the testing of other hypotheses than the ones which concern us in this study. The list of such variables used is (why each of them was included in the study will be discussed when the variables are related to the church participation variables in chapter 6):

8. Previous Denominational Affiliation
9. Size of Present Church
10. Relative Organizational Involvement[19]

3. The Church Participation or "Intervening" Variables

The most important questions for this part of the questionnaire were those used to construct the four basic indices related to the types of church orientation mentioned in chapter 1 (Nos. 1-4 below).[20] In addition to the questions used for this purpose, a number of other questions relating to church participation were also included. Thus the total list of church participation variables is:

1. Organizational Involvement
2. Religious Knowledge
3. Devotional Orientation
4. Belief Orientation
5. Church Attendance and Program Participation
6. Contributions to the Church
7. Reasons for Joining the Congregation
8. Expectations of Church Participation
9. Attitude on the Importance of Church Programs

10. Critique of the Institutional Church
11. Importance of the Elements of Worship
12. Critique of the Minister
13. Subjective Definition of "Christian"
14. Acceptance of Traditional Beliefs

The research design calls for studying the relation between the independent variables and several of the above listed church participation variables.

4. The Consequential Variables

Questions were included on a number of contemporary social, political and economic issues. These are what are often called the "dependent" variables, but since church participation is treated as being at least partially "dependent" on the "independent" variables, the term "consequential" has been employed throughout the study in preference to the term "dependent." From the perspective of the study, these are the issues for which the study is seeking relationships to the "Church Variables." What are the attitudinal consequences of the church participation of the respondent? Obviously, these areas of "secular" attitudes may as well be related to the "Independent Variables" as they are to the "Church Variables." Therefore when significant relationships between church variables and consequential variables are established, the design of the study calls for testing whether such relationships hold even when the independent variables are held constant. The point is to establish the extent to which the church variables become significant intervening variables between the independent variables and the consequential variables. The following are the consequential variables used for the study (the first five are indices, the construction of which will be explained in Part 3 of the study):

1. Attitudes Toward Federal Policies
2. Attitudes Toward Public Policy Issues
3. Relation of the Church to Issues of Public Policy[21]
4. Social Acceptance of Minorities
5. Attitudes Toward Civil Rights Issues
6. Attitudes Toward the Place of the Individual in Social Change
7. Attitudes Toward the Place of Collective Responsibility in Social Change

One final word is in order with respect to the repeated use of the term "consequential" for relationships which in this study will be simply statistical relationships between selected variables. It is clear to everyone familiar with sociological materials that it is a common fallacy to claim to have uncovered "causal" relationships when one has simply happened upon variables that are related to each other but may well be "causally" related to some as yet undetermined third variable. To remain strictly responsible to the discipline of sociological analysis, none of the relationships which will be established in this study should be referred to as more than statistical correlation. There are an infinite variety of variables which could "explain" the relationships and establish "causal" priority. However, the term "consequential" will be used with our understanding that it is largely a literary convenience and no "ultimate" meaning is intended. However, every effort will be made to eliminate "explanations" which have been established in previous literature as well as to fully describe the theory which supports our usage at any given point. Where the term is used in such a tentative fashion, we can only be pleased if subsequent research unearths "third" variables which go further than the present research in "explaining" the relationships.

Statistical Test of Significance

Throughout the first three sections of the study we will keep the presentation of the data at as low a level of abstraction as possible, and we will introduce statistical and theoretical amplification only where necessary. It is important to note that though a great deal of statistical material is necessary for the examination of the hypotheses, we will not utilize several of the commonly employed forms of statistical manipulation of the data. We are searching for "patterning" of responses and a too sophisticated utilization of statistical techniques tends to obliterate the relatively unsophisticated means which contemporary sociology is forced to use in the data-gathering process. That is to say, to perform certain statistical manipulations on materials gained by the usual survey research methodology is unjustified since the material is not substantial enough to support such manipulation.

We are convinced that modern technology related to computer usage has "lured" researchers to attempt a great deal of statistical manipulation of data which is not justified either on the grounds of any supportive theory or on the grounds of the "richness" of the data. We will therefore refrain from using a number of familiar statistical tools of analysis. We will utilize data only in accord with the basic design of the study, will seek for "tendencies" and "patterns" rather than strict "causal chains," and will amplify theory (prior to chapter 11) only where absolutely necessary to give guidance for seeking additional relationships between variables. Wherever the construction of the table makes it possible, the "chi square" test of significance has been employed and the 5 percent level of significance has been used as the criterion for acceptance of the table.

Chapter 3—Description of the Survey Population

Introduction

This chapter, as the title signifies, will examine the social and economic characteristics of the respondents to the survey. The intent is to utilize primarily those variables which, for the purposes of the study, are considered "independent." The relation of these variables to church participation variables and secular issues will be examined in Parts 2 and 3 respectively. This chapter opens with an overall description of the survey population, the middle sections examine the way in which each of the primary subsamples utilized in the study do or do not deviate from the general pattern, and it closes with an examination of the ways in which several of the "independent" variables are related to one another.

From the review of previous research in the opening chapter there are several expectations one would have about the social and economic characteristics of the population responding to this survey. Since the denomination from which the sample is drawn has a constituency two thirds of which came from a denomination shown in previous research to be above average in social class, this sample should manifest a number of the characteristics associated in America with social privilege and wealth. However there should also be a fair representation of the relatively nonprivileged.[1] We would expect our sample to have more women and older people in it than would be the case for a representative sample of the total American population.[2] Given the essays which have been written concerning the identification of American churches with general American middle and upper-middle class values,[3] one might well expect that the survey population will show "model" patterns with respect to marital status and family life. The respondents will probably come from home-owning families with two or more children. On the basis of previous research, we should expect the respondents to be "joiners" of a variety of types of organizations since America has been known as an "overorganized" culture.[4]

The expectations are not so clear in terms of how the various subsamples might be expected to deviate from the above pattern. In terms of rural-urban differentiation, one might expect the more rural respondents to manifest a narrower range of social class difference than do the urban respondents, given the assumption that cities are generally felt to be more heterogeneous than rural areas and small towns. However, whether or not the "selective" factors that are believed to operate in terms of who participates in churches (the *very* rich and the *very* poor being felt to be outside of its influence) will offset this expectation is not known. Also, will the migration of young people to cities make the rural samples "older" or will this too be offset by the "selection" process of church participation? Can one expect the urban respondents to be better educated than their "country cousins"? Do town and country people join organizations more or less often than the urban people? Some would argue that urban people have more freedom to concentrate on special personal interests or even to refrain from joining *any* organizations than would be the case in more "conformist" villages[5] while others would expect cities and villages to be very similar in terms of patterns of organization.[6] Again we are faced with the question of whether the "selective" appeal of churches will offset whatever might be relative differences between cities and more rural communities.

There are also a great many extant theories concerning the differences which exist between cities in various regions of the country. Some argue that urban American culture has a kind of "sameness" about it which tends to eliminate regional characteristics while others hold that regions continue to make cities within them very different from one another. Now of course the answer to such a debate is partly in terms of *what kind* of characteristics one is discussing. However, in terms of the independent social variables we are using in this study, the question is whether our different subsamples from different regions of the country differ from one another or not. There is little research on church participants to point to such expectations, and one simply has to raise the question and examine it for this sample. If difference is found between the subsamples one will want to look at various types of "regional characteristics" for some explanation, but if the subsamples are similar, one cannot know if this is due to the church "appealing" to similar people in all of the different cities or if it is due to the fact that the cities themselves are in fact very similar in terms of those characteristics being tested. In any event the research design cannot really answer the question of *why* the difference (or lack of it); the question here is simply *whether* it exists.

What are we to expect in terms of the two "special" samples? The authors expected that the Negro subsample would be very similar to the patterns of the majority of the white respondents in terms of social characteristics (not necessarily in terms of certain social attitudes). The reason for the expectation is research which has shown the way the Negro community is heterogeneous in cities and those who would choose to identify with a predominantly white upper-middle class denomination would be expected to be upper-middle class in social characteristics.[7] By definition the "university church" subsample should be more affluent and more educated, but how it will differ in other social characteristics is uncertain.

General Characteristics

Overall, the sample of United Church of Christ parishioners can be described as a middle-aged, upper-middle class group. The typical respondent is married, has children, a white collar job, earns approximately $8,100 a year, has gone to college, grew up in the type of community in which he now lives, and owns his own home.[8] Thus the average respondent is a "successful establishment-type" American.

The median age reported by the respondents was 45 years of age with the distribution of ages falling in the pattern of a normal curve around that figure with the notable exception of a higher frequency of those in the older years rather than in the younger. Over 14 percent of the sample was 65 years of age or older while less than 10 percent were under 25.

The sample was approximately 60 percent female and nearly 80 percent of the respondents were married. Seven out of ten of the respondents were people with children, one out of ten was single, and about one out of ten was either widowed, separated or divorced. Compared with the adult population of the United States, our respondents were overrepresented in the married group (67.4 percent for the U.S.), and substantially underrepresented in the single group (22 percent for the U.S.). The proportion who are widowed and divorced is approximately that of the population as a whole.

Approximately one third of our respondents were housewives and 43 percent of the respondents were employed full-time. Eight percent reported that they were retired.

If the pattern of the typical American family is that it moves often (a common statistic being that one family out of five moves each year) then our sample deviates significantly from that stereotype. They are a very stable group. Nearly 63 percent of them have lived in their present community for 10 years or more and the same percentage has lived in their present homes for five years or more; 80 percent of the respondents own their own homes. The low rate of mobility and the high rate of home ownership may in fact be a function of the age of the sample population. When one is older one is less likely to change jobs and more likely to own one's home.

In terms of education, income and occupation, the sample is a relatively advantaged group. Fifty percent of the respondents had some formal education at the college level with 32 percent having graduated from college. Only 18 percent had less than a high school education. This same advantaged position is reflected in income and occupation. Nearly one third of the respondents had an annual family income of more than $10,000 and 40 percent of them were professional, technical, or managerial workers. Seven out of ten were "white collar" workers.

In order to study relationships between socio-economic factors and other crucial variables in this research, an Index of Socio-Economic Class (hereafter referred to as ISEC) was developed. It utilized two variables: income and occupation. Any index based on the gross measurements available in a study of this type is not useful except in studying general patterns. The ISEC is no exception. The broad census categories which each respondent used to label his own occupation can be ordered in a general way in terms of social class by reference to the categories of other studies in social stratification.[9] This was done, and then the respondent's income classification was correlated with the occupational breakdown, and the respondent was assigned an ISEC classification according to Table 3-A and the distribution of ISEC scores which resulted is found in Table 3-B.

The question of why an index is necessary for measuring social class can quite logically be raised. Why not simply use income? The answer to the question is found by reference to theories and research related to social stratification. It is clear that a complex society does not order

TABLE 3-A: Numerical Categories Assigned for the Index of Socio-Economic Class

Occupational Group	$15,000 and over	$10,000–$14,999	$7,500–$9,999	$5,000–$7,499	Under $5,000	NR	N
Professional and Technical	4	4	4	3	3	3	2,777
Proprietors and Managers	4	4	3	3	3	2	1,050
Farm Managers and Farmers	4	3	3	3	2	2	679
Clerical and Sales	3	3	3	2	2	2	1,367
Operatives and Craftsmen	3	3	2	2	2	1	1,207
All others	3	2	2	2	1	1	623
Not Reported (NR)	2	2	2	1	1	0	846
N.	1,096	1,820	1,564	1,842	1,818	409	8,549

TABLE 3-B: Distribution of Respondents on the Index of Socio-Economic Class

Category	Number of Respondents N = 8,549	Percentage of Respondents
Upper (4)	2,683	31
Upper middle (3)	2,298	27
Lower middle (2)	2,483	29
Lower (1)	1,085	13

itself only on the basis of monetary income. Issues of prestige, possessions, social interaction, values, etc., all play a part in the American class system.[10] A discussion of all of the issues involved is beyond our purpose here, but the reason for choosing the two particular variables described needs to be justified. This justification is crucial for the whole research design, and it is necessary to engage in a brief "excursus" on a particular theory of social class before proceeding to other general characteristics of the survey population.

In a very important essay,[11] Max Weber made some crucial distinctions which have not been considered seriously enough by many students of social stratification. In that essay he distinguished class from status by relating class to the "marketplace," the acquisition of goods and services, while status was more related to "social honor." Class is one's economic "life chances" or how one "produces," while status is more a matter of how one "consumes" or the "life style" one adopts. Though there is of course a great deal of interrelationship between class and status, it is important to differentiate the two *especially in the context of the present study.*

Weber pointed out that class is more closely related to the "mass" characteristics of the society, while status is more related to one's "communal feelings." There is a sense then in which one could speak of a kind of "priority" being given to class issues (one cannot consume if he does not earn), even as one recognizes that he is talking about social conditioning and is not adopting a kind of "Marxian" economic determinism. Now, given the present study's design (assuming certain socially "given" factors, relating those to church participation, and then seeing how both the factors and the participation are related to certain public issues), class is more nearly a clear "social factor" than is status. In fact, it is precisely the point that churches are seen as "status" institutions, which is crucial in the study! What kind of status institutions are they and how do they relate to social attitudes? Hence for our design purpose we must seek to keep class and status issues as separate as possible, given the fact of their interrelationship. Churches do seek to influence the "style of life" of their participants, and we are concerned to see just how they do, if at all.

Weber goes on in his essay to argue that the economic factors (class) are related to the social factors (status) and they in turn are related to the political factors (party). The "social" conventions eventually become institutionalized structures and laws. It is not too far afield to argue that there is a clear parallel in Weber's essay to the research design underlying this study. What are called in this study independent variables are informed at many points by economic issues and "life chances"; indeed we have used the terms socially privileged and socially deprived. The "intervening" variables of church participation are being examined to see how they are affected by "economic" factors and how they appear to influence the attitudes on public issues. They are parallel to the place Weber assigns to the "status" issues, and what are being called here the "consequential" variables (the public issues) are "political" in the sense Weber uses that term in the "party" section of his essay. They relate to issues of social structure and laws. They deal with issues of legalized social convention.

What this excursus has shown is that for an "independent" variable we are most interested in stressing "class" rather than "status." Therefore income can be used in the ISEC as well as occupation (a form of "life chance"). Education would not be as suitable for inclusion since, though it does affect one's life chance and occupation, it also is more clearly related to consumption and life style. The man who chooses to advance his life chances through education is influenced by social forces as well as economic forces. It is interesting to see whether this distinction between the ISEC and education will be significant when we discuss relationships found between the three types of variables in our study.

Having completed this excursus, let us return to examine some characteristics of the survey population which are of a slightly different order from those discussed above. These are the characteristics which, as was pointed out in chapter 2, have a mixed character about them. They are both independent and also related to church participation. First, we will examine organizational involvement.

The active American middle-class image is upheld by our respondents in terms of their membership in outside organizations. More than half of the respondents belonged to two or more outside organizations (see Appendix, question 38) and the types of organizations chosen most frequently by the respondents reflect middle-class values. Our respondents are more likely to belong to the PTA, lodges and social clubs than they are to belong to political party organizations, civil rights groups, labor unions, or even business organizations (see Appendix, question 39).

An interesting issue related to organizational behavior is whether or not our respondents were more involved in "outside" organizations or in church organizations. In order to address this issue, an Index of Relative Organizational Involvement (IROI) was constructed. The number of church organizations the respondents belonged to was related to the number of "outside" organizations in which they claimed membership, and a numerical category was assigned to each respondent according to the pattern shown in Table 3-C. The distribution of IROI scores which resulted is found in Table 3-D. More than 50 percent of the respondents are more involved in "outside" organizations than they are in the church. The majority of our respondents are American "joiners" who seem to prefer to be busy in social and "not-too-demanding" service organizations.

TABLE 3-C: Numerical Categories Assigned for the Index of Relative Organizational Involvement

Outside Organizations	Church Organizations						
	0 or NR	1	2	3	4	5	N
0 or NR	0	5	5	5	5	5	2195
1	1	3	4	4	4	4	1685
2	1	2	3	4	4	4	1728
3	1	2	2	3	4	4	1211
4	1	2	2	2	3	4	656
5 or more	1	2	2	2	2	3	1074
N =	4054	2758	1332	311	58	36	8549

TABLE 3-D: Distribution of Respondents on the Index of Relative Organizational Involvement

IROI Category	Number of Respondents N	Percentage of Respondents
0 = Not involved in either	1220	14.3
1 = Outside organizations only	2834	33.2
2 = More involved in outside organizations	2185	25.6
3 = Equally involved in both	955	11.2
4 = More involved in church organizations	380	4.4
5 = Church organizations only	975	11.4

A final issue describing the survey population is that of denominational background. In what denominational tradition were the respondents "brought up"? Not surprisingly, the most frequently mentioned denominations were Congregational Christian and Evangelical and Reformed (23 percent and 20 percent respectively), *but* together they account for *less than half* of the respondents. More than half of the respondents are not "birthright" members of the United Church of Christ (in terms of having come into one of the previous denomina-

47

tions as a child). Three denominations claim more than 10 percent of the respondents as childhood members: Methodist 17 percent, Presbyterian 12 percent and Lutheran 10 percent. An interesting question will be to determine if "denominational background" appears to be related in any significant way to any other variables. If there is a significant difference, we will want to see if one can explain this through any theory of social conditioning or theory of church participation.

How have our findings matched with expectations based on previous research? Every expectation mentioned in the introduction to this chapter has been fulfilled. What this tells us is that there is some reason to expect that our sample, which was drawn on a "purposive" sampling plan, *may* have more possibility of being considered "representative" of a certain segment of American Protestantism than was originally suggested. We *may* be able to say that the "internal analysis" we are undertaking can be generalized beyond the group of respondents themselves. However before one is able to affirm the validity of such possible generalizability of the findings more will need to be known than has thus far been described concerning how the sample population compares with other studies on similar issues.

We are now in a position to compare each of the major subgroups of the sample with these overall statistics. In the remainder of the chapter the assumption will be that the subgroup in question is similar to the general sample unless a deviation is noted.

Rural-Urban Differentiation

On the basis of general characteristics of the type described above, our sample would tend to support the thesis that church participants in America are very similar whether they reside in small towns or metropolitan areas. The deviation between our subsamples on the rural-urban continuum was very minimal. Where there was any deviation it was modest and was as follows: with increasing urbanization, we found (1) a decrease in average age, (2) an increase in the number of female respondents, (3) an increase in the level of education, (4) increased income, (5) an increase in the ISEC index, and (6) a decrease in length of residence. Denominationally, the urban respondents were more frequently Congregational Christian and Presbyterian in background, and less frequently Evangelical and Reformed or Lutheran in background.

All the above differences were very modest, and in the direction one might expect in terms of the "stereotypes" one has of urban vs. rural people. The point is that the stereotypes are correct in terms of tendencies, but the differences are very slight among our respondents. Only one finding tended to be surprising to us, namely the fact that urbanization had no effect one way or the other on the organizational involvement of the respondents. The types of organizations tended to be similar all along the rural-urban continuum, and similar patterns of "Relative Organizational Involvement" were also observed. In terms of relative organizational involvement, the most urban subsample matched nearly perfectly the most rural subsample, and in the "middle-sized" cities one found a slight increase in involvement in "outside" organizations. In all subsamples the majority of the respondents were more active in outside organizations than they were in the church.

There was one other difference between rural and urban respondents, though it was not a very surprising one. The issue was that of the kind of community in which the respondent was raised (see Appendix, question 14). The figures showed that there was more migration from the rural areas to the city than the reverse. Forty percent of the most urban sample had grown up in communities of under 10,000 population, while only 9 percent of the most rural sample had grown up in cities of over 50,000 population.

We can summarize the rural-urban difference in the survey population by saying that the stereotypical pattern of difference can be discerned. However, either the church appeals "selectively," thus mitigating this difference, or the society is more homogeneous than the stereotypes assume. It could reasonably be argued that for this survey population, class and status as related to the influences of a mass society are more significant than population density.[12]

Differences Between Metropolitan Subsamples

As one examined the patterns of responses in the various cities where subsamples were drawn, it was apparent that for the respondents in this study one could more meaningfully discuss *regional* differences in contrast to differences between particular cities. Where deviation between the subsamples occurred, Cincinnati and Louisville would tend in one direction (in a few cases St. Louis followed the same tendency) and the other cities tended in the other direction. Thus we might refer to these three cities as being the "border" cities, that is, they are all on the "border" between North and South. The term was chosen since the deviations described below were often of a type which fits the popular image of differences between North and South. (San Francisco was always "northern" in its characteristics.)

The "border" subsamples had more respondents at the extremes of the age continuum, both the old and the young, and many of the other deviations were consistent with this difference. These "border" subsamples were less well-educated, earned less, had fewer professional and technical workers, had lower scores on the ISEC index, and were less frequently married than were the other subsamples.

It is important to repeat here that, as in the case of rural-urban difference, the deviations mentioned were not pronounced. Either the church draws "selectively" thus mitigating differences between regions of the country or else the regions are not as different as is often assumed. The point is that our subsamples are not greatly different one from the other.

The University Church Subsample

This specially drawn subsample had several characteristics which set it apart from the other subsamples. It had the highest percentage of persons between the ages of 15 and 19 years (18 percent vs. 3 percent for the total sample), it had the highest percentage of persons over 65 years of age (22 percent vs. 14 percent for the total sample), it had the highest percentage of persons with no children under 18 (67 percent vs. 32 percent for the total sample), the highest education (80 percent with education beyond high school), highest income (median income $11,325), and highest percentage of professional and technical workers (64 percent vs. 28 percent for the total sample).

It was the subsample which was most active in "outside" organizations, these organizations tending to be much more frequently of a professional or charitable sort. Interestingly enough, this organizational involvement was equally addressed to the church since they had the *lowest* percentage of persons who were active *only* in outside organizations.

The respondents from University Church were very stable residentially with 80 percent of them indicating they had lived in the same community for 10 years or more.

In terms of denominational background, the respondents in this subsample were much more frequently Congregational Christian in background than was the case for other subgroups.

One could summarize this subsample by saying that it had all the tendencies described for the sample as a whole, only it was "even more so."

The Nonwhite Subsample

The Negro parishioners who were drawn from the seven predominantly Negro churches exhibit the "middle class" characteristics referred to above to a greater extent than the average white parishioner. If our sample of Negroes is at all typical of Negro parishioners in the United Church of Christ they are *not* typical of the "average" American Negro. Our Negro respondents were slightly older than our white respondents, they were better educated, and more of them were employed in professional occupations. However, the consequences of job discriminations are reflected in the fact that in spite of his higher educational status, the average Negro respondent has an income which just barely equals the average white income, and this income is more often than not earned by more than one member of the family. The Negro subsample is the only one in which 50 percent of the families have more than one breadwinner. In all other subsamples only one third or less of the families have more than one person earning the family income. Thus, given the way the ISEC in this study was constructed (a combination of income and occupation), the Negro sample has a similar ISEC pattern to other respondents.

Only the "University Church" subsample exceeds the Negro subsample in "outside" organizational activity. The upper-middle class Negroes represented in our sample are active in a wide variety of types of organizations, but their prime interest is in civil rights organizations—65 percent of the Negro respondents indicated such membership, while the average for all other subsamples was 2.1 percent indicating such activity! In relation to the white respondents, the Negro respondents have a pattern in the IROI which indicates a lower percentage active only in outside organizations and a higher percentage active only in church organizations.

The Negro respondents were a very stable group residentially with 81 percent indicating they had lived in the same city as they now resided for ten years or more.

Not surprisingly, the Negro subsample is over represented in the percentage of respondents who were either Baptist or Methodist in denominational background. It should also be pointed out that all of the so-called "Negro" churches used in this sample were Congregational Christian churches prior to the union of the United Church of Christ, but only 15 percent of the Negro respondents gave that denomination as their denominational "background." Therefore a total of 75 percent of these respondents had been brought up as Methodists or Baptists and made a decision (associated with social mobility?) to join the Congregational or UCC churches.

Interrelation of the Independent Variables

Having examined our total sample in terms of the independent variables, and having compared those findings with each of the major types of "purposive" subsamples in our study, it remains to determine if there are any significant correlations *between* these variables. Then in Part 2 we will study the ways these are related to church participation variables.

Since we have already compared how rural-urban difference and race are related to the other independent variables, and since we are analyzing income and occupation through the combined ISEC, we must examine whether or not there is any relationship between some of the remaining variables: age, sex, education, ISEC, denominational background and IROI.

To begin with, as one might expect there was a very high correlation between education and the ISEC. Those with more education were much more likely to be rated as having a higher class standing. This of course supports the point mentioned earlier, that there tends to be an interrelationship between class and status. This relationship between the ISEC and education was sufficiently strong so that what is said below about the relationship between the ISEC and the other independent variables also holds true for education.

Women respondents tended to score lower social class index scores than the men, and tended to have lower education. Their pattern of relative organizational involvement was more church-oriented than was the organizational involvement of the men. However, neither males nor females were more likely to be categorized by the IROI as being "not involved in either church or outside organizations."

Those over 65 were clearly of a lower social class than the rest of the age categories and had less education. The most upper-class groups were those aged 35-64. These middle-aged groups were also the ones most likely to be active in both church and outside organizations. The only category of the IROI which showed a clear increase with each succeeding age group was the "church only" category. Thus there is some tendency for the older people to become more involved in church groups rather than outside organizations.

Education and socio-economic class were related to the IROI in an interesting way, somewhat predictable from the above statements. Those with the least education and lower class were more likely to be involved *only* in the church or else not be involved *either* in the church or outside organizations. Equal involvement in the church and outside organizations *or* more involvement in the church than outside organizations was found among those with "middle" social class scores and "middle" amounts of education. Involvement *only* in outside organizations or *more* in outside organizations than in the church was found among those with the highest social class scores and the highest education.

How was denominational background related to social class and to the IROI? On the basis of ISEC scores, denominational backgrounds could be ordered in the following way (from the highest average ISEC scores to the lowest): Presbyterian, Methodist, Congregational, Baptist, Lutheran and Evangelical and Reformed (the only denominational backgrounds with enough respondents to consider). The order is what one might expect from the previous studies mentioned on social class related to denominations, except that one might have expected the Methodists and Congregationalists to reverse their respective positions. However, it should be remembered that except for the former Congregationalists and former "E and R's" all other respondents in this study represent persons who have "changed" denominations. Therefore, the "Methodists" in this study for example are those Methodists who have chosen to change their denomination and thus a very selective factor is introduced which might explain why they are of a higher social class than other studies might predict. Are our "Methodists" those who have experienced vertical social mobility in an upward direction? This would at least be a likely possibility.

Finally, combining the findings of the two previous paragraphs, one can predict the relation of "former denomination" and the IROI. Baptists have IROI scores very close to the average for the total sample; Presbyterians, Methodists and Congregationalists are more likely to be involved in *both* the church *and* outside organizations; and the Lutherans and "E and R's" are more likely to be either involved *only* in the church or not to be involved in either the church or outside organizations.

Summary

The commonalities between the subsamples far surpass the few deviations which were found between the various subgroupings. The sample as a whole, and all of the various major subgroupings, represents a middle- and upper-middle class grouping in church participants. We can have some confidence, then, in using the sample to discuss the patterns of church participation, both in terms of its social conditioning factors and its consequences for such a grouping.

Part 2-The Sociology of Church Participation

Chapter 4-The Layman Faces the Church

Introduction

Since it has been established that our survey population is predominantly of an upper-middle class character but with an evident range of responses on all of the independent factors, we are now in a position to examine how this survey population viewed their church participation. This chapter will be devoted to gaining an overall perspective on the respondents' attitudes toward a variety of church-related issues and in evaluating their church-related behavior in some instances (attendance, offices held, contributions, etc.). Then chapter 5 will extract from these responses various criteria from which the four basic "church participation indices" will be constructed. Finally, in chapter 6, the relationship of the independent factors to the church participation variables will be examined.

Based on previous research, what would be the expected attitudes of our respondents to the church? Should we find that the respondents in this study "match" other findings, this will increase our possible freedom to generalize later findings. However, if they do not manifest the same church-related behavior and attitudes that were found in other studies of similar types of parishioners, we will want to see what particular theories might explain such a deviation.[1]

A number of studies done within the decade of the sixties can provide some "yardsticks" against which to compare our data. Argyle summarized some of this research by stating:

> Several careful observers of the American scene have recently remarked on the growing liberalism of belief, together with signs that there is now a gospel of happiness, adjustment, and acceptance of the American way of life; there is more tolerance, but also more secularism and a withdrawal of affect from religion, while the old ideas of sin and sacrifice are forgotten.[2]

These general observations about the place of religion in America are only heightened in intensity when one looks at the denominational comparisons made by Stark and Glock in their recent volume on a national random sample gathered in the same year as our study.[3] Consistently the "Congregational"[4] group was less orthodox in belief than most other groups, less likely to engage in religious practices, and less likely to feel that the church was making a significant impact upon their lives.[5] Thus it is quite reasonable to expect that our data will replicate such findings.

Schroeder and Obenhaus added an important fact to this general pattern when they sought to discover whether or not there was any evidence among laymen of open or latent hostility toward or criticism of the churches. They were not able to uncover any significant amount of criticism. Indeed, they found that most people were quite accepting of their churches and ministers.[6]

Before proceeding to the examination of our data to find its consistency (or lack of it) with these general findings, it is important to note again one of the major thrusts of Demerath's work. That is, while a single denomination has tendencies in certain dominant directions, yet it incorporates a fair degree of diversity within its constituency.[7]

Patterns of Church Behavior

When we examine those indicators from our study that measure the patterns of "church behavior" of our respondents, we find that on the average the participants in this study are stable supporters of an institutional church which is relatively close to their home. Seventy percent of them have been members of their congregation for over five years (question 1)[8] and the majority of them live within a two-mile radius of the church building (question 18). Sixty-four percent of the respondents attend worship "three or four times" a month (question 3) and the majority belong to at least one church organization (question 6). The types of church activity outside of the worship services that are the most popular are women's groups and family nights. Men's groups, social action groups, retreats and prayer groups appeal to a very limited proportion of the survey population (question 11).

Financially, the parishioners support their church with a median weekly pledge of $2.83 (question 9). In addition they make regular contributions to United or Community Funds (82 percent), and to medical research (50 percent). Only one parishioner in ten contributes to social reform movements such as the NAACP, CORE, or SCLC, and only one in twenty contributes to theological seminaries (question 10).

Patterns of personal friendship for the participants in this study were assessed by asking the respondents to tell how many of their five closest friends were also members of the same local congregation. The friendship patterns are predominantly outside of the local congregation. However, 31 percent of the people indicate that they had three or more of their five closest friends within the congregation. Later it will be important to see what characteristics are correlated with friendship pattern both inside and outside the congregation.[9]

Since the Stark and Glock study was done in the same year as our study, and since it was a carefully planned "representative" sample, it is interesting to compare the above findings on religious behavior with the Stark and Glock figures. They found that 45 percent of the "Congregationalists" attended worship "nearly weekly or better,"[10] while we found that 64 percent of our respondents did so. However, given the fact that we are using a UCC study rather than simply a "Congregational" sample, our figures are not much higher than one might expect by looking at some other Stark and Glock figures for other "former" denominational groups found in our sample (Stark and Glock's figures for American Baptists was 75 percent and for American Lutherans was 65 percent).[11] A figure between the two studies that compares even more closely is the figure on church organizations. Stark and Glock found that 54 percent of their "Congregationalists" belonged to one or more church organizations, while we found exactly the same figure among our respondents.

Our survey population appears to have an overall pattern of church behavior similar to such patterns found earlier for more "liberal" denominations. The fact that the sample is made up of persons from several denominational backgrounds may well explain why our figures do not exactly match the findings of other studies of Congregationalists. We will examine this possible explanation later.

Patterns of Attitudes Relating to the Church

A range of questions was included in the study in order to evaluate a variety of attitudes of the respondents toward the church and religious matters. The questions can be grouped into four types: (1) help desired from the church, (2) critique of the church in terms of its present program, (3) acceptance of traditional beliefs and practices, (4) views on the church's relation to certain issues of public policy. Inevitably there is overlapping between the groups, but in this chapter they will be presented as relatively discrete types and later the patterns of interrelationship between major church participation variables will be analyzed.

1. Help Desired from the Church

Help desired from the church can be evaluated both in terms of asking the respondent to reflect on why he joined the church in the first place, and by asking him what help he now desires from the church. Twelve "reasons for joining" were presented to the respondent and he was asked to indicate which of them seemed to him to have been important and which did not seem to be so. Table 4-A shows the percentages[12] who indicated that they felt the "reason" was "very important." The order of priority of responses indicates that the respondents are family oriented; they want to like the minister; and they like the denomination, the program, and the people in the church. Finding a place to serve others or having been invited to join appears to be less important. They want to help their own children but are not likely to be looking for a way to help "others."

When asked more directly to answer a question giving nine optional kinds of help desired from the church now (Table 4-B), the five most frequently chosen options all deal with personal and family life from a "positive" theological point of view (stressing God's love, "faith," "good moral foundations," etc.). On the other hand, the four least frequently chosen options are the ones which stress either the "social" character of Christianity or the "negative" theological issues (anxiety, conflict, etc.).

In terms of "help desired" our respondents follow expectations very closely indeed.

TABLE 4-A: Respondent's Reasons for Joining the Church (Question 5)

How important was each of these reasons for you personally when you joined your present church?	Percent of those answering the question who indicated the reason was "Very Important"
For the sake of my children	68
Liked the minister	60
Enjoyed form of worship service	60
Preferred the denomination	56
Church program appealed to me	42
Liked people I met in church	42
Grew up in the church school	42
Enjoyed its friendly atmosphere	39
Located conveniently near my home	33
A place to serve others	32
Invited to join by the minister	29
Invited to join by a member	19

TABLE 4-B: Kind of Help Which Respondents Desire from the Church (Question 8)

I want my church to help me to	Percent of those answering the question who desired "much help"
Raise my children properly	77
Build good moral foundations for my personal life	74
Strengthen my faith and religious devotion	73
Know of God's care and love for me	67
Find meaning for my personal existence	67
Work for justice in my community and in my world	53
Meet my personal problems of anxiety, conflict, etc.	48
Understand my daily work as a Christian vocation	47
Be aware of the needs of others in my community	42

2. Critique of the Church

In order to understand the "critique" of the church and its programs by the respondents, let us look first at the same list of options referred to when the respondent was asked to tell in which of the areas he had *actually received* "much help" (question 23). In no option did more people say they had received help than had earlier indicated they wanted it. And in general one can say that they felt they had received help in the areas where they said they wanted it. The same options are in the "upper half" of the list in both questions, and the same options are in the "lower half."

A similar type of criticism was sought, but with different options of choice, when the respondents were asked to tell where they thought the church had "not done enough" about certain areas of concern (question 13). It is interesting that not one option had a majority of the respondents indicating that the church had not done enough. The respondents as a whole are simply not very critical of their churches. The two most frequently chosen options were that the church had not done enough "teaching the Bible" or "helping young people." Only about one respondent in five indicated that he felt that the church had not done enough to "affect changes in our government policies," the least frequently chosen option.

The evaluation of attitudes thus far would indicate that the parishioners see the institution of the church as primarily serving their privatized needs, developing good moral foundations and family life. Apparently less help is expected, or received from the church in the public sector of the parishioners' life.

When we turn to look at how the sample population evaluated the worship service (question 20), we see that the majority of the parishioners find all parts of the traditional worship service "very helpful" except the prayer of confession, the music (other than hymns), and the offering. We could reasonably assume then, that the respondents were pleased with the general worship service, and again found the church most helpful in terms of a sense of their "goodness" rather than their "sinfulness" and they did not find it particularly helpful to "give" either to the institutions or to others.

A majority found only the boards and committees of the church to be "very important" among the church program options presented to them (question 12) and were very unlikely to find social action groups, retreats, or prayer meetings to be very important (less than one person in four chose such programs as important).

A final type of "critique" asked of the survey population was an evaluation of the way the minister is perceived to spend his time (question 22). When we look at what a small percentage of the respondents indicated that the minister spent "too little time" in any area, it is obvious that *no* area of the minister's work is felt to be significantly ignored. Only 15 percent of the respondents in the most frequently chosen option indicated that the minister spent too little time in that area and that was "calling on members." One can only conclude that, among the respondents, there is not a great deal of criticism of the way the minister spends his time, and where there is, the respondents want more personal care of the congregation.

3. Acceptance of Beliefs and Practices

Turning to the third area of religious attitudes, that of acceptance of traditional beliefs and practices, two questions were asked. The first asked the participant to pick from a variety of beliefs or practices those which he felt to be "absolutely necessary" for a Christian. Of the options given, only two were felt by the majority to be of such a character: "Believe in Jesus as Savior," and "Obey the Ten Commandments" (Table 4-C). Thus, though this sample draws from a relatively active group of church participants, the majority do not consider regular worship, baptism, daily prayer, or working for social justice, to be essential to the Christian life.

TABLE 4-C: Characteristics Considered to be "Absolutely Necessary" for a Christian (Question 19)

Christians are those who	Percent of those responding
Believe in Jesus as Savior	82
Obey the ten commandments	74
Have been baptized	45
Attend Sunday worship regularly	38
Work for social justice	36
Accept church creeds	36
Are active church members	36
Pray and read the Bible daily	28
Had a conversion experience	10

A second question on acceptance of beliefs took a group of traditional statements regarding the content of Christian theology and asked how many were "true," "probably true," "probably not true" or "not true." Table 4-D summarizes the "true" responses for each statement. Notice that, except for the beliefs concerning "sin" and "punishment," the majority of the respondents believe the statements to be true. The respondents again prefer a kind of "positive" theological view rather than one which stresses the "dark" side of life.

The above findings make it clear that our respondents are following expected patterns with respect to issues of belief.[13]

TABLE 4-D: Certainty of Belief (Question 24)

Statement	Percent of those reporting "True"
All men are equal in the sight of God	87
God revealed himself to man in Jesus Christ	81
Jesus rose from the dead	73
God answers prayer	71
The Bible is the word of God	67
We are justified by faith	66
There is life after death	59
Jesus was born of a virgin	57
The Church is the body of Christ	57
Sin is separation from God	49
All men are born guilty of original sin	28
Hell is a just punishment for sinners	18

4. The Church and Public Policy

A fourth and final area of attitude on the church which was pursued in the study was the relation between the church and selected issues of "public policy." These issues have a "mixed" quality about them, since they involve both one's view about the church *and* one's view about the social order. Therefore, the questions are of particular interest in a research design of the type underlying this study.

As in several of the other questions, the respondents were asked to select from among a group of options those issues where they agreed the church should "take a stand." The denomination under study has often taken a position on issues which it felt were both "religious" and "public." On some issues there is wide agreement, while on others the consensus at the local congregational level is lacking. In Table 4-E we see that the majority of those who responded to the questions supported four of the seven issues selected. There is near unanimity among those who responded on the issue of "open" church membership, but only six in ten of the respondents feel that the church should actively support the Negro's struggle for civil rights. The participants in the study are more willing to give the local minister freedom of the pulpit than they are to have the denomination issue statements on social and economic matters. The majority would allow prayers in public schools but only a very small minority agree that religion should be taught in the public schools. The patterns would seem to be that the majority of the respondents are in favor of a more "passive" role for the church in public policy. Thus, one can "open" the church but not get involved

TABLE 4-E: Respondents Views on Selected Issues of the Churches' Relation to Public Policy (Question 46)

Issue of Public Policy	Percent of those answering the question who agree
Church membership should always be open to people of all races and nationalities	90
Ministers have a right to preach on controversial subjects from the pulpit	72
Prayers should be allowed in the public schools	61
Churches should support the Negro's struggle to achieve civil rights	58
Denominations have a right to issue policy statements on social and economic matters	42
Christians should refrain from using alcoholic beverages	29
Religion should be taught in the public schools	15

in the struggle for justice, one can listen to a minister discuss controversial issues, but one does not wish to "go on record" by having a printed denominational "policy" statement, and one can permit people to "say their prayers" in public schools as an act of public piety but not permit the possibility that a teacher might actively "recruit" for some position or other in *teaching* religion.

Finally, temperance (i.e., refraining from using alcoholic beverages) as a "public policy" issue for Christians is salient for only three out of ten respondents.

Summary

When the participants in this study "look at the church," they tend to give a picture of a group of "church supporters" who are seeking personal help in a general area of faith and devotion. They are a group that appears to be quite contented with what they are receiving from the congregation to which they belong, and they do not wish to have the church become too involved in any specific area of "outreach" or public policy.

The study thus far supports the generalizations which have become so familiar in previous research work. The church as represented in this sample appears to be "captive" to the more "privatized" concerns of home and family life. Based on our findings in Part 1 which showed our sample population to be upper-middle class in composition and now our findings which show them to be men who prefer a more privatized and "liberal-positive" gospel, it would be quite easy to write a summary of the study stressing the same points made by previous researchers and essayists. The church as represented in this sample *is* captive to the American way of life. However, we are not finished with the analysis, for such dominant patterns may well tend to "gloss over" or "submerge" a more profound understanding of the multiple factors involved in the religious life of contemporary men.

We will, in the next chapter, take a number of the responses which have just been summarized and develop a set of four indices of church participation. Since the responses were rarely if ever unanimous in any of the questions, it becomes important to see whether there is a variety of "styles" present among the church participants which will help to understand the full "meaning" of church participation.

Chapter 5–A Typology of Church Participation

Introduction

As was shown in chapter 1, a great deal of the most productive research in the sociology of religion has been dependent on differentiating between a variety of "types" of church participation. Any person who reflects seriously upon the participation patterns of laymen in American churches realizes that not all participants in any particular congregation are drawn with the same intensity into any particular aspect of the life of that congregation. Some are more drawn to various organizations, some are more interested in the study of the meaning of the Christian faith, some find their religion to be most meaningful in terms of personal devotional life, while others would feel that the traditional doctrines of the church are at the "heart" of Christianity.

These differences are not, of course, easily separated one from the other. Indeed it is likely that there is a good deal of overlapping between "types," but nevertheless it is possible to see tendencies in one direction or the other among parishioners. It is important to stress that these "types" or "styles" are not necessarily conscious types from the point of view of the parishioners themselves. There may well be some degree of "consciousness" about the styles, for it is common to refer to people as "pillars" of the congregation (probably referring mostly to institutional activists). Moreover some parishioners may think disparagingly about fellow churchmen who "do not seem to really *believe*

65

in Christianity." But on the whole we suspect that most parishioners are fairly unreflective about the "style" which their own church participation takes.

Though researchers interested in this problem have tended to vary the number of "types" which they choose to "operationalize" (and have changed the terminology from time to time in identifying the types),[1] certain types have continued to prove meaningful for research purposes. Four types have been chosen for inclusion in this research. As they are described below, comparisons will be made from time to time to similar categories used by others.

In this chapter we are not concerned to explore any theories of "why" people tend to emphasize one "style" of church participation in preference to any other. In chapter 6, we will relate the "independent" factors to the four styles in the effort to see what are the characteristics of respondents who choose each of the types. Relationships will then make some reflection possible in terms of "why" people choose the various types. Certain overall assertions of theory will then assist in the ordering of the remaining sections of the volume.

Index of Organizational Involvement (IOI)

Lenski[2] defined "associational" involvement in terms of a person who either (1) attended the worship service of his church every week or (2) attended worship at least two times a month *and* attended at least one church-related group each month. Glock,[3] on the other hand, made a distinction between "ritual" involvement and "organizational" involvement. The first referred to attendance at the worship service or the service of Holy Communion while the second referred to participation in church-related organizations. There was a high degree of correlation found between Glock's two types of involvement.

Given the fact that the denomination being studied here stands broadly within the "free church" tradition and has had a historical aversion toward "ritual," it was decided that the definition of this facet of church participation should not seek to make a distinction between "ritual" and "organization." Indeed, within the Congregational tradition it was historically the case that worship services were often called "church meetings," the church building was referred to as a "meeting house," and it was not at all uncommon either in the past (or even now) to have congregational business meetings following the Sunday worship service.

Our purpose in this particular dimension of church participation was to find a measure of involvement which would help us locate those persons who were the most ardent supporters of what broadly might be called the "organizational activities" of the institutional church. Church attendance would not be a sufficient measure, since in every congregation there are regular attenders who are on the periphery of the "life" of the institutional church. Likewise, there are congregations which elect or appoint church officers from among "prominent" public figures who may hold membership in the church but are infrequent in their church attendance. Therefore, an index was devised which took into account the wide range of activities which are a part of the life of typical congregations. Nine different activities or responses on the questionnaire were selected as indicative of organizational participation: (1) attendance at worship services two or more times per month, (2) contribution of at least $2 per week to the church budget, (3) membership in men's or women's groups, (4) attendance at study groups or Sunday school classes, (5) attendance at family nights, (6) membership in a social action group in the church, (7) membership in some church board or committee, (8) attendance at church retreats or participation in a church prayer group, and (9) membership in two or more church organizations. Those persons who scored zero or one from among the nine options were labeled as "low" in the index of organizational involvement (IOI); those with scores of two, three or four were labeled "moderately low"; scores of five, six, or seven were labeled "moderately high"; and scores of eight or nine were considered to be "high" in organizational involvement. Table 5-A indicates the distribution of respondents in terms of this index.

TABLE 5-A: Index of Organizational Involvement (IOI)

Organizational involvement	N	%
Low (0–1)	2264	27
Moderately low (2–4)	2938	34
Moderately high (5–7)	2475	29
High (8–9)	872	10
Total	8549	100

Index of Religious Knowledge (IRK)

Schroeder and Obenhaus[4] found in their study that church participants were generally very uninformed at the cognitive level about their Christianity. That is, when questions were asked about the meaning of certain biblical stories or theological doctrines, the respondents were unable, for the most part, to give a great deal of content to how they understood these stories or doctrines. Therefore at the outset it was determined that any questions used to evaluate religious knowledge would necessarily be of a very limited and uncomplicated form. We wanted to avoid any kind of theological sophistication in the responses and confine ourselves to relatively simple facts which a church participant might be expected to know about Christianity. We determined to test knowledge and not find an "intellectual" orientation in the sense in which Glock used the term in his study[5] of Episcopalians. In that case he defined "intellectual" orientation in terms of whether the respondent read church periodicals, sought help from religious literature in times of crisis, and felt that the church has been a major influence on his ideas. Earlier, Glock had defined the "intellectual" dimension of religion closer to the definition we are using.[6]

The response to three questions in the questionnaire[7] were used to construct the Index of Religious Knowledge (IRK). One question was biblical, one church historical, and one contemporary. The biblical question asked the respondent to check which of the books listed could be found in the Old Testament; the second asked him to check which of the leaders listed were associated with the Protestant Reformation; and the third asked him to check which of the listed denominations had bishops in their organizational structure. There were nine correct answers in the three questions, and the respondents were listed according to the number of correct answers they checked, (wrong answers being subtracted from correct answers). A final score of 0 or 1 gave the respondent a "low" on the index, a score of two to four merited a "moderately low" index, five to seven was listed as "moderately high," and those who had a score of eight or nine were given a "high" Index of Religious Knowledge. The distribution of respondents into the various categories is found in Table 5-B.

TABLE 5-B: Index of Religious Knowledge (IRK)

Religious knowledge	N	%
Low (0–1)	1052	12
Moderately low (2–4)	2960	35
Moderately high (5–7)	3233	38
High (8–9)	1304	15
Total	8549	100

Index of Devotional Orientation (IDO)

Most conceptions of religion include a recognition that religion does have a highly personal "dimension" which deals with one's feelings of relationship with some "ultimate" aspect of reality. This "inner" dimension of religion is not exactly the same as earlier references to the "privatized" character of contemporary American religion. The use of "privatized" implies that the institutional church (and its supporters) has tended to focus concern upon family life, interpersonal relationships, and personal ethics as opposed to concern for social issues, institutional relationships, and social ethics. It *may* be that the "innerpersonal" character of religion does tend to make religious men more sensitive to "privatized" issues, but that does not seem to be a logical necessity. One's feelings of "personal" relationship with the "ultimate" basis of all reality could, at least logically, cause one to be concerned about social issues as well as "privatized" issues. Old Testament prophets, for example, often had a very personal sense of relationship to God and God's "speaking" to and through them, and they addressed their concerns to both social and "privatized" issues.

The problem of "operationalizing" this more "inner" dimension of religious life is a difficult issue for sociologists of religion. If we want to include at least some measure of this "solitary" character of religion in a typology, how do we "measure" it? We could, as some have done, ask questions like "How important is prayer in your life?" or "How often do you pray privately?"[8] It was decided, however, for this study that "indirect" questions relating to "devotional" life would be asked rather than using such direct questions. The opinion of the authors is that such an approach may be more defensible in this area of religion.

The responses of the survey population to three questions were used to construct an Index of Devotional Orientation (IDO). One question asked the respondent to be critical of a number of facets of congregational life.[9] Among other things, he was asked whether or not he felt churches in general had done enough to "foster the devotional life." If he answered that the churches have not done enough to foster the devotional life, the respondent was given one point toward his IDO score. Another question asked him about a number of ways of defining who is and who is not a Christian.[10] One part of that question defined a Christian as one who "prays and reads the Bible daily." If the respondent said that such activity was "absolutely necessary" in defining a Christian he was given one point toward his IDO score. The third measure used in this index was the response to a question dealing with the importance of a number of church activities,[11] one such activity being "prayer meeting." If the respondent indicated that he felt such programs were "very important" he was given a point toward his eventual IDO score.

On the basis of these three questions, the survey population was grouped into the four IDO categories: "Low" (no points), "Moderately low" (one point), "Moderately high" (two points), and "High" (three points). The distribution of the sample population is shown in Table 5-C.

TABLE 5-C: Index of Devotional Orientation (IDO)

Devotional orientation	N	%
Low (0)	3949	46
Moderately low (1)	2697	32
Moderately high (2)	1270	15
High (3)	633	7
Total	8549	100

Index of Belief Orientation (IBO)

The contemporary period of history is one in which there is a great deal of debate within the church on the meaning of traditional Christian doctrine. Leaders in the church such as Bishop John Robinson in England and Bishop James Pike in America have written and preached a form of Christian belief which is considered by many to be heretical. Professors such as William Hamilton, Thomas Altizer, and Harvey Cox have popularized a variety of theological argument which is appealing to many and deeply criticized by others. One can assume, with a fair degree of certainty, that the parishioners represented in our study have been subjected to a wide range of theological interpretations from the pulpits of their churches and from the various forms of mass media. Indeed, the options "available" to the contemporary Christian make it a difficult question to decide how to frame questions on belief. Phrases like "the death of God" and "secular Christianity" have nuances of meaning which one suspects are lost by most laymen who have heard the terms used.

It is possible, of course, to enunciate several traditional Christian statements which represent a type of "belief" which may or may not have been accepted by a wide cross section of Christians at an earlier point in history. These statements have nuances of meaning which are debated by theologians and these nuances may also be lost by most laymen, but the statements have the advantage of more familiarity among a cross section of churchmen. Thus one could expect most churchmen to at least have an opinion with respect to them. It has been shown that by using these more traditional Christian statements one can order the main denominations along a "conservative-liberal" continuum.[12] However, it has also been shown that *within* a particular denomination there is a variation along the same kind of continuum.[13]

In the present study it was decided that the use of relatively traditional theological statements would make it possible to construct an index of "belief" which might differentiate groups within the survey population which were different from the groups being identified by the other church participation indices. As was seen in chapter 4 (Table 4-D, and the Appendix, question 24), the majority of our respondents considered nine of the twelve statements used to be true. As was pointed out there, the majority rejected only the statements which stressed sin and judgment.

From these twelve options, the Index of Belief Orientation (IBO) was constructed. Persons who selected three or fewer beliefs as "true" were labeled "low" in the IBO; those who selected four, five, or six statements as "true" were designated "moderately low" on the IBO; the designation "moderately high" was applied to those selecting seven, eight, or nine statements as "true"; and persons who selected ten, eleven, or twelve of the statements as being "true" were considered to be "high" believers. The distribution of the sample population is shown in Table 5-D.

TABLE 5-D: Index of Belief Orientation (IBO)

Belief orientation	N	%
Low (0–3)	1978	23
Moderately low (4–6)	1717	20
Moderately high (7–9)	2633	31
High (10–12)	2221	26
Total	8549	100

With respect to such an index and the way in which it was constructed, it should be emphasized that the index is simply an operational definition of "belief" and the authors recognize that those persons with a low IBO may of course be strong "believers" in a much different interpretation of Christianity than what has been used in these questions. We suspect that if the clergy of the denomination were sampled, many would have a low or moderately low IBO. This does not necessarily mean that they would be "unbelievers," *except* in terms of such very particularized statements of the Christian faith.

The Interrelation of Church Participation Indices

Having established some operational measures of a variety of styles of church participation, it is important to know the extent to which there is any interrelationship between the styles. Each of the variables was related to the other variables in turn, and of the six possible interrelations, all were found to be of a positive type. That is, increasing participation on any one of the variables would imply increasing participation on any of the other variables. Such a finding is hardly surprising, since it was suggested earlier that there was "overlapping" of types and it was argued that the types are probably unconscious for most people. However, the mere fact of positive relationships being found between all of the four variables does not imply that they are measuring the same thing. It would be a temptation to develop a "composite" index since there is such interrelationship. However, as will be seen later, the different styles of participation are correlated in different ways with attitudes on a variety of subjects. They are also correlated differently with the independent variables.

The degree of interrelationship varies between the various indices, ant they can be ranked in terms of the amount of interrelationship (as tested by the application of the chi-square test). The highest correlation was found between Belief Orientation and Devotional Orientation and the lowest correlation was found between Belief Orientation and Religious Knowledge. The order of degree of correlation from highest to lowest was:

Belief Orientation and Devotional Orientation (Table 5-E)
Organizational Involvement and Religious Knowledge
Organizational Involvement and Devotional Orientation
Religious Knowledge and Devotional Orientation
Organizational Involvement and Belief Orientation
Religious Knowledge and Belief Orientation (Table 5-F)

We are now in a position to examine the relationship between the independent factors and the church participation indices.

TABLE 5-E: Interrelation Between Belief Orientation and Devotional Orientation Indices in Percent of Respondents

Index of Belief Orientation	Low	Mod. Low	Mod. High	High	Total
Low	73.0	21.4	4.6	1.0	100
Moderately low	53.1	33.8	9.4	3.7	100
Moderately high	39.8	35.5	17.2	7.5	100
High	24.6	34.2	25.3	15.9	100
Total Sample	46.2	31.5	14.9	7.4	100

(Index of Devotional Orientation across columns)

TABLE 5-F: Interrelation Between Religious Knowledge and Belief Orientation Indices in Percent of Respondents

Index of Religious Knowledge	Index of Belief Orientation				
	Low	Mod. Low	Mod. High	High	Total
Low	30.4	20.8	30.4	18.3	100
Moderately low	24.5	19.6	31.7	24.2	100
Moderately high	20.7	19.7	30.5	29.1	100
High	20.2	21.6	29.8	28.3	100
Total Sample	23.1	20.1	30.8	26.0	100

Chapter 6–Some Factors Affecting Church Participation

Introduction

From the foregoing analysis, it is apparent that our survey population manifests most of the characteristics which we have been led to expect from previous research and analysis. The population is an upper-middle class group which is oriented to its denomination in a somewhat uncritical way, supportive of dominant American values cast in a "theological" framework. They are "active" both in the social order and in the church, they prefer theological statements which stress God's love and care for them rather than those statements which stress man's "sin" or God's "judgment," and they prefer the church to concern itself with those aspects of life which center in home and family rather than in more "public" issues.

Such general summary statements, true as they are, tend to submerge the differences which exist within the survey population. All parishioners in the sample were not upper-middle class, all of them did not prove to be uncritical of the church and its programs, they were not all active in the social order and/or the church. Some indicated acceptance of theological statements stressing sin and judgment, and there were those who felt that the church should have a concern for the more "public" issues of life. What patterns of relationship can one find between the various social factors used to describe the survey population and the church participation indices which were used to differentiate the various ways people relate to the church? One of the most common errors in statistical analysis of any set of responses to survey research is to assume that because one finds dominant pattern manifest in two different sets of variables there must be a positive correlation between the two variables. This assumption could be applied to the present research by arguing that one would expect all variables relating to social class to correlate positively with all of the church participation variables. Each of the church participation variables correlated positively with the other three such variables, and they all were developed for a basically upper-middle class group of fairly "active" church participants.

There is a certain kind of logic in such an argument, but it needs to be tested by the empirical data. This chapter is just such a test. Here we will relate each of the major independent variables in turn to the indices of church participation, in order to find whether or not we have any "deviant" cases of relationship. Following such an analysis, we will be in a better position to make predictions about how both the independent variables and the church participation indices are likely to be related to some of the social issues which were a part of the survey research.

It was noted earlier (chapter 1), that by combining the first and second hypotheses of this study, we could expect that "privileged social groups will choose organizational and religious knowledge orientations to religion, while socially deprived groups will choose belief and devotional orientations." This expectation grew out of previous research that tended to show that socially privileged groups are oriented toward religion in a way related to cultural values while socially deprived groups prefer religion that acts in some way as a form of "compensation" for the social deprivation. What is interesting to note at this point in the study is that *all four* types of orientation correlated *with each other*. There could be several explanations for this: (1) the questions chosen for the IDO and the IBO in this study do not "really" measure this type of "compensatory" religion, (2) *within* a single denomination these differences between the socially deprived and the socially privileged are not so severe as they are *between* denominations,[1] or (3) the correlations are submerging differences which are in fact still present. Only empirical examination will help to make a choice between these options.

To assist in the presentation of the findings, we will continue to use the combined hypothesis mentioned above and will consider each of the variables as a form of social privilege or social deprivation whenever possible. Since Argyle[2] both summarized much of the research in the twentieth century on factors affecting religious behavior and also made use of the social privilege-deprivation theory, his work will form the particular "backdrop" for comparative purposes in this chapter.[3]

Age

1. The Church Participation Indices

In summarizing a number of studies relating age and church participation, Argyle commented, "There is a sharp decline in all aspects of religious activity (following an interest in religion early in life), the years 30-35 being the lowest point in the life cycle. There is a steady increase from about 35 until old age, which is marked by widespread belief in God and the afterlife."[4] Notice that the summary statement utilizes both religious "activity" and religious "belief." Are they both lowest at 30-35 and highest at 65 and over?

In the present study, support was found for both sentences in the above summary statement but there is *a difference* between the pattern for "activity" and the pattern for "belief." Table 6-A shows the percentage of respondents having a "high" or a "moderately high" scores on each of the indices by age-group. Notice that religious "activity" (IOI)

TABLE 6-A: Age Related to the Church Participation Indices

Age-groups	N = 8549	Organizational Involvement	Religious Knowledge	Devotional Orientation	Belief Orientation
Under 20	448	36	43	21	49
20-34 years	1719	29	46	20	57
35-49 years	2953	46	53	22	55
50-64 years	2149	42	57	24	58
65 years and over	1242	36	59	24	61
Nonresponses on Age	38	24	13	26	34

Percent Scoring High or Moderately High on Index of:

77

does have its lowest point at ages 20-35, (as does the Index of Devotional Orientation), but its highest point is for the group aged 35-49, not for those over 65. As Argyle also suggested, "belief" (IBO) does have its highest point among the oldest group, but its lowest point is *not* among the 20-34-year-olds. In fact, each of the indices appears to have a somewhat different relationship to age. Strangely enough, the Index of Religious Knowledge has the clearest relationship. The percentage of respondents with a high or moderately high IRK increases with each age-group. Devotional orientation appears to be the least clearly related to age of all of the indices. There is some decline in the age-group 20-34 but otherwise it appears to have a slight increase with each age-group. Belief appears to be a function of age, older people believing more, except for the slight decline among the 35-49-year-olds (that group with the highest IOI scores!).

In summary, we could argue that three of the indices tend to be a function of age (IRK, IDO, and IBO), while the fourth index is not (IOI). Organizational involvement reaches its peak in that age-group which is in some sense in the "prime of life." Those who are 35-49 have probably established themselves in their occupations, they have begun to accumulate possessions, they are raising their families, and they have not yet experienced the "after 50" decline.

Using phrases like "prime of life" implies that in some sense one can relate "social privilege and deprivation" to age. If America is a "youth-oriented" culture, as many social commentators have argued, then older people *are* deprived of a form of status by our culture. Our original "combined" hypothesis would have predicted our findings in terms of three of the indices (IOI, IBO, and IDO), but the Index of Religious Knowledge becomes a "deviant" case. Is religious knowledge somehow different from knowledge in general so that it is not a "cultural value" in the same way as other knowledge? Is it in some way related to "belief" so that one who "believes" in religion also tends to "know" about it?[5]

At the moment, one deviant case is not enough to completely abandon the hypothesis which "explains" most of the findings. We simply must note that the IRK may be "misplaced" in expecting it to be related to social privilege, or it may be that age is in some way a special factor which for unknown reasons is related to the IRK in a "deviant" way. Further empirical evidence is necessary before deciding between these alternative explanations of the findings.

The reader will recall that in chapter 4 a number of questions relating to church attitudes and behavior were asked (beyond those utilized for the four church participation indices). These questions were grouped according to four types: (1) help desired from the church, (2) critique of the church, (3) acceptance of traditional beliefs and practices, and (4) relation of the church and public policy. For each of the independent variables treated in the present chapter, we will examine how the variable tended to affect response to the first three of these types of church attitudes. (The effect of the independent variables upon issues of "church and public policy" will be treated in Part 3, especially in chapter 8.) We turn now, to an examination of age as it is related to each of the three types of church attitudes.

2. Help Desired from the Church

In terms of the "help desired" from the church, age did have a significant relation to both the reasons for joining the church (question 5) and in terms of asking for help from the church (question 8). Without exception, every reason for joining the church and every kind of help desired was more likely to be picked by older groups than by younger groups. However, the *order* of preference between the options remained the same for *all* age-groups, almost without exception.[6] On the basis of such a finding we could argue that with an increase in age there is an increase in all types of help being desired from the church, but as age increased the *order of preference* for the various types of help desired does not seem to change. Such a finding fits our social privilege-deprivation hypothesis very well. If one tends to be more "deprived" as one gets older in a youth-oriented culture, one will desire all types of "help" from the church. However, in an "affluent" culture people in all age-groups have a *relative* preference for personal and theologically "positive" help rather than help for "public" or theologically "negative" issues (anxiety, conflict, etc.).

3. Critique of the Church

Given the above findings on how age is related to "help desired" from the church, the findings on the relationship between age and "church critique" are quite predictable. When asked how much help they had actually received from the church (question 23), younger people indicated they had received less help than did the older age-groups. But, as in the case with "help desired," age did not tend to affect the relative position of each option within any age-group. That is, for all age-groups, the same options tended to appear more frequently. For example, all age-groups indicated they had received *more* help on "strengthening my faith and devotion" than they had on "being aware of the needs of others in my community," but the older the age-group, the more frequently both options were chosen. When asked to tell where they felt the church "had not done enough" (question 13), the different age groupings made almost no difference at all in either the ordering of the responses or the frequency of response. There were two notable exceptions to this general rule: (1) young people were more likely than older people to say that the church had not done enough "working for racial justice and equality" and (2) older people were more likely to say the church had not done enough "caring for the needs of older people."

Older people tended to find all parts of the worship service more helpful than did younger persons (question 20), but again the relative position of most helpful and least helpful parts of the service did not change between the different age groupings.

Older people were also more likely to feel that all of the various church programs were more important than younger people (question 12), except in the case of "retreats" and "social action groups." Younger people were more likely to prefer those two particular types of program than were older people. Younger age-groups put "women's groups" and "men's groups" at the bottom of their lists, while older age-groups tended to put these two types of activities very high in importance.

These findings fit general patterns already described in terms of the privilege-deprivation hypothesis we are using to organize the empirical data, except that for the first time we have emerging a special kind of critique among the younger age-groups, those under 35 years of age. These respondents have indicated some desire for the church to take a more active role in "public" issues. More data than these few isolated illustrations will be needed before any attempt is made to find a place for such findings through elaboration on our basic hypotheses.

4. Acceptance of Traditional Beliefs and Practices

We already know from relating age to the IBO that younger age-groups tend to be less believing than older age-groups (Table 5-A). The question here is whether young people tend to prefer *certain* beliefs more often than older people. The use of an index will submerge such differences.

When age was related to the responses on questions 19 and 24 (how one "defines" a Christian and what traditional theological statements are believed to be "true"), it was found that every option on both questions was more likely to be accepted by older groups than younger groups. Furthermore the relative position of the various options in terms of frequency of choice did not change from age-group to age-group.

5. Summary

If we consider that older people are in some sense socially deprived in contemporary American culture, then the empirical data from this survey population supports the hypothesis that the socially deprived identify with the church through more acceptance of traditional Christian beliefs and a more "devotional" orientation to the church. Older respondents scored higher on both the IBO and the IDO, they desired more help from the church, and they were less critical of it. Those in the prime of life (the socially privileged) are more likely to be organizationally oriented toward the church.

Two divergent patterns emerged which are more difficult to account for through our operating hypothesis, that is: (1) why did the older people manifest higher scores on the Index of Religious Knowledge and (2) why did the younger age-groups tend to prefer the church to be more involved in public issues? Either these "divergent" findings will prove to be too isolated to matter to the general hypothesis, or else some elaboration of the hypothesis may become necessary later in the study. One probable explanation for these two divergent patterns is to point to "epochal" shifts in a culture. Older people were raised in a less secular era, and younger people have been raised in a time when the culture has become very conscious of its most fundamental social problems.

Sex

1. The Church Participation Indices

It will be remembered from the general description of the survey population that there was a larger percentage of female respondents than male. Is it also true that women score higher on all of the church participation indices than men? The findings which Argyle reviewed would lead us to expect that such would be the case. He said, after reviewing a number of studies, "Women are more religious than men on all criteria, particularly for private prayer, also for membership, attendance and attitudes, while differences in beliefs are small."[7]

In Table 6-B, the respondents' sex has been related to index scores of "high" or "moderately high" for the four church participation indices. Females have higher index scores on three of the indices (IBO, IRK

TABLE 6-B: Sex Related to the Church Participation Indices

Sex	N = 8549	Organizational Involvement	Religious Knowledge	Devotional Orientation	Belief Orientation
Male	3364	41	48	18	50
Female	5175	38	56	25	62
Nonresponses	10	0	0	30	30

Percent Scoring High or Moderately High on Index of:

and IDO—the same three on which older people tended to score more highly), while on the Index of Organizational Involvement they score just slightly below the males. How can this seeming discrepancy between Argyle's summary and the present study be explained? There is in fact no discrepancy, for he speaks of "membership" and "attendance" as the measures of what has been called "organizational involvement" in this study. The IOI is simply more inclusive than membership and attendance (in our study women *were* higher in both membership and attendance at Sunday worship, but they were not higher in the IOI where there are nine factors involved and not just the two).

What about the findings with respect to the operating hypothesis of privilege-deprivation and church participation then? In spite of all of the progress which has been made in recent generations toward "equality" for females, it would need to be said that females still suffer relative social "deprivation" when compared with males. Congress in recent years felt it necessary to include "sex" as a category where it was forbidden to discriminate in employment. It is difficult for women to gain certain kinds of prestige positions (Nixon for example had no women in his first cabinet appointments), and certain prestige colleges and universities are only slowly beginning to recognize the place of women in their student bodies. Thus it could be argued that our data follows the "expected" hypothetical pattern in the case of three indices, with women higher in the IBO and IDO ("compensatory" types of participation) and lower in the IOI (a form of identification mirroring the social values). As in the case of age, the pattern found between sex and the IRK does not follow the hypothesis. Again, we must ask whether it was wrong to assume that religious knowledge would be associated with social privilege, or whether some elaboration of the overly simplified hypothesis is necessary to explain this "deviant" finding.[8]

In summary it should be stressed that the differences found above are all of a relatively slight nature (the maximum difference in percentage points being 12 in the IBO). It appears that women are more active in churches in general, *but* once people are active, the sex differences are modified. The slight differences found are not very significant in themselves, but may become significant when the patterns are compared with other patterns found in the study.

2. Help Desired from the Church

Of the twelve options given in question 5 as reasons for joining the church, not a single one was picked more often by men than by women. The women considered all of the reasons to be more important than did the men. Also in the case of types of help desired from the church (question 8), women again picked every option more often than men. It is interesting however that the difference in frequency of choice is greatest (22 percentage points) in the case of the option "meeting my personal problems of anxiety, conflict, etc." and is least (5 percentage points) in the case of the option "work for justice in my community and in my world." The "deprived" are more likely to want help in all areas, but by comparison with the "privileged" do they want more help in personal problems than in social issues? Again, the finding is too isolated at this point to make very much of it, but will it combine with other findings in similar patterns or not?

3. Critique of the Church

In all options of question 23 (asking the respondents where they had actually received help from the church) women were more likely than men to say they had received help. The greatest difference came in the option "Know of God's love and care for me" (16 percentage points difference), and strangely enough the least difference was in "helping me to raise my children properly" (5 percentage points difference).

When respondents were asked to tell where they thought the church had "not done enough" (question 13), women picked five of the options more often, and men picked four of the options more often. Those options that were picked more often by men, and those that were picked by women do not follow any discernible pattern. In fact the differences were very slight indeed (the greatest difference being under six percentage points).

Women found all parts of the worship service to be more helpful than men, and they were more likely than men to indicate that they thought all types of church programs were important. The order of priority given to parts of the worship service and to the various church programs remained virtually unchanged for men and women.

This is simply more evidence for the fact that women are less critical of the church than men.

4. Acceptance of Traditional Beliefs and Practices

In defining a Christian (question 19), women picked all of the options more frequently than men with one exception (being active church members). With this same exception, the order of priority of the various options remained unchanged for men and women. It is interesting that this one exception fits with our finding that the only index in which women were lower than men was the IOI index. The sex differences in behavior are thus matched by differences in attitude.

We already know that women are higher "believers" than men based on the IBO, but do they differ in terms of which beliefs they prefer? The answer is no. The order of preference given to all of the beliefs remained unchanged when sex was held constant, and women simply tended to prefer *all* beliefs more frequently than men (there was one exception, they were less likely to believe that "hell is a just punishment for sinners," but since that was the least believed option for both males and females it did not affect the order of preference of beliefs).

5. Summary

From relating sex to church participation indices and attitudes we have found that sex differences are quite modest, but when they do occur they tend to support the hypothesis of privilege-deprivation with which we are working. The IRK remains a difficult variable to fit into the hypothesis.

Educational Achievement

1. The Church Participation Indices

Research on religious behavior has tended to collapse the distinction between class and status which was noted earlier. The reason for this is quite clear since there is so much interrelationship between the two types of measure for social privilege. In this study, we are stressing educational achievement as more "status" oriented, while we use the ISEC (income and occupation) as the more "class" oriented variable.

Argyle pointed out that differences one finds in religious behavior based on educational criteria are likely to be confused with differences due to social class or intelligence.[9] However he also summarized the effect of education by saying, "American students show a temporary decline in religious activity during the middle years of college, (but) there is little overall effect of education as such."[10]

Since status and class are but different forms of social privilege, our expectation based on our working hypothesis would be that both education and the ISEC would be positively correlated with the IOI and the IRK, and they would be negatively correlated with the IDO and IBO. Table 6-C shows that our expectation, with respect to education at least, was fulfilled. Even the Index of Religious Knowledge followed "expected" patterns for the variable of educational achievement. It is interesting to note that of the two "positive" correlations, the correlation between education and the IRK is stronger than between education and the IOI. Likewise in the two "negative" correlations one is much stronger than the other (education and the IBO stronger than education and the IDO). Will this pattern of "relative strength" be the same for "class" as for this measure of "status"?

TABLE 6-C: Educational Achievement Related to the Church Participation Indices

Educational Achievement	N = 8549	Organizational Involvement	Religious Knowledge	Devotional Orientation	Belief Orientation
8th grade or less	936	32	45	28	69
9th-12th grade	2158	35	43	25	69
Attended or graduated from trade school	952	41	48	25	68
Attended or graduated from college	2618	41	58	19	50
Post-college or graduate work	1774	45	67	19	39
Nonresponses	111	23	26	24	53

Percent Scoring High or Moderately High on Index of:

The findings concerning education and the indices are very important for this study. Argyle said that there was *no* particular influence of education one way or the other, and others have argued that increased education means a *lower* relationship to the church.[11] Our data states that education means a difference in "style" of participation, not an "overall" decline.

2. Help Desired from the Church

When educational achievement was held constant in relation to the reasons given for joining the church (question 5), the order of preference among the reasons given did not alter significantly, but there was a tendency for persons with more education to indicate less importance being attached to *all* of the reasons than did the persons with less education.

In terms of types of help desired from the church (question 8), the people with more formal education tended to desire less help of all types and again, the order of preference did not change very much with different amounts of formal education.

3. Critique of the Church

People with more education not only desired less help from the church, they also indicated that they had received less help (question 23). Furthermore, when the respondents were asked to tell where the church had "not done enough," (question 13) those with more education tended to choose every option more often than did the people with less education. As we have so often found however, the order of preference between the options did not change for the various educational groups in either question.

People with less education were more likely to find all parts of the worship service more helpful than were people with more education (question 20), there being only one exception to this generalization. The more educated the respondent was, the more likely he was to find "music other than hymns" to be helpful.

Education appears to have little influence on the relative importance attached to various types of church programming (question 12), with one exception. Social action groups are likely to be more highly valued by the respondents with more formal education.

4. Acceptance of Traditional Beliefs and Practices

All definitions of a Christian were seen to be less necessary the more education one had, except for the one option in question 19 which stated "Christians are those who work for social justice." In that case, the more education the respondent had, the more likely it was to be seen as being "absolutely necessary." All of the "beliefs" given in question 24 were less likely to be seen as "true" the more education one had, however, the differences were less among the more "preferred" beliefs than they were among the less frequently chosen beliefs. For example, for the most frequently chosen belief (see Table 4-D), namely "All men are equal in the sight of God," of those with an eighth-grade education or less 89 percent said this was true, while for those with postgraduate education 83 percent said it was true (a difference of only 6 percentage points). *But* for the least frequently chosen belief (in all educational groupings), "Hell is a just punishment for sinners," 37 percent of those with an eighth-grade education or less thought this was true while only 9 percent of those with postgraduate education thought this was true (a difference of 28 percentage points).

5. Summary

Education is the first "independent" variable which has fully matched expectations in terms of relating to the four church participation indices in the "expected" way. People with more education are more likely to be oriented toward the church in terms of organizational involvement and religious knowledge. However, they are less likely to be oriented toward traditional beliefs or devotional life, less likely to expect or receive help from the church, and less likely to feel the various church programs are as important as do the people with less education.

In two instances we had slight deviations from these generalizations which might prove of interest in later analysis. People with more education valued social action groups more highly and they were more likely to feel that a Christian should work for social justice.

Socio-Economic Class

1. The Church Participation Indices

Relating the respondents' scores on the Index of Socio-Economic Class to their scores on the church participation indices (Table 6-D) indicates that those with higher "class" standing are more oriented toward organizational involvement and religious knowledge, while those with lower "class" position are more likely to be oriented toward the church in terms of devotional life and traditional beliefs. This pattern is the same as was found for education, and it indicates the

TABLE 6-D: Index of Socio-Economic Class Related to the Church Participation Indices

ISEC Category — Percent Scoring High or Moderately High on Index of:

	N = 8549	Organizational Involvement	Religious Knowledge	Devotional Orientation	Belief Orientation
Low	1085	26	46	28	65
Moderately low	2483	33	46	27	70
Moderately high	2298	41	53	22	58
High	2683	49	62	17	40

high degree of overlap between the two variables, giving added support to our operating hypothesis of social privilege and deprivation as it relates to church participation.

However, notice that there is a difference between education and the ISEC in terms of which of the two "positive" church participation indices is affected to a higher degree. Education was more strongly related to religious knowledge while the ISEC is more strongly related to organizational involvement. The question is whether this is simply an "oddity" of statistical analysis, or is it a "clue" to further elaboration of our basic hypothesis which may be necessary?

2. Help Desired from the Church

Those with higher social class were less likely to say that *any* of the reasons for joining the church (question 5) were "very important," but relative order of choice for the options remained unchanged for the various ISEC categories.

The same pattern of relationship held between ISEC scores and the "help desired from the church" (question 8).

3. Critique of the Church

Those with a higher social class not only desired less help from the church, they also indicated they had received less help (question 23). Furthermore when they were asked to tell where the church "had not done enough" (question 13), the respondents with higher social class tended to choose every option more often than did the people with a lower social class. The order of priority, however, remained relatively unchanged between the various social class groupings.

People of lower social class were likely to find all elements of the worship service (question 20) more helpful than were those of higher social class groupings. Again the order of "preferred" elements of the worship service remains relatively unchanged for the different social class groupings.

Social class seems to have less influence on opinions about the various types of church programming (question 12), though there is a tendency for higher social class groupings to see less importance in all of the church programs. This difference is not a marked one. Again the order of "preferred" programs remains relatively unchanged for the various class groupings.

Those of higher social class groupings are thus more likely to be less approving of the church and its programs, but they have similar "orders of preference" to those of lower class groupings.

4. Acceptance of Traditional Beliefs and Practices

All definitions of a Christian (question 19) were seen to be less necessary by those of higher social class groupings, but there was one noticeable shift of order of preference. For the lowest social class grouping, "working for social justice" was the eighth "most necessary" element, while for the highest social class grouping the same option was the third most frequently chosen.

All of the statements of theological doctrine (question 24) were less frequently believed by the higher social class groupings, and there was no significant change in order of preference. As was the case for education, there was less difference between the social class groupings on the more "preferred" beliefs than there was on the least "preferred" beliefs.

5. Summary

Social class tends to follow a very similar pattern to that followed by education when it is applied to attitudes toward the church. The only real difference between the two variables is that people of high social class are more likely to be oriented toward the church through organizational involvement, while those with higher education have a stronger correlation with the Index of Religious Knowledge. Also there was the slight indication that those of higher social class put more emphasis on "working for social justice."

Rural-Urban Differentiation

1. The Church Participation Indices

From the description of the sampling plan employed, it will be remembered that one of the "purposive" elements in that design was the concern for rural-urban differentiation. For purposes of appraising the significance of this criterion, the respondents were grouped in the following ways: (A) residents in communities of under 10,000 population, (B) residents in communities of 10,000-49,999 population, (C) residents in "Great Plains" communities of over 50,000 population and (D) those respondents residing in the seven "metropolitan" communities mentioned earlier.

What "prediction" of results from such a grouping could be assumed? Argyle pointed out that the studies he surveyed indicated less religious activity in cities than in more rural areas.[12] However, he also notes that this variable is a difficult one with which to work since it might or might not be "causal." He suggests that the difference may simply be one of "culture lag" with more rural areas being "behind" cities in terms of "decline in religious activity," as such areas tend to be "lagging" in other aspects of contemporary life.

In Table 6-E, the rural-urban categories are related to the four church participation indices in terms of those scoring "high" or "moderately high" on the indices. Three of the indices tend to show a decline with urbanization, while the Index of Organizational Involvement shows an increase with urbanization. Thus, one would want to modify Argyle's summary and argue that for church participants, there is a

TABLE 6-E: Rural-Urban Differentiation Related to the Church Participation Indices

Rural-Urban Category	N = 8549	Organizational Involvement	Religious Knowledge	Devotional Orientation	Belief Orientation
0–9,999	1433	30	56	32	70
10,000–49,999	1059	39	55	25	61
Great Plains' Cities	1326	45	55	17	55
Seven City Groups	3444	43	49	23	60

Percent Scoring High or Moderately High on Index of:

decline in devotion, religious knowledge and belief with urbanization, but there is an increase in organizational activity as measured by the IOI.

How do these findings fit with the privilege-deprivation hypothesis? We would need to establish deprivation in some sense with respect to rural-urban difference. If the thesis of Vidich and Bensman is correct,[13] namely that small towns in a mass society tend to have their destiny controlled outside of themselves, we would have to argue that urban people in a predominantly urban culture are more "people of privilege" than are nonurban people. If this is correct, we would expect decline in the IDO and IBO with urbanization, and would expect increases in the IOI and the IRK. Thus our findings again fit with the thesis except for the IRK. Again we have to ask questions about why this particular measure does not "follow expectation." Is the Index measuring something which we have not yet explained, or is the hypothesis deficient?

2. Help Desired from the Church

Of the twelve options given to the respondents concerning the reasons for joining their present church, four of the options indicated a rising importance as the sample became more urban (question 5). These four were the location of the church near the home, whether or not the respondent liked the minister, whether or not he enjoyed the worship service, and whether or not he liked the people he met. Notice that all four of these categories imply needs growing out of the urban situation which stresses secondary relationships. By contrast only one option showed a relative decrease as the sample became more urban, namely whether or not the respondent grew up in the church school.

When the size of city was related to the help desired from churches (question 8), it was found that generally the more rural the sample the more persons expected the church to be helpful in all areas. However the greatest decline in importance with increasing urbanization was in desiring help in working for justice, the only case of a decline of more than 20 percent. This finding gives some support for the hypothesis that the more urban church members feel a need for more privatized religion rather than a religion with social significance. It may also be that racial justice is an "abstraction" in nonurban places, for in another question (no. 49), when rural-urban differences were compared with it, it was found that metropolitan people manifested less acceptance of Negroes than did the rural samples. But, the rural samples manifested less acceptance of American Indians than did the metropolitan sample. People seem to be prejudiced against minority groups with whom they come in contact, not against minorities they do not really "know."

3. Critique of the Church

The respondents' evaluation of how helpful the church has actually been to them (question 23) showed little influence of urbanization except in the matter of being aware of the needs of others. Here the more urban respondents felt the church had been of less help to them than did the more rural respondents.

Urbanization had little effect upon the responses of the sample population to the question dealing with where the church had not done enough work (question 13). Likewise rural-urban differentiation made little difference in the evaluation of the value of the parts of the worship service (question 20). There was also little difference in the evaluation of various church programs (question 12) except that urban respondents were slightly less convinced of the value of the adult church school or prayer meetings and were slightly more convinced of the value of social action groups.

4. Acceptance of Traditional Beliefs and Practices

As would be expected from the findings of the effect of urbanization upon beliefs, it is the case that in nearly all issues where the respondents were asked to tell which beliefs and practices they felt were essential for Christians, the more urban respondents were less likely to consider that the item in question was essential as a definition of who is a Christian (question 19). The same point is true for specific beliefs used in the construction of the Index of Belief Orientation (question 24) except for the first option (belief that all men are created equal). In this case there is an increase with urbanization, and of course this is a basic belief of the "American Creed."

5. Summary

The rural-urban categories proved to have some support for the basic hypothesis with which we are working, except for the case of the IRK. It appeared to have less effect on most of the other questions of church attitudes. When it did have an effect, it seemed to be somewhat contradictory. Urban respondents appear in some instances to be more socially liberal (they are more convinced of the value of social action groups and believe all men are created equal), but in another instance they indicate they do not want more help than do more rural respondents in "working for social justice."

Race

1. The Church Participation Indices

It is difficult to know how to make predictions with respect to findings on the relation between race and the church participation indices. The reason for the difficulty is that nonwhites are certainly socially deprived in the American culture. Yet the Negroes in this sample were found to be Negroes who had a higher socio-economic class position than one would predict for Negroes as a group in America. Thus, would *these* Negroes manifest church participation characteristics associated with their class or their race?

Table 6-F indicates that more often than not they manifested the

TABLE 6-F: Race Related to the Church Participation Indices

	N	Organizational Involvement	Religious Knowledge	Devotional Orientation	Belief Orientation
Total Survey Population	8549	39	53	22	57
Negroes	176	47	37	35	61

Percent Scoring High or Moderately High on Index of:

church participation characteristics of social deprivation (race) rather than social privilege (class). They were higher than the survey population as a whole in the IDO and the IBO and lower in the IRK. However it is interesting that the Index of Organizational Involvement showed an increase rather than a decrease for Negroes. It appears that they "believe" more, are more "devotionally oriented" as well as "organizationally oriented," but they are not as likely to possess religious knowledge. Here, for the first time the IOI does not fit the hypothesis. Is such an orientation due to the class position of these Negroes, or is it simply that the church has had a special place in the life of American Negroes?

2. Help Desired from the Church

The Negroes in the study tended to join the churches for similar reasons to those chosen by the other participants in the study, except that they were far less likely to join "for the sake of their children" and more likely to join because of the church program. They also were far less likely to seek help from the church in raising their children but were much more likely to seek help in working for justice.

3. Critique of the Church and Acceptance of Beliefs

The Negroes were critical of the church in many ways for its failure in the struggle for social justice. They did not feel that they had been given the help they should have been given in this area, they felt that the church as a whole had not done enough in this area, they were much more likely to feel that social action groups were important, and they considered working for social justice to be the third most important characteristic in defining a Christian (68 percent of them chose this option as being "absolutely necessary" while only 36 percent of the sample as a whole considered this characteristic to be "absolutely necessary").

4. Summary

In most matters, other than the issue of social justice, the Negro subsample tended to respond to church participation questions in a manner similar to the rest of the sample. However, given the deviations found in the church participation indices and in the matter of social justice, race will need to be considered later in the study in terms of the consequences of church participation.

Denominational Background

We turn now to the first of three "independent" variables which were noted in chapter 2 as being of a "mixed" variety. They are "givens" from the point of view of the design of this study, but by definition they involve "church participation" in a sense and are therefore different from the other variables which have been discussed above. For each of these three variables, no attempt will be made to relate them to all of the types of church participation questions which have been discussed above. They will be related only to the four main church participation indices of the study.

It will be recalled from chapter 3 that there were six "former" denominations represented in the study which were frequently mentioned by respondents as being the denominations in which they were raised as children. At that time, it was indicated that when the Index of Socio-Economic Class was related to a respondent's former denomination, the denominations could be ordered by social class hierarchy in the following order: Presbyterian, Methodist, Congregational, Baptist, Lutheran and Evangelical and Reformed. (Baptists were almost exactly average for the survey population in the ISEC.) This order differs somewhat from expectation based on other studies of class and denomination, but the differences may well be explained on the basis of the fact that, except for Congregationalists and former Evangelical and Reformed members, the respondents in the various denominations have chosen to change denominations and therefore may be "socially mobile" people.

The list also differs slightly from a list based on "theological camps" which was developed by Glock and Stark. They spoke of a "new denominationalism" in which they grouped a variety of denominations in terms of "theological camps."[14] They spoke of five camps: (1) liberals: Congregationalists, Methodists, and Episcopalians; (2) moderates: Disciples of Christ and Presbyterians; (3) conservatives: American Lutherans and American Baptists; (4) fundamentalists: Missouri Synod Lutherans and Southern Baptists; and (5) Roman Catholics (a special case similar to the "conservatives" but not relevant in the present study). As a result of their groupings, they raised questions concerning the viability of many contemporary mergers between denominations. The issue is interesting here because we are studying a "merged" denomination from "camps" 1 and 3.[15]

In the present study we found more than 500 respondents from only six denominational backgrounds. One of those denominations (the Evangelical and Reformed Church) was not a part of the Glock and Stark analysis. However one would hypothesize that had they been included in the earlier research they would have been similar to Glock and Stark's "conservative" category. This hypothesis is based on the fact that in terms of ethnic background and socio-economic status they have been shown to be similar to American Lutherans. Thus in this study we have two "liberal" denominations (Congregationalists and Methodists), one "moderate" denomination (Presbyterian), and three "conservative" denominations (Evangelical and Reformed, Lutheran and Baptist). It should be pointed out that given the way the question on denominational background in this study was constructed it is impossible to separate "American" Lutherans from "Missouri Synod" Lutherans or "American" Baptists from "Southern" Baptists. Undoubtedly there are some "fundamentalists" in our sample, but one would suppose that Missouri Synod Lutherans and Southern Baptists would be unlikely to join United Church of Christ congregations. One cannot of course be sure of this.

In terms of the four main church participation indices, what differences do we find in terms of the denominational background from which the present participants in these United Church of Christ congregations came? The question will be whether or not denominational backgrounds can be grouped as Glock and Stark supposed or whether it is even a significant variable for persons who in fact change denominations, as in the case for four of the six denominations in question here. A further question is whether our privilege-deprivation hypothesis is upheld or not when denominations are ordered according to the ISEC scores.

Table 6-G related the denominational background to the indices. The Organizational Involvement Index reveals that the highest involvement tends to be among those groups which were *"converts"* to the United Church of Christ, the Presbyterians, Baptists and Methodists. Only the Lutherans have a lower index than the Congregationalists and the Evangelical and Reformed respondents. Do "new" participants involve themselves more fully because they have made a more self-conscious choice to "pick" the denomination in which they participate?

Religious knowledge on the other hand, as measured by the IRK, is

TABLE 6-G: Denominational Background Related to the Church Participation Indices

Denominational Background	N	Organizational Involvement	Religious Knowledge	Devotional Orientation	Belief Orientation
Presbyterian	855	43	58	20	49
Methodist	1255	42	54	21	52
Congregational	1963	35	54	20	46
Baptist	541	44	52	29	61
Lutheran	910	36	48	25	67
Evangelical and Reformed	1632	41	54	26	75
Total Sample	8549	39	53	22	57

Percent Scoring High or Moderately High on Index of:

found to be highest among the Presbyterians and lowest among the "Lutheran" participants, without much difference between the other groupings. The Baptists, Lutherans and Evangelical and Reformed respondents reveal the highest index scores in terms of the Devotional Index.

It remains, however, for the Index of Belief Orientation to make the largest discrimination between the denominational groupings. Here we find that there is some support for the groupings proposed by Glock and Stark, a grouping based on "theological" concerns. The highest belief is found among the "conservatives" (Evangelical and Reformed, Lutheran and Baptist), with descending amounts of belief found in the Methodists, Presbyterians and Congregationalists respectively. Only the "Methodists" are "out of order" in terms of the Glock and Stark categorization.

In terms of the privilege-deprivation hypothesis, three denominations followed "expected patterns," Presbyterian, Methodist and Lutheran (that is if they had above average ISEC scores they should have had above average IOI and IRK scores and below average IDO and IBO scores, and vice versa). We can discount the Baptists for this hypothesis since they had almost average ISEC scores and hence it would be difficult to predict their church participation index scores. The interesting fact is that the two major denominations of the study, the ones which went to make up the UCC, did not follow expectations! The former Evangelical and Reformed participants were above average in *all* church participation index scores, and the former Congregationalists had lower than average IOI scores. Exactly how and why the "former denomination" influences scores the way it does is not yet clear. Perhaps later patterns and analysis will clarify this matter.

The point remains that the denominational background of the respondent does appear to be a discriminating variable especially with respect to Belief Orientation, and later in the study, when consequential variables are considered in relation to church participation, denominational background will need to be considered as a "control variable."

Size of Local Congregation

In spite of early hypotheses on the part of the authors that the size of local congregation would be a useful independent variable, and indeed designing the sample so that such a variable could be carefully checked, it was found that this was perhaps the least useful independent variable of all those tested. In only one place did any differences emerge which are even worth reporting. That was in the case of reasons respondents gave for joining their present congregation. Here, the members of larger congregations reported a significant increase in evaluation of "liking the minister," enjoying the worship service, and approving of the church program. These differences could be expected since in a large congregation the place of the minister is heightened in importance for the visitor contemplating membership, and the secondary features of church program and worship service style are likely to influence his decision to join.

Otherwise, there was simply a slight decline in the Organizational Involvement Index in the larger churches, but in nearly all instances, size of church was simply not a productive variable to use for analysis.

Index of Relative Organizational Involvement

In chapter 3 the construction of the Index of Relative Organizational Involvement (IROI) was explained, and in the present chapter we are interested to know the extent to which involvement in "outside" organizations appears to have an effect on church participation (Table 6-H).

TABLE 6-H: Index of Relative Organizational Involvement Related to the Church Participation Indices

IROI Category	N	Organizational Involvement	Religious Knowledge	Devotional Orientation	Belief Orientation
A-Not in Either	1220	16	38	22	61
B-Outside Organizations Only	2834	23	48	16	49
C-More Outside Organizations	2185	53	63	22	53
D-Equal Involvement	955	56	57	28	66
E-More Church Involvement	380	91	67	31	72
F-Church Organizations only	975	48	56	31	67
Total Sample	8549	39	53	22	57

For ease of communication, a letter designation will be assigned to each category used in the IROI as follows:
- A: Not involved in either church or outside organizations
- B: Outside involvement only
- C: More outside involvement
- D: Equal involvement
- E: More church involvement
- F: Church involvement only

With respect to the IROI, it should be noted first of all that the distribution of IROI scores showed the survey population to be typically upper-middle class in terms of being highly organizationally involved in "outside" organizations. Thirty-three percent of the respondents were categorized by the IROI as "outside involvement only" and 26 percent were categorized as "more outside involvement" than involvement in the church.

The influence of relative organizational involvement upon the Index of Organizational Involvement is of less importance since the IOI was developed with heavy weighting being given for involvement in the church. Thus as is true almost by definition, the highest IOI is found among those respondents categorized as "E" respondents (more involvement in church organizations).

The highest religious knowledge is found among those persons who have some church involvement (all categories except "A" & "B"). High belief however is found among groups "A," "D," "E," and "F." Belief apparently drops significantly when the person has either most or all of his involvement in outside organizations. This would be precisely what one would expect if the culture is seen as an influence toward secularization. Finally, devotional orientation is found to be highest among those with all or most of their involvement in the church. In all four of the church participation indices it was the category "more involved in church organizations than in outside organizations" which achieved the highest index score. Thus church participation of all four styles is highest among persons who have *some outside* organizational involvement rather than among those who have *only church* involvement.

Many students of the subject, including Argyle, have of course pointed to the fact that social group membership influences religious behavior and attitudes, but the point to be made here is that *lack* of church group membership is associated with high belief orientation to the church but with low orientation in all of the other three types of church orientation. Thus, for this relatively socially privileged denomination, one would have to argue that a "social isolate" is high only in belief and does not seek solace in other forms of church orientation. Finally, the fact that the highest scores on all four indices of church participation tend to be achieved by those who are more involved in the church but are also *somewhat* involved in outside organizations, will need to be kept in mind when a theoretical construction is attempted later in the study and when the practical implications for the churches are reflected upon in chapter 12.

Thus the IROI appears to be a variable which does relate in significant ways to church participation and will be treated later in the study as a control variable, when testing for the influence of church participation upon consequential variables.

Toward a Theory of Church Participation

At this point it is appropriate to pause and seek to ascertain if any coherent patterns are emerging from the summaries of the data. In order to test for patterns let us rephrase our hypothesis by using two common arguments which have been advanced concerning different types of "social causation" in relation to church participation. One of the arguments is the "country club at prayer" or "suburban captivity" argument. The privileged classes relate to the church for personal satisfaction and support of the status quo. The church does not transform the culture of the participants; the church adapts to the culture of the participants. The second common argument is usually advanced in relation to church participants from the opposite end of the social class spectrum. It is the "religion as the opiate of the people" argument usually applied to sectarian movements. The church is a "balm" to frustration experienced in the "real world." Religion is used to compensate for losses or deprivation experienced in a lower social position and it has a tendency, according to Marxian kinds of argument, to keep people from working for real social change and revolutionary upheaval to "right the world's wrongs." Such an oversimplification of the arguments hardly does them justice, but such a statement is sufficient to use as a guiding principle to organize the findings expressed thus far. Where deviations emerge in the empirical data, we will later look for more sophistication in the argument.

The overall patterns of responses found in this study of a relatively privileged denomination clearly give support to the first argument. However, since the variables tested (both independent and church participation) have "higher" and "lower" scores, the data should be able to support both arguments.

Let us review how the independent variables were related to social privilege and social deprivation. The first independent variable, *age*, was difficult to relate to privilege and deprivation with any degree of precision, but it was stated that the American culture is "youth-oriented" and does not esteem old age. It would be possible to argue that the "golden years" are those of expectation and beginning achievement, when majority has been reached but the aging process has not yet begun to take a visible toll, namely from 20-35. The years 35-50 could be called the years of "accomplishment." These are the years of peak economic productivity and social respect. After 50 the decline clearly begins to take place and the older groups are in some sense "socially deprived" in our society. *Women* have gradually been able to discard a "second-rate" citizen position, but there is still evidence for social deprivation being experienced by females. Full equality of the sexes remains a goal rather than an accomplishment. *Education* is obviously highly respected and those with higher educational achievement can expect to experience high social approval. *Socio-economic class* is obviously another set of words for speaking of the topic we are discussing. *Urban* society is more associated with "trend-setting" and social power than is rural society. Clearly the *nonwhites* continue to experience social deprivation in the American society.

Turning then to the church participation variables, they can be related to the two arguments in the following way: In terms of the first argument, namely the "social captivity of the church" argument, one would expect increasing social status to be associated with increasing organizational participation. Thus if the church is simply expressing the views of the dominant social classes, it would be expected that the privileged social groups would find satisfaction in associating with the church in its programs and organizations. On the other hand, one would expect social deprivation to be associated with higher participation in terms of devotion and belief in the traditional doctrines of the church. The socially deprived individual would take consolation from a personal relation to God and would find the orthodox beliefs a form of consolation and separation from the dominant secular culture which has caused the deprivation. The fourth style of church participation used in this study, namely religious knowledge, is difficult to relate to the two arguments. A case could be made for associating increased religious knowledge *either* with the first argument *or* the second argument. One could argue that religious knowledge is simply another form of knowledge and therefore one would expect that those who have had more education (and therefore more prestige) would also be expected to know more about religion. Therefore religious knowledge would be seen as a function of education and one would expect any measures which correlate with increased education to correlate with increased religious knowledge, or in terms of our first argument, those with more social privilege could be expected to have more religious knowledge. On the other hand an equally persuasive case could be made that religious knowledge is related to beliefs. Therefore the man who has high beliefs would be expected to "know something" about religion, and thus have higher religious knowledge than the man who does not "believe" in religion. This form of argument would take the position that if churches of the upper classes are nothing but secularized clubs their members would not be expected to believe anything about the Christian faith *or* to know anything about it. Persons following such an argument would expect increased religious knowledge then to be associated with the various forms of social deprivation. Which is true? Is increased religious knowledge associated with social privilege or social deprivation?

Testing the arguments against the relation of independent variables to the church participation variable, let us look first at the Index of Organizational Involvement. The social captivity argument is supported by nearly all of the variables (age, sex, education, socio-economic status and rural-urban differences). The most involved are the 35-49-year-olds, males, the most educated, those with highest socio-economic class, and the more urban respondents. The argument is not supported by "race" and "former denominations." The former "E and R" members are not less involved, the former Congregational members are not more involved, and the nonwhites are more involved rather than less involved.

The person interested in supporting the first argument is likely to object to these "deviant" variables by saying that a case could be developed for each one of them. The "deviant" variables are the more ambiguous variables rather than the obvious ones. The difference on the issue of former denominational identification is very slight indeed and after all three denominations followed the "expected" pattern while only two were at variance with the argument. Also the nonwhites in this study are probably people of some considerable social mobility and even though their overall socio-economic scores are just average this is caused by differential pay for Negroes and so one should expect *these* Negroes to have high IOI scores. In summary we would have to say that there is a certain validity in these explanations and the pattern of the relation between independent variables and IOI scores does seem to give considerable credence to the first or "social captivity" argument. We simply note that the support is not without ambiguity.

What happens with the independent variables as related to the Index of Belief Orientation? Here there is almost no ambiguity in support of the second argument. The socially deprived do seem to be getting solace out of increased traditional beliefs. The oldest groups get the highest IBO scores, females score higher than men, the lowest educational groups have the highest IBO scores, the Index of Socio-Economic Class is inversely correlated with the IBO scores, higher belief is found in the more rural samples and the denomination with the lowest present ISEC scores and vice versa. The only possible ambiguity is introduced by the IBO scores of the nonwhites. In the previous paragraph it was argued that these were "special" Negroes and hence one could "expect" high IOI scores. Then here we should expect lower IBO scores and in fact they were higher for Negroes. We might well argue that these "special" Negroes can be expected to have a "special" pattern of index scores.

The case of the relation of the independent variables to the Index of Devotional Orientation is also very supportive of the social deprivation argument. Every single variable is related to the IDO in the expected direction based on a theory which says the deprived will be more devotional than the privileged. The elderly are more devotional, the females are more devotional, the highly educated and those with high ISEC scores are less devotional, the rural respondents are more devotional, the denominations with lower ISEC scores tend to get higher IDO scores and vice versa, and the nonwhites have higher IDO scores than was the average for the total sample.

What about the Index of Religious Knowledge related to the independent variables? This was difficult to defend in terms of one argument or the other. Which argument gets support from the empirical findings? If IRK scores are largely a function of education in general (and thus social privilege in some sense), we find that the results of the variables of education, ISEC and race support such a contention. Those with higher education and scores on the Index of Socio-Economic Class tend to have higher IRK scores, and the nonwhites have lower IRK scores than the average for the sample. Likewise the pattern of IRK scores for the former Presbyterians, Congregationalists, Methodists, and Lutherans support the contention, for the Presbyterians, Methodists and Congregationalists are above average in their ISEC and IRK scores, while Lutherans are below in both types of scores. However, if one contends that religious knowledge is related to belief (and thus to special social deprivation in some sense), the results from the variables of age, sex and rural-urban difference would support the argument. For, we find that the older respondents, women and nonurban residents have the highest IRK scores. Also the IRK and ISEC scores of the former Evangelical and Reformed respondents support the same contention. The former E and R's have a lower than average ISEC score but a higher than average IRK (and IBO) score. Thus we see that the variable of religious knowledge remains a problematic variable. Sometimes it seems to support one contention (social captivity of religion) and sometimes it seems to support the other contention (religion as compensation for social deprivation).

Thus far, then, what is the position of our theory? The relatively simple statement that religion is largely an expression of social captivity for people of privilege while it is largely an expression of compensation for social deprivation for underprivileged people seems to be working out fairly well. The point is that we have shown that people of privilege prefer organizational religion, while people of deprivation find devotional and traditional beliefs more helpful. Support is clearly emerging for part of the first hypothesis mentioned for the study, namely differences in an individual's social situation do result in different modes of religious orientation. Our theory is hardly complete however, for one of our "modes" of religious orientation does not fit very well into the theory, and we do not yet know how much either the modes of religious orientation *or* the social situation appear to affect secular attitudes (our second and third hypotheses from chapter 1). Before turning to an examination of the findings with respect to social attitudes, let us finally note some of the less critical findings which emerged in the present chapter. Interestingly enough they nearly all related in one way or another to social attitudes.

It was found that there was a slight tendency for those under 35 to prefer a more "public" stance on the part of the church. Also it was found that women preferred more help on private problems rather than public issues. More educated people gave a slightly higher standing to social action groups and to the place of "working for social justice" in the definition of who is considered Christian. Likewise those with higher ISEC scores felt "working for justice" was more important. Rural-urban differentiation yielded conflicting findings on issues of social justice.

Thus we shall see some indication that in this survey population, it is the "people of privilege" who are manifesting more concern for the "public" expression of the churches' role. (The Negroes are an exception to this generalization.)

Finally there was the pattern of IROI scores which showed a tendency for some "outside" involvement on the part of church participants to be associated with an increase in all of the "styles" of church participation.

We are now in a position to examine relationships between all of our variables and some issues of public concern.

Part 3-Church Participation Related to Social Issues

Chapter 7-The Layman Faces the World

Introduction

Part 3 of this study could well have been entitled "Consequential Analysis of Church Participation," for the intention in this part is to examine the ways in which church participation appears to have "consequences" for a variety of social beliefs and/or attitudes. However, the more modest title was chosen for two reasons. The first is that the design of the study permits only an examination of relationships between church participation variables and a small sample of attitudes on social issues. We will not be able finally to establish that the social attitudes and/or beliefs are fully the "consequence" of church participation in the sense of being "caused by" such participation. We will, of course seek to control for the influence of some of the more obvious variables usually associated with social attitudes, but in the final analysis, even where we establish some remaining relationships between church participation and social attitudes, we will not be sure that some as yet unsuggested variable could account for the relationship. However, to clarify what the relationships are will have been an important undertaking, even if the word "consequences" will always have to remain within quotation marks. As sociological researchers, we have chosen to operate with a model suggesting causal relationships, but as social "philosophers" we are sufficiently convinced of the complexity of human nature to refrain from the assumption that a modest study of this sort will do any more than merely uncover some interesting relationships which will need to be integrated into a much larger perspective.

The second reason for the choice of the more modest title is that the "consequences" of church participation are undoubtedly much wider than the few illustrative social attitudes we have chosen to examine. Are there psychological correlates of church participation? Does church participation correlate with certain kinds of practices in family life and child rearing? These would be but two examples of a whole range of issues which this research was simply not designed to study.

The range of social issues chosen as "consequential" variables for this study emerges out of certain very important themes present in contemporary American church life. These themes are most apparent to persons acquainted with the life of denominations drawing their constituency predominantly from the middle and upper-middle classes, the so-called "main line" denominations. Within the last decade, there has been a growing concern for the way in which the church should be related to issues of public policy and social concern. Some observers would see this growing concern as the "last gasp" of an increasingly "secularized" church struggling to find a reason for existence. Others would see this as a "return" to "true" religion, away from the "comfortable pew" which such observers believe has characterized "main-line" denominations in recent history. There is a wide range of opinions and variations of opinion on just what is happening in this growing concern for the "social relevance" of the Christian faith.

This growing concern was becoming evident during the time when this study was being designed and the questionnaires were administered. Now, at the time of publication of the findings, the concern has reached such a point that even the secular mass media find it "profitable" to devote space and time to a description and accounting of it. Readers of national news magazines know that ministers have been "ousted" from their pulpits over issues relating to race. Television viewers know of clergy who have "marched" because of the social concerns growing out of their understanding of what the church "should be about." Local parishioners know that their denominations "take stands" on a variety of social issues, and as a result some ask their ministers why the church "doesn't stop giving out statements and *really do* something" while others want to know from their ministers "what in the world all of that has to do with the gospel!"

In the midst of this growing concern very little research has emerged. This study seeks to add one kind of knowledge to the discussion about the issues. How does church participation appear to be related to certain types of social attitudes? The primary concern of the study is not the specific questions or issues which are examined, but to seek to discern *patterns of relationship*. Obviously pattern of relationship cannot be discerned without addressing specific issues through particular questions, but equally obviously specificity is by definition very ephemeral or at least seasonal. Any reader of public opinion polls knows that such findings are out of date even before the newspaper story about them is printed. However, any astute politician also knows that certain *patterns* which are uncovered in "poll taking," if carefully analyzed, can be utilized for purposes of election eight years hence! We are seeking just such a careful analysis of the data revealed by this study.

Exactly where the issues may have shifted since the questions were asked will be important for the analysis, but the fact that they *have* shifted does not substantially affect the validity of the patterning present. Readers may have forgotten what was on the front pages of the newspaper a year ago, they may even have forgotten how they reacted to it. But anyone who knew their reaction and studied it carefully could make some very responsible predictions about how those same readers will react to tomorrow's headlines.

The specificity of our questions suggest three groupings. Some questions were related to public policy issues, a number of the questions were related to the racial crisis of America, and some questions were related to how people felt social change should be brought about. Part 3 of the study will be organized around those three types of questions. In the present chapter we will examine how the survey population as a whole responded to each of the types. In chapter 8, we will look only at the first type of question, questions of general public policy, and the examination will center on how both the independent variables and the church participation variables appear to be related to those questions and attitudes. Chapters 9 and 10 will examine the other two types of questions in the same way. The goal is to determine the validity of the third and most crucial hypothesis of the study. Do "different church participation orientations have different consequences for behavior and attitudes on social issues" or not?

Public Policy Issues

The respondents to the study were presented with two lists of public policy issues (questions 44 and 45) on which they were asked to give their opinion. They could indicate that they were in favor of each policy, were opposed to it, were not sure about it, or they didn't really know about the issue. In all, there were thirteen issues ranging over a fairly wide area of concerns. Some issues were selected because they were highly controversial issues, while others were selected because they represented a policy which was known to have a wide basis of support among Americans. Some issues were very "topical" and related to policies being discussed in the mass media at the time the questionnaire was mailed, while others had either been discussed at an earlier time or were more "long range" in their implications. Some issues were clearly related to urban problems, while others would be of more interest to residents of "town and country" America.

Table 7-A lists all thirteen of the issues in order of the percentage of those answering the questions who favored the policy. Of the thirteen issues, only four received two-thirds or more support from the respondents. None of those four would normally be considered very controversial policies.

TABLE 7-A: Public Policies, Percentages of Respondents Favoring

Public Policy	Number Responding to Question (Total N = 8549)	Percent Favoring
1. U.S. Participation in the United Nations	8070	86
2. Soil Conservation	7950	80
3. Food for Peace Program	7842	67
4. Preservation of Family Farm	7894	66
5. Federal Nondiscriminatory Employment Legislation	7854	55
6. Medical Care for Aged Through Social Security	8161	50
7. Farmer Cooperatives	7818	45
8. Federal Nondiscriminatory Housing Legislation	7836	44
9. Ban on Nuclear Testing	8021	43
10. Federal Aid to Public and Private Education	7972	39
11. Cabinet Post for Urban Affairs	7746	30
12. Govt. Price Support Program (Agricultural)	7842	21
13. Collective Market Bargaining	7694	21

Among the less popular policies, Medicare and a cabinet post in urban affairs were not realities at the time the survey was being conducted. Half of the respondents favored Medicare while less than one person in three was in favor of the urban addition to the President's cabinet. Federal laws enacted to eliminate or control discrimination against minorities have more support (just over 50 percent) when applied to job situations than when applied to housing situations.

Only about one person in five is in favor of the government supporting agricultural prices, and also only about one person in five feels that collective market bargaining for farmers is a worthwhile policy. At the same time two thirds of the respondents are in favor of "preserving the family farm." One wonders what means of preservation would be approved by the respondents when they so overwhelmingly reject two policies normally directed toward the goal of preserving the family farm.

In looking over the responses to the policy questions, the authors come to the conclusion that the survey population taken as a whole manifests a rather conservative posture on social issues.

It is appropriate to remind the reader of the position taken by the respondents with respect to the churches' relation to matters of public policy. The issue was discussed in chapter 4, and at that time it was pointed out (Table 4-E) that the respondents preferred a "passive" role of the church in relation to public policy. They favored "open" church membership but did not want the church involved in the struggle for justice; they were willing to let their ministers discuss controversial issues but they did not want the denominations to issue policy statements. And they were willing to have prayers in public schools, but did not want their children subjected to religious "teaching" in the public schools.

From the pattern of responses to the policy questions and the questions concerning the church's relation to policy issues, one does not see the sample population as a very dynamic group dedicated to social change.

From among the policy questions the authors chose four questions to construct an index labeled: "Index on Federal Activity" (IFA). These questions were chosen from among the thirteen options because they were not clearly identified as "urban" or "rural" questions (therefore all respondents could be expected to have opinions on them), because they did not deal with the racial crisis (which will be treated through other indices later), and because they ranged from highly approved to highly controversial issues. The four issues chosen were (1) U.S. participation in the United Nations (an international relations policy which was already being practiced), (2) the ban on nuclear testing (a policy involving national security and international relations which had not yet been solved and a policy on which there was considerable difference of opinion in the American population), (3) federal aid to public and private education (a national issue, highly controversial, involving states' rights, and covertly involving the church-state question since the bulk of "private" education is clearly "parochial"), (4) medical care for the aged through social security (a national issue involving the individual and "private enterprise" not yet a policy, and somewhat controversial in the population at large).

Each respondent was given a score of from "0" to "4" depending on how many of the items he approved. The respondents who did not reply to the question at all were discounted in the percentages of responses given in Table 7-B. The summary table clearly shows that the survey population falls generally into a "normal curve" pattern with respect to this index. In the next chapter it will be important to discover which independent variables tend to correlate positively with this index. Is the tendency for people of social privilege or people of social deprivation to prefer the forms of federal activity represented in this index?

TABLE 7-B: Index on Federal Activity in Percentage of Respondents

IFA Category	Percent of Respondents (N = 8237)
Low (0)	8
Moderately Low (1)	23
Moderate (2)	31
Moderately High (3)	26
High (4)	13

The Racial Crisis

Given the importance of the problems surrounding the Negro's struggle for social justice in the contemporary period, a number of questions were asked in the study related to this problem. For presentation purposes the issue is separated from other public issues.

One question used was a modified version of the Bogardus Social Distance Scale, an instrument long used by social scientists to measure racial and ethnic prejudice. The respondent is asked "To which steps in the scale below would you admit people in the various racial and nationality groups listed at the right?" Englishmen, American Indians, Italians, Mexicans, Negroes and Orientals were the racial and ethnic groups used in our questionnaire.

The scale itself consisted of the following seven steps: (The order given below reflects respondents' order of prejudice. The order in which the options were given in the questionnaire is found in question 49.)

1. To close kinship by marriage
2. To my club as personal chums
3. To my street as neighbors
4. To my home as guests
5. To employment in my occupation
6. To my church as members
7. To citizenship in my country

The scale assumed that if one were to admit a person to all steps in the scale he reflected no prejudice, whereas if he admitted a person only to "citizenship in my country," he was giving expression to a high degree of prejudice. For our total sample, the result of this scale is reported in Table 7-C.

TABLE 7-C: Summary of Responses to the Social Distance Scale

Social Distance Scale	Percent of respondents who would admit					
	English	Indian	Italian	Mexican	Negro	Oriental
1. Close kinship by marriage	82	30	49	20	9	19
2. My club as personal chums	79	52	60	43	38	48
3. My street as neighbors	85	63	73	52	45	62
4. My home as guests	85	72	76	64	58	69
5. Employment in my occupation	81	71	73	67	66	69
6. My church as members	85	78	79	74	71	76
7. Citizenship in my country	87	82	81	79	79	80

When the results of the social distance scale are examined, we see immediately that the responses of our sample of parishioners differ significantly both in degree and kind, depending on the ethnic group to which they are applied. Since nearly all respondents in our total sample are white, it is understandable that the least amount of social distance is reflected toward Englishmen. On the other hand, only half of them would admit Italians "to close kinship by marriage" and only 60 percent would admit them to their social clubs.

The greatest degree of social distance is reflected toward the Negro. Less than one person in ten would admit Negroes "to close kinship by marriage," and less than half of them into their "club as chums" or on their "street as neighbors." To a lesser degree, the majority would not admit Orientals and Mexicans to their clubs or to close kinship by marriage.

From the social distance scale questions with respect to Negroes, an Index of Social Acceptance (ISA) was developed. Since there were seven options to which a respondent might indicate he would agree to "admit" Negroes, each respondent was coded in terms of the number of "steps" to which he was willing to admit Negroes. If the respondent was not willing to admit Negroes to any of the "steps" indicated on the scale, or if he was willing to admit them to American citizenship or membership in his church but to nothing else, he was categorized as having "low acceptance." Those who were willing to admit Negroes to employment in their occupation, as guests in their homes or as neighbors were categorized as having "moderate acceptance," and those who were willing to admit Negroes to their social clubs or to close kinship by marriage were categorized as having "high acceptance." The results of such a procedure for the entire sample population are shown in Table 7-D.

TABLE 7-D: Index of Social Acceptance by Percent of Respondents

ISA	Percent of Respondents N = 7614
Low Acceptance	22
Moderate Acceptance	38
High Acceptance	40

A second index was developed from questions dealing with the racial issue and this index was labeled the Index of Civil Rights (ICR). Three questions were used in its construction, the two questions dealing with nondiscriminatory federal legislation in jobs and housing (mentioned earlier above, question 44), and the question from the series on the church and public policy (question 46) which asked whether or not the respondent agrees that "churches should support the Negro's struggle to achieve civil rights." Thus a person could agree with none, one, two or three of the questions and be given a score of "0," "1," "2," or "3" accordingly. The results of this index for the sample population as a whole are shown on Table 7-E.

TABLE 7-E: Index of Civil Rights by Percent of Respondents

ICR	Percent of Respondents N = 8219
Low (0)	30
Moderately Low (1)	22
Moderately High (2)	15
High (3)	33

In addition to the questions on social distance and the two indices just described, attitudes on civil rights were also measured by presenting the respondents with a series of twelve statements which have been commonly made by both supporters and opponents of the civil rights movement. They were asked to indicate whether they agreed or disagreed with each statement (question 51). The results of this inquiry are summarized on Table 7-F.

The reader will notice in glancing over this list that some questions are those with which a man of "prejudice" would be expected to agree, while others are questions with which a "civil rights advocate" might be expected to agree. Still other questions are difficult to place in terms of whether a "civil rights advocate" would be expected to agree or disagree with them. Thus, because there are different "types" of questions in the list, the presentation of Table 7-E (descending order of approval) is not a very useful type of presentation for giving us a "picture" of the attitudes of the survey population on issues of civil rights. The problem of deciding which items a civil rights advocate would approve and which he would disapprove is complicated by the growth, since the time of the administration of the questions, of the

Black Power movement. Several "goals" of "civil rights advocates" have changed drastically in a few years. For example, many are now saying that integration is wrong rather than a goal to be sought. The point is that the policy a civil rights advocate "approves" has proven to be a question with very ephemeral answers.

To sort out this complicated problem, let us return to our purpose in the chapter. Our object is to present a description of the social attitudes of our survey population taken as a whole. At one level, Table 7-F is such a description. However, such a table needs to be summarized according to some principle, and we wish to use the principle of "civil rights advocacy," because in recent years this has been a critical

TABLE 7-F: Civil Rights Issues in Percent of Respondents Agreeing

Statement	No. Responding	Percent Agreeing
1. When Negroes move into white residential areas, property values tend to go down	8233	63
2. The Negro is right in demanding his full civil rights now	8135	56
3. Negroes are trying to move too fast to obtain justice and equality	8197	51
4. On the whole, Negro children receive inferior education in comparison to white children	8184	51
5. Negroes are happier in Negro churches and Negro schools	8199	47
6. Restaurant owners have a right to refuse service to a person because of his race	8236	22
7. On the whole, American Indians are better off living on reservations	8158	19
8. Negro leaders today are working for the eventual mixture of races through intermarriage	8188	18
9. We owe the Negro some kind of compensation for past injustices	8128	17
10. Negroes should be given jobs in proportion to their numbers in the population	8107	16
11. In general, the government's policies toward the American Indian have been just and fair	8053	16
12. Negroes should now be hired even if they are not fully qualified to make up for discrimination against them in the past	8216	4

issue in American churches. We wish to know the degree of "civil rights advocacy" one finds in our survey population.

On the issue of civil rights, then, one can safely assume that a "goal" for Christians would be to "love one's neighbor" and be "unprejudiced" in dealings with one's neighbor regardless of the color of his skin. One way to describe a group of Christians would be to show how far they fall short of such a goal. The difficulty comes in knowing which policies indicate "love" and a "lack of prejudice" and which policies indicate the opposite. We shall use two means of sorting out the issues. The first means will be to use the nonwhites who were a part of the survey population as a "standard" for deciding what is a statement which "should" be approved and what is a statement which "should" be disapproved. It seems reasonable to assume that if a majority of those against whom prejudice is addressed agree with a statement, one who is interested in civil rights advocacy might be expected to agree with the statement, and vice versa. Table 7-G groups the statements from Table 7-F according to whether the majority of the nonwhite respondents agreed or disagreed with each statement. The percentages of agreement and disagreement for the nonwhite respondents is given in each case as well as the same percentages for the white respondents.

Looking at Table 7-G helps to give a summary picture of our survey population on civil rights. With respect to the Negro respondents, notice that with the exception of statement "L," there was great unanimity on feeling about the statements. In nearly all of the other statements three fourths or more of the Negro respondents felt the same way about them. Notice furthermore in comparing white responses with Negro responses that there is only one statement ("F") in which the white's attitudes exceeded the Negro's feelings. That statement is an interesting one, since it is a statement about a policy which some particularly "radical" civil rights advocates were suggesting at the time of the administration of the questionnaire. Moreover, the policy has since come to be adopted in somewhat modified form in many places of employment as a type of "on the job training." It is not surprising that our white respondents disagreed to the extent that they did in 1964, and it is also not surprising that our "somewhat privileged" Negro respondents also generally disapproved of such a policy. After all, they had probably gained the impressive educational and other types of qualifications they had at some considerable sacrifice and would feel that others should at least "be qualified" for the jobs they want.

Comparing the white and Negro responses overall in Table 7-G, we see that in seven of the twelve statements, the white majority viewed the statement in the same way as the Negro majority (statements "B," "D," "E," "F," "I," "J," and "K"). To be sure, in nearly all of those seven cases (the notable exception being statement "F"), the white majority is considerably smaller than the Negro majority. However, what the table does show is that, within the survey population white majority, there is considerable variation in attitudes toward civil rights issues. When we combine the findings of this table with the Index of Social Acceptance and the Index of Civil Rights, we find that the

TABLE 7-G: Civil Rights Statements Ordered by Disapproval and Approval of Respondents in Percent

Part 1 Statements with Which Nonwhite Respondents Disagreed

Statement	Nonwhite Respondents Number Responding	Nonwhite Respondents Percent Disagree	White Respondents Number Responding	White Respondents Percent Disagree
A. Negroes are trying to move too fast to obtain justice and equality	174	98	8197	29
B. Restaurant owners have a right to refuse service to a person because of his race	170	97	8236	65
C. Negro leaders today are working for the eventual mixture of races through intermarriage	175	89	8188	47
D. On the whole, American Indians are better off living on reservations	171	83	8158	56
E. In general, the government's policies toward the American Indian have been just and fair	162	81	8053	60
F. Negroes should now be hired even if they are not fully qualified to make up for discrimination against them in the past	175	75	8216	84
G. When Negroes move into white residential areas, property values tend to go down	173	75	8233	18
H. Negroes are happier in Negro churches and Negro schools	173	73	8199	20
I. Negroes should be given jobs in proportion to their numbers in population	160	70	8107	61

Part 2 Statements with Which Nonwhite Respondents Agreed

Statement	Nonwhite Respondents Number Responding	Percent Agree	White Respondents Number Responding	Percent Agree
J. The Negro is right in demanding his full civil rights now	172	87	8135	56
K. On the whole, Negro children receive inferior education in comparison with white children	171	83	8184	51
L. We owe the Negro some kind of compensation for past injustices	169	51	8128	16

respondents include people with great prejudice against Negroes, people with fairly strong feelings of acceptance and a desire to help the Negro in his efforts toward civil justice, and people with very mixed feelings on the subject.

There is a second way to summarize the attitudes in civil rights among our respondents. This would be to select from among the questions asked in the study, those questions which parallel questions asked in other studies of the American population. Are our respondents on the whole more or less prejudiced than other groups of the American people? Both Glock[1] and Argyle[2] have suggested that religious people are more prejudiced than nonreligious people. Certain problems in Glock's study will be commented upon in chapter 9, but Argyle's summary statement is worth repeating at this point. He said:

> Regular and devout church members tend to be less prejudiced than nonattending members, though religious people in general are more prejudiced than nonreligious people. Catholics are the most prejudiced, closely followed by the major Protestant denominations; Jews and sect members are the least prejudiced.[3]

Argyle went on to explain this finding on the basis of Adorno's theory of the authoritarian personality.[4] In chapter 9 we will examine just what differences the types of church participation appear to make in the levels of prejudice in our survey population. But it is important at this point to determine, if possible, whether or not our population is as both Argyle and Glock would suggest: "in general" religious people are more prejudiced than the population as a whole.

As a base line for such comparison, two national studies done by Louis Harris and William Brink (1963 and 1966) for *Newsweek* magazine will be used.[5] It is fortunate that these studies bracket, in time of administration, the present research. Several questions used by Brink and Harris parallel closely questions used in this study. Table 7-H has made comparisons between this study and the Brink and Harris study on questions which were not worded exactly in the same way but which were sufficiently close to warrant comparison without undue modification. From that table it appears that both our white respondents and our Negro respondents are if anything "more liberal" or "less prejudiced" than the population as a whole.[6] Only in statement 2 of Table

TABLE 7-H: A Comparison of Findings with Respect to Prejudice

Issue	Brink and Harris		Campbell and Fukuyama	
(Page numbers refer to Brink and Harris study)[5]	Negro Attitudes in Percent	White Attitudes in Percent	Negro Attitudes in Percent	White Attitudes in Percent (q = questions in Appendix)
1. Negroes are moving too fast (agree) (p. 258 and 220)	3 (1963) 4 (1966)	64 (1963) 70 (1966)	1 (q. 51)	51 (q. 51)
2. Would not be upset at having Negroes in their neighborhood (p. 109)		48 (1966)		45 (q. 49)
3. Is there discrimination against Negroes (p. 125)				
(Agree)		61 (1966)		84 (q. 48)
(Disagree)		28 (1966)		5 (q. 48)
4. Negroes should be given job preference (p. 278)				
(Agree)		3 (1963) 4 (1966)		4 (q. 51)
(Disagree)		93 (1963) 90 (1966)		81 (q. 51)
5. Negroes prefer to go to Negro schools (p. 234)				
(Agree)	10 (1963) 11 (1966)		8 (q. 51)	
(Disagree)	70 (1963) 70 (1966)		73 (q. 51)	

7-H do we find the respondents in the present study "more prejudiced" than the population at large.

Before leaving the subject, however, one other finding of the Brink and Harris study needs to be included in the analysis. They found that there was a tendency for more affluent people to have more liberal views on the issues of civil rights. Thus it is not quite fair to compare our sample (which tends to be upper-middle class) with the American population as a whole. Table 7-I compares questions between the two studies taking "affluence" into account.

Two interesting things emerge from this table. Brink and Harris defined the "Affluents" as the "one quarter at the top,"[7] but since the present survey population is "privileged" on the whole, yet hardly all in the "top quarter" of the American class structure, the two studies are not totally comparable. However, even granting these difficulties of comparison, two interesting additions to the description of our survey population emerge from an examination of Table 7-I. In the first place, our survey population is more "liberal" than the "Affluents" in one statement, equal to or slightly less "liberal" than the "Affluents" in the second statement (see note at the bottom of the table), and less

TABLE 7-I: A Comparison of Findings on Prejudice Among the Affluent

Issue	Brink and Harris (p. 136) All Whites (in percent agreeing)	"Affluents" (in percent agreeing)	Campbell and Fukuyama Those Responding (in percent agreeing)
1. Negroes are discriminated against	60	78	84 (q. 48)
2. Object to Negroes living next door	51	41	41* (q. 49)
3. Negro education worse than white	40	58	51 (q. 51)

* (Note: The way the question was worded in the two studies makes comparison a bit difficult. The Campbell-Fukuyama study asked if one would "admit" Negroes to one's neighborhood, while the Brink-Harris study asks if one "objects" to having Negroes live next door. The figure given above for the C-F study was obtained as follows: 45 percent said they "would admit Negroes," 14 percent did not respond to the question. Assuming that all of the nonrespondents would admit Negroes to the neighborhood, the remaining 41 percent presumably "object." Thus the figure of 41 percent is a "low" figure for the C-F study since one cannot assume that all nonrespondents would be willing to admit Negroes. In all probability most of them would not.)

121

"liberal" than the "Affluents" on the third statement (though still more liberal than the total American population). Secondly, since statement "2" of Table 7-I is the obverse of statement 2 of Table 7-H this is clearly a statement where the present survey population was more prejudiced than the population at large.

In summary, the comparison with Brink and Harris findings raises some question concerning the easy judgment that religious people are more prejudiced than nonreligious people. However, much more importantly for the purposes of this study is the question of the relative importance of one's social position for one's social attitude as well as for one's style of religious participation. Social position appears to make a great difference in such issues as those treated in this section on civil rights.

As in the case of the other "public" issues, treated in the section above it appears this survey population is very diverse in attitudes on racial questions. Overall it is hard to argue that it is more "prejudiced" than the population at large, but it is also not very impressive in its overall "liberality." We simply must know much more about the influence of the various factors present in the survey population before we can make very meaningful judgments about church participation and social issues.

The Means of Achieving Social Change

Before turning to an examination of the influence of the various types of factors upon social attitudes, there is yet a third category of "social attitudes" which needs to be explained. It is of a slightly different order from the two categories of social attitudes which have been explained above. It involves one's attitudes toward the church as well as toward social issues. Assuming that one is interested in social change, how should *Christians* go about achieving such social change? The introduction to this chapter pointed out how much difference of opinion there is in the contemporary church over social issues, and a good deal of that difference of opinion is related to the question of just what the "church" should *do* about social issues.

Given the fact that some parishioners at least believe that certain changes are desirable in various areas of our secular life, the question remains as to the role which it is appropriate for the church to play in relation to such changes. Many different opinions have been held with respect to this question, but one common distinction is between those who believe (a) that the church exerts its change upon individual members and they in turn have the responsibility to work for change in the social order, and those who believe (b) that the church should act with its institutional "power" directly upon the social issues in need of change.

Persons holding the first position often are willing to have small groups of Christians (such as a social action committee of a local congregation) act in cooperation with each other toward some social end which they believe to be desirable, but they do not want the church to act as "a body" in relation to any particular social issue. The usual argument put forth by such persons is that any social issue is too complicated and ambiguous to be certain exactly which answer is the "Christian" one. Therefore, Christians should indeed be encouraged to work for social change, but they act as individuals (or small groups of individuals) and there is no implication that the "church" or Christianity would interpret the solution to the problem in the way in which they do. A related argument for this position is a more pragmatic one which simply recognizes the diversity which one finds present within churches on nearly all matters of social policy and therefore argues that, short of those few places where there might be overwhelming agreement on a social issue, it is simply institutionally unwise to suggest group action by the "whole" church. Such efforts will only lead to the death of the institution or at the very least the unwelcome control of the institution by a particular type of "activist" minority.

The alternative position ("b") on the other hand, also has been defended along both theoretical and pragmatic lines. The theoretical argument often employed points to the "prophetic" strain within the Judeo-Christian tradition which has called for major social change when evidence of injustice was rife within the society. Therefore the church should "speak out" and "act" as it has at various periods of history. The church must always be concerned lest it become "captive" to its surrounding culture and respond to the culture's "calls" rather than to the "call" of God. The more pragmatic argument tends to point out that in a highly complex society such as twentieth-century America, individuals and small groups are not able to effect any significant changes. Like it or not, the church is a large institution in an institutionalized social order, and if one honestly expects to accomplish any significant change one must direct institutional strength toward institutional solutions. Not to act is to put the strength of the institution behind the "status quo."

It has been shown in previous studies[8] that only a very small minority of church members are very sophisticated about such issues or have given very much thought to them. However, in all probability most parishioners have some "feelings" on these matters and would have a "tendency" to react one way or another to questions which dealt with the issues. In order to test such a hypothesis, several of the questions which have been discussed previously in this report were grouped in terms of whether they indicated attitudes similar to those of position "a" or position "b." In each case three questions were chosen and an index was constructed and each respondent was given his appropriate index score.

The index related to position "a" above was designated the "Index of Individual Conscience" (IIC) and it was constructed from the three following responses: (1) when asked about the types of help the respondent desired from the church he indicated he wanted "much" help to "work for justice in my community and in my world" (Appendix, question 8), (2) when asked to evaluate a variety of types of church programs the respondent indicated that he considered social action groups to be "very important" (Appendix, question 12) and (3) when asked to indicate his attitudes on a series of characteristics considered to be "absolutely necessary" in defining who is a Christian he chose "Christians are those who work for social justice" (Appendix, question 19). Depending on the number of these questions to which the respondents replied affirmatively, he was given an IIC score of "0," "1," "2," or "3." The results of this index being applied to the total survey population are found in Table 7-J.

The index related to position "b" above was designated the "Index of Collective Social Responsibility" (ICSR) and it was constructed from the three following responses: (1) when asked to be critical of the church in a number of areas the respondent had the attitude that

TABLE 7-J: **Index of Individual Conscience in Percent of Respondents**

IIC	Percent of Respondents N = 8549
Low (0)	40
Moderately low (1)	29
Moderately high (2)	21
High (3)	10

the *church* had not done enough in "working for racial justice and equality" (Appendix, question 13), (2) when asked whether or not the church had done enough in "affecting changes in our governmental policies" he affirmed that the church had not done enough (Appendix, question 13), and (3) when asked about his attitudes on the questions relating the church to public policy he agreed that "denominations have a right to issue policy statements on social and economic matters" (Appendix, question 46). Again the respondent could then be given ICSR scores of "0," "1," "2," or "3." The results of this index for the survey population are shown in Table 7-K.

TABLE 7-K: Index of Collective Social Responsibility in Percent of Respondents

ICSR	Percent of Respondents N = 8549
Low (0)	40
Moderately low (1)	32
Moderately high (2)	18
High (3)	11

From examining the results of both of these indices, one can argue that, either (1) the participants in this survey are, for the most part, not very interested in social change either by individuals or the institutional church, or (2) the questions were not adequate to measure interest if it was present.

Interrelationship Between Social Issues Variables

Before proceeding to examine the ways both independent variables and church participation variables appear to influence the opinions of the respondents on the above range of social issues, it is important to see whether or not there is any correlation between the various social issues indices which have been described in this chapter. Do the same people achieve "high" scores on all of the indices, or are we dealing here with a variety of subgroups within the survey population?

We will begin by examining the extent to which there is correlation between the two civil rights indices. One would certainly expect that a person who achieved a high score as a "civil rights liberal" would also be one who would be likely to achieve a high score for "social acceptance." When the Index of Civil Rights was related to the Index of Social Acceptance there was a positive correlation. High scores on one index are very likely to imply a high score on the other. However, though there is a high degree of interrelationship between the two variables, we are not dealing with exactly the same persons when we speak of the "high" subgroup for each index.

Is it also likely that one who is in favor of civil rights and/or who is high in "social acceptance" will be "high" in the Index on Federal Activity? Since the questions used in the Index of Civil Rights were ones which advocated federal intervention in civil rights, one would expect that there might be a high correlation between the ICR and the IFA, and this proved to be the case. The Index on Federal Activity also correlated positively with a high positive correlation between the two indices.

Each of the three indices already discussed were then tested for their relation to the two indices concerning the means for social change (IIC and ICSR). In every case a positive correlation was found. However, in the case of each of the three original indices there was a stronger correlation with the Index of Collective Social Responsibility than with the Index of Individual Conscience. That those who are in favor of various forms of social change are also in favor of the means of social change is hardly a very surprising finding. But the fact that correlation is higher with change by institutional means than with change by individual means would be modest evidence indicating a preference within the survey population for position "b" on social change which was discussed above.

Summary

Two findings emerge clearly out of the examination of the reactions of the total survey population to the series of social issues discussed in this chapter. First, as a total body one would be very hard pressed to argue that the social attitudes of the participants in this study were of a very "radical" sort. The participants in this study were shown in Part 1 of the study to be a stable middle and upper-middle class group reflecting the characteristics of such people. Thus far, in Part 3, we have found that their social attitudes are on the whole of a fairly conventional variety.

However, the second important finding is that one cannot argue that the group is monolithic. One can support the generalization of "conservatism" only by pointing to majority responses to the questions. There is nearly always a sizable minority which deviates from the "normal" responses to the questions used in the study. The question is, what seems to cause, or effect, this deviation? Since Part 2 of the study showed that there was significant variation on the church participation variables, let us now turn to an examination of the relation between these variables and the social attitudes.

Chapter 8—Church Participation and Public Policy

The Developing Theory

At the end of Part 2, we found that our empirical findings supported in most instances a simplified theory of social privilege and deprivation. Parishioners of social privilege tended to relate to the church through certain styles of participation while those of social deprivation had a tendency to utilize other forms of participation. Certain "deviant" findings were noted, but they were not of sufficient magnitude that the theory needed to be abandoned. Rather, it was suggested that certain enrichment of the overly simplified theory may be necessary in order to deal with the "deviations."

Now we can explore the adequacy of the simple form of the theory in dealing with issues of church participation in relation to public policy. In this and the following chapters, we will again be parsimonious with respect to theory. The most minimal theory will form a background for presentation of the data, and instances of "deviation" will be noted when they occur. Later (in Part 4) when a more amplified theoretical explanation is undertaken, the "deviations" from Parts 2 and 3 will be incorporated into the discussion.

How then, would the simple form of the privilege-deprivation theory "predict" social attitudes? We need to recall that the hypotheses of this study have been stated in a relatively "neutral" form. That is, it has been hypothesized that "differences in an individual's social situation result in different modes of . . . social outlook" and "different church participation orientations have different consequences for behavior and attitudes on social issues." No content is provided in the hypothesis for predicting the *direction* or *form* of influence upon social outlook by either the "social situation" or the "church participation orientations." Is it possible to develop some simple theory which will suggest "direction" or "form" of influence?

Since the privilege-deprivation theory proved to be so adequate earlier in the study, it is a promising theory to be utilized here. A relatively simple, and commonly accepted, form of the theory would be to state that the socially privileged and the socially deprived have strong "self interests" which will condition social attitudes. Thus, the socially privileged have been regarded as supporters of the "status quo" (they "like" being in a privileged position and do not want it changed), while the socially deprived would prefer to see social change which will improve their social position.

A problem emerges in seeking to apply such an "obvious" theory to a complex society. It is not exactly clear which attitudes represent "status quo" and which represent "social change." For example, take the attitude of approving an "open society" which encourages social mobility for its members. If a society has been developed with such an attitude as a rather fundamental notion (as many would want to argue about the American society), do persons who hold such a notion support the "status quo" or are they in favor of "social change"? Or, take the attitude toward "social change" itself. If we live in a period of rapid social change (as most commentators would want to suggest is the case), then what is a "status quo attitude" and what is a "social change attitude" *about* social change?

One answer would be to discuss the *direction* of the change. If changes which are presently underway tend to be for the benefit of persons who are already privileged (the rich are getting richer), then we might argue that slowing down the change or reversing its direction is to the advantage of the socially deprived. In such a situation, to favor present direction of change becomes a "status quo" attitude, while favoring a decline in social change becomes a "social change" attitude.

Such a brief excursus into the ambiguities and confusions of applying an "obvious" theory to a complex society should suggest why more "neutral" forms of the hypotheses were utilized at the outset. What in fact are the social attitudes found among the socially deprived and the socially privileged? After these have been established other amplifications can be attempted.

Given the complexity of the public issues which were included in the questionnaire, it is not always readily apparent which attitudes will be more common among the socially privileged and which ones will be more common among the socially deprived. Therefore, the present chapter will first examine how the independent variables are related to the public issues, and then it will examine the extent to which the church variables are correlated with certain public-issue attitudes. It will conclude by discussing the adequacy of the simple hypothesis that the privileged prefer one set of social attitudes while the deprived prefer the opposite attitudes.

The Independent Variables and Public Policy

1. Introduction

If our hypothesis on privilege and deprivation has any merit, we should find that older persons, females, persons of lower education, those with lower ISEC scores, inhabitants of more rural areas, and nonwhites should have a tendency to view issues in one way. And in contrast, younger people, males, the more highly educated, those with higher ISEC scores, urban persons, and whites should tend to view issues in a different way. This is a very "mixed" group of variables to be using to test the privilege-deprivation hypothesis. However, it is the logical extension of the hypothesis used thus far in the study.

We will examine each of the variables in turn with respect to its relation to the Index on Federal Activity (IFA), its influence upon the individual public policy issues, and its relation to the issues of "the church and public policy."

2. Age

When we compare the age groupings with the various categories on the IFA (Table 8-A) it becomes clear that there is a tendency for older people to be less in favor of federal activity than younger people. However, we must ask whether this tendency is a result of the particular issues chosen to construct the IFA or whether the tendency for younger people to favor federal activity is true in all issues in this study. When age was related to all of the options used in questions 44 and 45 of the questionnaire, on nine of the thirteen issues involved there was a tendency for the younger respondents to be more in favor of the policy. The only issues where more favor was found among the older respondents were four of the six "agricultural" issues. It appears quite clear that older people tend to be more opposed to federal "solu-

TABLE 8-A: Age Related to the Index on Federal Activity in Percent of Respondents

Age	N	Low 623	Moderately low 1886	Moderate 2558	Moderately high 2119	High 1051	N.R. 312	Total 8549
0–19	448	5	16	28	33	17	1	100
20–34	1719	5	21	31	28	14	1	100
35–49	2953	6	21	32	26	13	2	100
50–64	2149	9	23	29	25	11	4	100
65+	1242	12	27	25	17	9	11	100
N.R.	38	11	11	32	16	11	21	100
Total	8549	7	22	30	25	12	4	100

tions" to public issues. They are even less in favor of Medicare, although it is an issue of "self interest" for them.

The clear weight of evidence is in support of the thesis that older people are generally less in favor of federal "solutions" to problems than are younger people. Will they also be less in favor of the "church" being involved in public issues?

When age was related to church and public policy issues (question 46) a confusing pattern resulted. The older respondents were more in favor of five of the seven issues, and less in favor of "open church membership" and a "free pulpit." How can a person not support an open church membership but wish to support "the Negro's struggle to achieve civil rights"? Or how does a person favor denominations issuing policy statements but oppose a "free pulpit"? The *pattern* of age related to church and public policy issues is a contradictory pattern. The relation between age and "church and public policy" issues is not clear.

3. Sex

When the sex of the respondents was related to the Index on Federal Activity, no meaningful relationship was found (Table 8-B). Sex apparently does not affect one's attitude in this index one way or the other.

Moreover, when sex was related to the thirteen individual issues, no meaningful pattern resulted. Of the ten issues which have some federal activity implied in them, females are more in favor of exactly half of them. Of the other three (nonfederal activity issues) they are

TABLE 8-B: Sex Related to the Index on Federal Activity in Percent of Respondents

Sex	N	Low	Moderately low	Moderate	Moderately high	High	N.R.	Total
		623	1886	2558	2119	1051	312	8549
Male	3364	9	23	28	24	13	3	100
Female	5175	6	21	31	25	12	4	100
N.R.	10	20	0	20	20	10	30	100
Total	8549	7	22	30	25	12	4	100

more in favor of one of them. Sex is simply not a very meaningful variable for predicting opinion on the thirteen public issues.

It is also difficult to establish any meaningful relation between sex and the attitudes on issues of the church and public policy. Females are more in favor of three issues, less in favor of three issues, and exactly equal to males on the seventh issue. They are less in favor of a "free pulpit," denominational policy statements, and religion in the public schools. But they are more in favor than males, of open church membership, helping Negroes in the struggle for justice, and in refraining from alcoholic beverages. It appears that sex must be rejected as a meaningful variable in predicting social attitudes among our survey population.

4. Educational Achievement

Table 8-C shows a modest tendency for people with more education to be more in favor of federal activity. However, this relationship between educational achievement and the Index on Federal Activity is not very pronounced.

When educational achievement was related to each of the thirteen issues in questions 44 and 45, those with higher education tended to be more in favor of ten of the issues. Only price supports for agriculture and Medicare were less favored by them. Education appears to be unrelated to opinions on "preservation of the family farm." The burden of the evidence falls on the side of persons with more education being more in favor of federal activity as a "solution" for public issues. When one considers that the more educated persons were also more in favor of farmer cooperatives and collective market bargaining for agriculture, there is some reason to suppose that the more educated people in the sample tended to favor "collective" solutions to public issues and not just federal activity.

TABLE 8-C: Education Related to the Index on Federal Activity in Percent of Respondents

Education	N	Low	Moderately low	Moderate	Moderately high	High	N.R.	Total
		623	1886	2558	2119	1051	312	8549
0-8th grade	936	14	22	25	22	9	10	100
High School	2158	8	20	30	27	11	3	100
Trade School	952	7	21	34	24	11	3	100
College	2618	7	26	31	23	11	2	100
Graduate School	1774	5	20	29	27	18	2	100
N.R.	111	14	22	15	14	5	32	100
Total	8549	7	22	30	25	12	4	100

How does educational achievement relate to opinions on issues of the church and public policy? Four of the seven issues are more favored by those who have higher education: open church membership, freedom of the pulpit, church support for the Negro civil rights movement, and denominational policy statements. The three that are less favored by those with higher education are: prayers in the public schools, religion in the public schools, and refraining from the use of alcohol. It would be quite possible to summarize such a grouping by contending that higher education is correlated with increased concern for the social relevance of the church, more certainty about the separation of church and state, and less concern for "moralistic" issues (in this case abstaining from alcohol). In all of the ways in which it was tested, education showed a fairly consistent pattern of influence upon social attitudes.[1]

5. Socio-Economic Class

The pattern of responses for the Index of Socio-Economic Class exactly parallels the pattern for education (see Table 8-D for example). Higher social class, like higher education, is associated with a tendency to approve federal activity and church involvement in public issues.

6. Rural-Urban Differentiation

The relationship between rural-urban differences and the Index on

133

TABLE 8-D: Index on Socio-Economic Class Related to the Index on Federal Activity in Percent of Respondents

ISEC				Index on Federal Activity				
		Low	Moderately low	Moderate	Moderately high	High	N.R.	Total
	N	623	1886	2558	2119	1051	312	8549
Low	1085	13	22	24	19	9	13	100
Moderately low	2483	8	21	30	27	11	4	100
Moderately high	2298	6	22	32	26	11	2	100
High	2683	6	23	30	24	16	1	100
Total	8549	7	22	30	25	12	4	100

Federal Activity showed a modest tendency for urban people to be more in favor of federal activity (Table 8-E). When rural-urban differences were compared with the thirteen individual issues, five issues had a rise with urbanization in the percentage favoring; five had a similar decline and three showed no relationship. All five of the issues showing a decline with urbanization in the percentage favoring were "agricultural" issues. It would seem that this is a clear case of opposing federal activity (or collective activity of any sort) if the activity is not in one's self interest.

The relationship between urbanization and the church and public policy table was inconclusive. The more urban samples were less in

TABLE 8-E: Rural-Urban Differentiation Related to the Index on Federal Activity in Percent of Respondents

Rural-Urban Category				Index on Federal Activity				
		Low	Moderately low	Moderate	Moderately high	High	N.R.	Total
	N	623	1886	2558	2119	1051	312	8549
0-9,999	1433	10	24	30	20	8	8	100
10,000-49,999	1059	7	23	35	25	7	3	100
Great Plains' Cities	1326	6	21	27	25	16	5	100
All Others	4731	9	22	29	26	11	3	100
Total	8549	7	22	30	25	12	4	100

favor of open membership, refraining from alcohol and having religion taught in the schools and more in favor of a free pulpit, prayers in the schools and denominational policy statements. Urbanization did not affect attitudes on supporting the Negro's civil rights struggle.

In general we conclude that rural-urban differentiation was not a very meaningful variable affecting social attitudes in any patterned way. This lessening of importance found in rural-urban distinction undoubtedly reflects the increasing dominance of urban values in our society, a consequence in large part of the impact of the mass media and high rates of mobility.

7. Race

When the Negroes were compared with the total survey population on their scores for the Index on Federal Activity (Table 8-F), it was found that they were considerably more in favor of federal activity than were the whites. It should be remembered that this index did not involve any questions which were clearly related to the race issue.

When race was related to each of the thirteen public policy issues, nonwhite were more in favor of every public policy issue except "preservation of the family farm" and "farmer cooperatives." Likewise, the nonwhites were more in favor of every "church and public policy" issue except refraining from the use of alcoholic beverages.

It is clear that nonwhites are generally more in favor of collective activity (both on the part of government and the church) in the solution of social problems. Our findings would support what has generally been acknowledged in the past. The federal government has generally been more responsive to their grievances than have individuals or local groups.

8. Former Denomination

We turn now to the first of two "mixed" variables (involving some

TABLE 8-F: Race Related to Index on Federal Activity in Percent of Respondents

Race	Index on Federal Activity					
	Low	Mod. low	Moderate	Mod. high	High	Total
Total Sample Population	8	23	31	26	13	100
Nonwhite Sample	1	4	14	49	32	100

aspect of church participation but treated as "independent variables") in order to examine the relation of such variables to the public issues under question in this chapter.

In Table 8-G, the denominational backgrounds of the respondents are related to the Index on Federal Activity. The denominations have been ordered in the table according to their respective scores on the Index of Socio-Economic Class (explained in chapter 6) going from the "highest class" denomination to the lowest. Examination of that table shows that there appears to be very little relation between "former" denomination and approval or disapproval of federal activity. We notice some tendency for former "Baptists" to be above average in their approval of federal activity, and there is a modest tendency for the former "E and R's" to be below average, but the rest of the denominations are very close to one another. According to ISEC scores, the "Presbyterians" should have been most in favor of federal activity, not the "Baptists." The curiously high scores of the "Baptists" are at least partially explained by remembering how high the nonwhites were in the IFA scores and noting that a very high percentage of nonwhites

TABLE 8-G: Denominational Background Related to the Index on Federal Activity in Percent of Respondents

Denominational Background	N	Low 623	Moderately low 1886	Moderate 2558	Moderately high 2119	High 1051	N.R. 312	Total 8549
Presbyterian	855	7	23	30	23	13	3	100
Methodist	1255	7	22	30	25	13	3	100
Congregational	1963	6	25	30	24	12	3	100
Baptist	541	7	17	27	30	19	2	100
Lutheran	910	9	21	30	23	13	5	100
Evangelical and Reformed	1632	9	23	30	25	8	5	100
Entire Survey Population	8549	7	22	30	25	12	4	100

in this survey were "former Baptists" (13 percent of all "Baptists" in the survey are nonwhite).

When former denomination was related to the individual public policy issues, we found a tendency for former Presbyterians, Methodists, Congregationalists and Baptists to be more in favor of the issues than the former members of the Lutheran and Evangelical and Reformed churches. However, that *exact* pattern applied to only five issues: participation in the UN, soil conservation, food for peace, nondiscriminatory housing legislation, and nondiscriminatory employment legislation. Another way to describe the pattern is to point out that the Baptists were more in favor on all issues except farmer cooperatives and collective market bargaining (the influence of the high percentage of nonwhites among the Baptists?), Presbyterians favored 9 issues, Methodists 8, Congregationalists 6, Lutherans 5, and Evangelical and Reformed 3 (preservation of the family farm, Medicare, and government price supports for agriculture). Again, then, Baptists seem to be most in favor of the issues and "E and R's" least in favor.

Turning to the issues of "church and public policy," what was the pattern? The more "upper class" denominations were more in favor of open membership, a free pulpit, churches supporting civil rights issues, and denominational policy statements. The other issues tended to be mixed in pattern except that the more "lower class" denominations were more in favor of religion being taught in the public schools.

We could summarize the "influence" of former denomination by saying that the denominations associated with higher class position tend to be more in favor of collective action on social issues. The strength of influence is not very strong and not without its ambiguities.

9. Relative Organizational Involvement

When the Index of Relative Organizational Involvement (IROI) is compared with the Index on Federal Activity (Table 8-H) there is not a clear indication of relationship between the two variables. There is some tendency for the "extreme" categories (A and F—those not involved in either outside or church organizations and those only involved in the church) to be less likely to favor federal activity, but it is a very weak tendency.

When IROI categories were compared with the individual issues in questions 44 and 45, we found that those persons who tended to be involved in both the church and "the world" are the most likely to favor federal or collective activity.

TABLE 8-H: Index of Relative Organizational Involvement Related to the Index on Federal Activity in Percent of Respondents

IROI Category

Index on Federal Activity

	N	Low 623	Mod. low 1886	Moderate 2558	Mod. high 2119	High 1051	N.R. 312	Total 8549
A. Not Involved in Either	1220	11	19	26	25	11	9	100
B. Outside Involvement Only	2834	8	22	29	25	13	2	100
C. More Outside Involvement	2185	6	24	32	24	13	2	100
D. Equal Involvement	955	6	22	31	27	12	3	100
E. More Church Involvement	380	4	23	34	25	11	3	100
F. Church Involvement Only	975	8	21	30	24	10	7	100
Total	8549	7	22	30	25	12	4	100

When we looked at the relationship of the IROI and the "church and public policy" questions (question 46), we found a somewhat confusing pattern of relationship. In terms of being above or below average in favoring the particular policies, most of the IROI categories do not follow any "reasonable" pattern. We can only note some interesting patterns for two of the categories. Those not involved in either outside organizations or the church (social isolates) were above average in three issues (prayers in schools, abstaining from alcohol, and religion being taught in the schools). These are the issues that those of higher education or higher ISEC were likely to favor *less*. Are the social isolates "people of deprivation"? Also, the respondents who were involved *only* in outside organizations were the ones more in favor of two issues (open membership and free pulpit). These are the only issues which received more than two-thirds support from the total survey population. They are the issues that involve relatively "passive" attitudes toward social issues and the church. (Recall that a "passive" social attitude for the church approves having open membership policies but does not support the Negroes' struggle for social justice, and it permits a free pulpit but does not allow denominations to "go on record" advocating a particular social position.)

10. A Theory Reexamined

At the outset, it was recognized that attitudes on social issues involve a complex interplay of factors. However, in keeping with the operating hypothesis of Part 2, it was decided to deal with social attitudes in terms of a social privilege-deprivation polarity. Without making use of terms such as "liberal" or "conservative" because they appear to have such transient and invidious meanings in a complex social order, it was suggested that the socially privileged people will look at issues from one point of view and the socially deprived could be expected to take an opposite point of view. We have now compared a variety of social factors (most of which involve some form of privilege or deprivation within them) to the social issues of the questionnaire. What has been the result, and are we now in a position to put some content into phrases like "status quo" and "social change"?

Our operating theory suggested that younger people, males, the more highly educated, those of higher class, the more urban residents, and the white respondents should view social issues in a similar way. That is, they should all have tendencies to favor the same issues.

Examining our findings with respect to the Index on Federal Activity, we found the following results:

Correlated with Higher IFA Scores	*No Correlation Discernible*
Younger Respondents	Sex
Higher Education Categories	
Higher ISEC Scores	
Urban Categories	
Negro Respondents	
Former "Baptists"	
"Middle" IROI Categories (weak correlation)	

These are very interesting results. Generally, one finds a pattern similar to expectation, but there are exceptions. Are they important exceptions? The fact that sex did not correlate one way or the other suggests that females may not be as "deprived" as we had earlier supposed, and the fact that our "mixed" independent variables (former denomination and IROI) did not completely follow the "expected" pattern may simply suggest that we will want to look at the church participation variables in the next section with some care. However, to have Negroes as an exception to "expectation" seems at first glance to be more important. Are the "privileged" Negroes who are a part of this study accepting a "privileged" point of view on social attitudes in spite of their "deprived" racial position?[2] We would want to ask why Negro parishioners sometimes tend to take a more "deprived" orientation with respect to church participation. Is the church a compensation for their "deprivation" and their orientation on social issues a reflection of their "privilege"? We can only say at this point, that this group appears to be a fascinating exception to traditional observations and that they will need to be kept in mind as we proceed with the analysis.

We attempted to discover if a meaningful pattern could be found by relating each of the individual items in questions 44, 45, and 46 to the various independent variables we have been discussing. We did find that there was some support for the thesis that privileged people tend to react one way while the deprived react in opposite directions. However, the number of exceptions to the hypothesis causes us to hold it very tentatively. It appears that a great many factors interplay in attitudes on social issues. We could not find clear indications of a few dominant factors that tend to influence attitudes.

The Church Participation Variables and Public Policy

1. Introduction

Given the complexity of relationships already found when the independent variables were related to public policy questions, we wonder just how effective the church participation variables will be in predicting attitudes on the variety of public issues under examination. However, since there was some slight tendency for measures of social privilege to be related in one way to public issues while measures of social deprivation were related in another way, we can begin by asking this question: Will the two church participation variables associated with social deprivation (the Index of Devotional Orientation and the Index of Belief Orientation) be associated with one type of social attitude and the Index of Organizational Involvement with another type of social attitude? The fourth church participation variable, the Index of Religious Knowledge, should be more closely associated with social privilege (and the IOI), though that association has already been found to be less reliable.

2. The Church Participation Indices and the Index on Federal Activity

Based on our previous findings the following expectations are the most logical ones:

A. Social Privilege Indices
   1. Higher IOI associated with *higher* IFA
   2. Higher IRK associated with *higher* IFA
B. Social Deprivation Indices
   1. Higher IDO associated with *lower* IFA
   2. Higher IBO associated with *lower* IFA

Each of the church participation indices was related to the Index on Federal Activity in turn, and the results were:

A. Social Privilege Indices
   1. The IOI had *no association* of any kind with the IFA
   2. Higher IRK associated with *higher* IFA (Tables 8-I and 8-Ia)
B. Social Deprivation Indices
   1. Higher IDO associated with *higher* IFA (Tables 8-J and 8-Ja)
   2. The IBO had *no association* of any kind with the IFA

To have the empirical findings result in *only one* index (the IRK) associated in the "expected" way with a measure of social attitudes, and to have one other index (the IDO) associated in a manner *opposite*

TABLE 8-I: Index of Religious Knowledge Related to the Index on Federal Activity in Percent of Respondents

IRK Categories	N	Low	Moderately low	Moderate	Moderately high	High	N.R.	Total
		623	1886	2558	2119	1051	312	8549
Low	1052	10	20	24	25	10	11	100
Moderately low	2960	8	22	29	26	11	3	100
Moderately high	3233	6	23	32	24	12	2	100
High	1304	6	22	31	24	16	2	100
Total	8549	7	22	30	25	12	4	100

TABLE 8-Ia: Index of Religious Knowledge Related to the Index on Federal Activity (Collapsed Categories) in Percent of Respondents

IRK Categories	N	Low 2509	Moderate 2558	High 3170	N.R. 312	Total 8549
Low	4012	30	27	36	7	100
High	4537	28	32	38	2	100
Total	8549	29	30	37	4	100

TABLE 8-J: Index of Devotional Orientation Related to the Index on Federal Activity in Percent of Respondents

IDO Categories	N	Low 623	Moderately low 1886	Moderate 2558	Moderately high 2119	High 1051	N.R. 312	Total 8549
Low	3949	7	23	29	24	13	4	100
Moderately low	2697	8	23	31	24	11	4	100
Moderately high	1270	7	19	30	28	13	3	100
High	633	6	20	31	26	13	4	100
Total	8549	7	22	30	25	12	4	100

TABLE 8-Ja: Index of Devotional Orientation Related to the Index on Federal Activity (Collapsed Categories) in Percent of Respondents

IDO Categories	N	Low 2509	Moderate 2558	High 3170	N.R. 312	8549
Low	6646	30	30	36	4	100
High	1903	26	30	40	4	100
Total	8549	29	30	37	4	100

of "expectation," suggests two possible interpretations. First, one could argue that the "expectation" was based on such slight tendencies in the previous findings that it really was not a very strong "expectation" in the first place. Therefore, to have "deviant" findings is not too surprising. Such an interpretation would have a great deal to commend it, *if* the above findings are isolated patterns. That is, if we find no other examples of such "unexpected" patterning of the variables, then we simply would assign these examples to the category of "statistical oddities." However, another interpretation which would be equally plausible is that, in spite of the weak previous associations on which the expectation was based, perhaps the IRK and the IDO are two types of church participation variables that are very significant in any analysis of the influence of religious institutions.

As has been shown several times in the study, most research on church participation has tended to concentrate on some form of organizational involvement (attendance, membership, etc.), or on some form of "belief" (acceptance of traditional doctrines, etc.). To have those two variables *not* function in this first test of influence upon social attitudes is a critical finding. The operating theory of privilege and deprivation certainly does not account for the findings and the fact that it does not cause us to become hesitant about it. We certainly desire more patterns that will assist in deciding what amplifications of the theory are necessary to explain such interesting "deviations."

3. The Church Participation Indices and the Public Issues

Each church participation index was related to each of the thirteen public issues, in order to see if there was an increase or a decrease in the percentage favoring the issue associated with increased church participation. The results of such comparison are summarized in Table 8-K. In this table it is assumed that there was increased approval of the issues with increased church participation except where a "minus" sign appears. In those cases there was a decrease of approval associated with an increase in the church participation index.

The table shows some interesting results. In the first place, the IOI and the IRK results almost exactly match the results produced when the variables of education and social class were related to the public policy issues. The only exception is the issue "preservation of the family farm." That is the only case where the relationship associated with the church variables differed from the relationships associated with the independent variables. Thus it appears that social attitudes associated with certain types of privilege are the same, whether measured by

TABLE 8-K: Public Policy Issues Related to Church Participation Indices

Public Policy Issue	Church Participation Index			
	IOI	IRK	IDO	IBO
A. U.S. Participation in the United Nations				—
B. Soil Conservation Program				—
C. Food for Peace Program				
D. Preservation of the Family Farm				
E. Federal Nondiscriminatory Employment Legislation				—
F. Medical Care for Aged Through Social Security	—	—		
G. Farmer Cooperatives				—
H. Federal Nondiscriminatory Housing Legislation				—
I. Ban on Nuclear Testing				—
J. Federal Aid to Public and Private Education	—	—		—
K. Cabinet Post for Urban Affairs				—
L. Government Price Support Program (Agricultural)	—	—		
M. Collective Market Bargaining (Agricultural)			—	—

"church" variables or "independent" variables. This might be some support for the assertion that church participation simply reinforces social attitudes associated with one's social position.

The second interesting fact can be stated in two ways. Either we can point to *how often* increased belief orientation is associated with a decline in approval of the issue, or we can point to *how seldom* increased devotional orientation is associated with a decline in approval of the issue. If we stress the first way of making the point, we would note that only for the following issues was increased belief not associated with a decline in approval: food for peace, preservation of the family farm, Medicare, and agricultural price support. If we stress the second way of putting the point, we note that only on the issue of collective market bargaining for the farmer does increased devotional orientation not mean increased approval. Either way of stating the issue, the point is the same: devotional orientation and belief orientation do *not* have the same influence upon attitudes toward social issues.

Since the IBO pattern tends to be the opposite of the pattern associated with the most reliable indices of social privilege (education and class), we can support the hypothesis that belief is associated with social deprivation as a style of church participation and in terms of social attitude. Why does the IDO differ? We are left once again with the bulk of the evidence supporting our hypothesis, but with a rather noticeable "deviation." The relationship between three of the church participation variables (IOI, IRK, and IBO) and social attitudes is according to "expectation," but the IDO does not fit the pattern.

4. The Church Participation Indices and the "Church and Public Policy" Issues

Each of the church participation variables was related to the church and public policy issues in order to determine if there was an increase or decrease in the percentage favoring the issue that could be associated with increased church participation. The results of this comparison are summarized in Table 8-L. In this table it is assumed that there was an increased percentage favoring the issue in question associated with each index unless a "minus" sign appears. In those cases there was a decrease of approval of the issue associated with an increase in that particular church participation index.

In seeking to interpret the table, let us recall what was found on these same issues when they were related to the independent variables. There it was found that those with higher education and higher social class (the most reliable indicators of social privilege) tended to be more in favor of all issues except prayer in the public schools, religion in the public schools, and refraining from the use of alcohol. In the present table notice that the Index of Religious Knowledge comes closest to duplicating that pattern, and the Index of Belief Orientation is exactly the opposite of that pattern. The patterns of the other two indices (IOI and IDO) are "mixed" when compared with the pattern associated with social privilege.

In summary, this table appears to show that persons oriented toward the church in terms of religious knowledge hold views on church and public policy issues similar to those held by people of privilege (hardly surprising since earlier we found that the IRK tended to be associated

TABLE 8-L: Church and Public Policy Issues Related to Church Participation Indices

Church and Public Policy Issue	IOI	IRK	IDO	IBO
1. Church membership should always be open to people of all races and nationalities				—
2. Ministers have a right to preach on controversial subjects from the pulpit			—	—
3. Prayers should be allowed in public schools		—		
4. Churches should support the Negro's struggle to achieve civil rights				—
5. Denominations have a right to issue policy statements on social and economic matters				—
6. Christians should refrain from using alcoholic beverages				
7. Religion should be taught in public schools		—		

positively with social privilege). Likewise, the findings on the IBO follow expectations. Since that index was negatively associated with social privilege, it therefore should be negatively associated with social privilege in terms of attitudes on church and public policy issues. But why did the IOI and the IDO *not* follow the "expectations" in this instance?

5. Summary

In chapter 6 we found that two of the most reliable indicators of social privilege (higher education and higher social class) were both associated with higher scores on the Index of Organizational Involvement and the Index of Religious Knowledge. Recalling this, we should expect that persons holding those two styles of church participation would tend to hold social attitudes associated with those same two indicators of social privilege. That expectation was substantiated by the empirical findings in some instances and was unsubstantiated in other instances. The following is a summary of the findings. (An asterisk appears next to instances where the expectation was followed.)

A. With respect to the IFA:
   1. The IOI showed no pattern of relationship
   *2. The IRK followed the pattern of social privilege
   3. The IDO followed the pattern of social privilege
   4. The IBO showed no pattern of relationship
B. With respect to the individual public policy issues:
   *1. The IOI followed the pattern of social privilege
   *2. The IRK followed the pattern of social privilege
   3. The IDO followed the pattern of social privilege more often than not
   *4. The IBO followed the pattern of social deprivation more often than not
C. With respect to the church and public policy issues:
   1. The IOI did *not* follow the pattern of social privilege in three issues
   *2. The IRK tended to follow the pattern of social privilege
   3. The IDO did *not* follow the pattern of social deprivation in three issues
   *4. The IBO followed exactly the pattern of social deprivation

This summary is quite significant. Notice that only the IRK followed the expected pattern of relationship in all three types of social attitudes. The IBO followed expectation twice, the IOI followed expectation once, and the IDO *never* followed expectation. In total we had six cases meeting expectation and six which did not.

At the conclusion of chapter 6 there was some uncertainty about the relationship between the IRK and social privilege. The findings of this chapter add substantially to the assurance that the IRK is indeed closely associated with social privilege. Moreover, we find that two out of three times the IBO continues to reflect its relationship with social deprivation. Does the fact that the IOI is not more strongly related to the social attitudes associated with social privilege reveal something about the nature of the influence of Organizational Involvement or is it simply that the questions were not very meaningful ones? It is impossible to say at this point. Finally, the Index of Devotional Orientation takes on new importance in this chapter. Why is its influence so clearly contrary to expectation? Again, is it that Devotional Orientation is a special form of church participation which is not yet explained? Or, is it that the questions were not meaningful measures of social attitudes? The pattern is not yet clear and so eventually we must look at other social attitude questions if we are to clarify the pattern.

Before turning to a summary of this chapter, one last task must be completed. Since the IRK was the only variable associated in an "expected" way with the IFA, we need to apply some tests to see whether or not that relationship was so weak that it will disappear if the measures of social privilege are held constant while the IRK and IFA are related to each other. The test was performed with the following results:

1. With age held constant a positive relationship continued between the two variables for all five age categories.
2. With education held constant a positive relationship continued between the two variables for two of the five categories (the least educated and the most educated).
3. With ISEC held constant a positive relationship continued between the two variables for three of the four ISEC categories (all except the "moderately high" group).

Therefore, in more than half of the categories (ten out of fourteen) the relationship continued to hold. Education came closest to eliminating the relationship. We now have some reason to assume that a religious knowledge type of church participation orientation is *reinforcing* social attitudes held by socially privileged people. Will such a finding be repeated in the case of other social issues?

A Theory Under Pressure

In this chapter, where for the first time we have put the entire theory of the study to a test, the result has been ambiguous. Up to this point a theory of privilege-deprivation had adequately served as a means of "explaining" the empirical findings of the study. The privileged were tending to relate to the church in certain "styles" and the deprived tended to adopt different styles for their church participation. This is not to say that there were not minor ambiguities in the earlier findings, but they tended to be of such a character that we had no reason to suspect that modest additions to the theory would not handle them. We were finding that differences in an individual's social situation were resulting in different modes of religious orientation. Our first hypothesis was being upheld.

However, this chapter has been the first test of whether "difference in an individual's social situation" would result in "different social outlook." And even more importantly, would "different church participation orientations have different consequences for behavior and attitudes on social issues"? We were also interested in whether the social situations associated with the religious orientations "explain" the social attitudes associated with the religious orientations.

In using a wide range of social issues to test all of these hypotheses and our theory, we found out several things:

1. Social attitudes are a very complex matter in terms of their relation to certain social factors. The social factors are not so easily grouped as they were in earlier sections of the volume. They do not tend to fall into just two types: the measures of "deprivation" and the measures of "privilege." Different "types" of deprivation appear to be related to social attitudes in different ways. Because one is an older person does not mean that such a form of "deprivation" will result in attitudes parallel to the attitudes associated with being a woman (which appears to be a different "type" of deprivation). Urban "privilege" and the attitudes associated with it are not the same as social class "privilege" and attitudes associated with that type of privilege. Just who is in favor of what "social change" and for what reason proved to be a very complex matter indeed. How one defines "conservatism" or the "status quo" in terms of attitudes, is shown to be a matter of considerable complexity and not easily summarized by a simple hypothesis.

2. Almost by definition, educational achievement and social class are measures of "privilege" and "deprivation." We may argue just how "deprived" older people are, or women, or rural residents, but we cannot really argue about whether those without education and with "lower" class are "deprived" in contemporary America. Thus, not surprisingly, education and social class were found to be associated with very similar patterns of social attitudes. Indeed, it will be remembered that they were in fact the *only* two variables which in Part 2 were *always* associated in "expected" ways with all four church participation variables. It is thus legitimate now to refer to these two variables as the "most reliable" measures of privilege and deprivation for the purposes of continued use of our hypothesis.

3. The relationships between church participation orientations and social attitudes proved to be a much more complex matter than the simple "working hypothesis" had suggested. Only the IRK followed "expectations" consistently. The IBO proved to be the next most "consistent" church participation variable. However there were some problems explaining the social attitudes associated with devotional and organizational orientations.

4. Race proved to be a somewhat unpredictable variable in this chapter. The sample of relatively "socially privileged" Negroes used in this study tended to be related to all of the variables in a somewhat "unique" way. In some ways the Negroes of this study are oriented to the church like "deprived" people and in some ways they are oriented to the church in "privileged" ways. They have some social attitudes that are similar to the "privileged" and some that are similar to "deprived" attitudes. They are, in short, a very "special" case which will need to be examined carefully in future sections before they can be incorporated into any consistent theory.

What, then, is the standing of our hypotheses and theory at this point? All of the hypotheses originally stated for the study are being upheld. Different social situations *are* resulting both in different church participation orientations *and* in different social attitudes. Different church participation orientations *are* resulting in different social attitudes. *But* in just what way the church participation variables are proving to be "intervening" variables between social situations and social attitudes is proving to be a complex and difficult matter. Our simple "working" theory about social privilege and deprivation is being tested rather severely. It still "functions" more often than not, but there is a significant number of "exceptions."

In conclusion it must be stated that the social issues used in this chapter were a complex group. It may well be that the difficulty of finding clear patterns of relationships is related to the use of too many issues. In order to see whether that is the case, we turn now to a concentration upon a single issue: the racial crisis. This is of course also complex, but most people have fairly strong feelings about the issue and the issue has a clarity for purposes of this study which many of the issues do not have; namely, that the United Church of Christ has taken some rather clear "positions" with respect to the issue. Do we then, find more clarity of relationships in this issue?

Chapter 9–Church Participation and the Racial Crisis

The Racial Crisis and the Churches

Though many denominations have from time to time addressed themselves to a wide variety of social issues, the problem of racial justice stands in a class by itself in terms of contemporary church life. As America has become conscious of the deep rifts in our society along racial lines, many major denominations have been involved at several levels in seeking solutions to the numerous dilemmas surrounding the actualization of social justice for Negroes. The United Church of Christ has been one of the most active denominations in this struggle.

Historically, the Congregational churches were active through laymen and clergy in working for the abolition of slavery. The Congregationalists established a number of schools and colleges for Negroes in the South and for many years the Council for Social Action has been active in working for racial justice. In more recent years, the United Church of Christ has been supporting the movement toward racial equality through a denominational campaign on "open church membership," through a national denominational fund raising effort called "Racial Justice Now," and by giving financial and leadership aid to a variety of national and local Negro protest movements. Local ministers and laymen, congregational social action committees, and the national instrumentalities of the denomination have participated in marches,

151

economic boycotts, and a variety of campaigns to assist in the efforts toward a just society.

The question is, just how much has this effort on the part of the church resulted in attitudinal change on the part of participants in local congregations? Do we find that the attitudes on civil rights have a clearer relationship to the various styles of church participation than was the case when we examined the public issues in chapter 8, issues in which the denomination has not exerted as much effort?

It was clear from the findings of chapter 7 that the overall picture of the survey population taken as a whole was hardly that of a very "radical" group on racial justice. However, it is obvious from our study that all participants in the denomination are not likely to be affected in the same way or to the same degree by any social issue. We would therefore expect that racial justice would be no exception, and we will expect to find certain patterns emerging. In order to understand the patterns, we will first examine which of the independent variables appear to be related to certain types of racial attitudes, and then we will examine how the church participation variables are related to these same attitudes. Finally, we will want to know if holding the independent variables constant will eliminate the relationships between the church participation variables and the racial attitudes. Let us begin then by examining the relationship between the independent factors and the racial attitudes.

The Independent Variables and the Racial Crisis

1. Introduction

Making predictions about racial attitudes is not a simple matter. Recent events have shown how complex are the feelings of Americans with respect to the place of Negroes in our culture. On the one hand, "liberty and justice for all" is a fundamental part of the American Creed, but on the other hand most Americans have appeared to be content to have Negroes in a position of "second-class" citizenship. In the midst of such a complex social pattern can we make any prediction based on a simple thesis about social privilege and deprivation? It is clear that enlarging the rights of Negroes represents a change in American patterns of behavior, but is it clear which social groups could be expected to hold at least an attitude advocating such a change? Certainly the Negro will be expected to advocate such a change, but which groups of whites are most likely to support him?

From one point of view it would be quite possible to argue that all whites are "privileged" with respect to race, and all Negroes are "deprived," and therefore *no* whites are going to be very enthusiastic about a change in the status quo in racial matters. After all, any rise in the position of the Negro represents either an immediate or a long-range "threat" to the position of whites. Negro improvement of social position "threatens" in an immediate way the job security and homes of the lower classes of whites, but it also is a kind of long-range "threat" to the social position of more upper class whites. In any event, the cause of racial justice is an issue in which the "self-interest" of any group of whites is involved. Reinhold Niebuhr has correctly observed many years ago that "the white race in America will not admit the Negro to equal rights if it is not forced to do so."[1] Social privilege and power is not usually given up voluntarily, even if in an expanding economy it is not necessarily the case that increased "privilege" for a minority group means less "privilege" for the majority.

However, it could be expected that those not immediately "threatened" by an improvement in the social position of Negroes might be the ones most likely to have attitudes consistent with the creed of "liberty and justice for all." Indeed, the research of Brink and Harris showed that the "affluents" among the whites had less prejudiced attitudes with respect to Negroes than did the "low income" whites.[2] Will all of the variables in this study which represent "privilege" in its various forms (except for race itself of course) correlate with attitudes more in favor of justice for Negroes, or will we find that the factors are more complex than that?

We will examine each of the variables in turn to see how they are related to the two indices concerned with racial issues, the Index of Social Acceptance and the Index of Civil Rights.

2. Age

Looking first at the question of age, we found that there was a strong negative correlation between increasing age and increasing social acceptance as measured by the Index of Social Acceptance. The older respondents are less accepting of Negroes than are the younger respondents. The negative correlation pattern was true also with respect to age and the Index of Civil Rights, but the negative relationship was not as strong in this instance. Remembering that we earlier discussed the possibility that older people can be considered in some sense "deprived" in the American culture, it appears that in the case of this first factor the more "privileged" (the younger respondents) are most likely to support the Negro in his struggle for justice.

3. Sex

The sex of the respondent did not prove to be a meaningful variable in predicting attitudes with respect to the racial crisis. Females tended to have lower scores in the Index of Social Acceptance, but they had higher scores on the Index of Civil Rights. Thus, sex must be rejected as contributing significantly to our understanding of racial attitudes.

4. Educational Achievement

We found that age was negatively related to the two measures of racial attitudes, but educational achievement was related positively to the same two variables. Here is a clear case of the "privileged" being more concerned about civil rights issues.

5. Socio-Economic Class

As has so often been the case in this research, the Index of Socio-Economic Class followed the same pattern as that reported for educational achievement. Those with higher social class scores were more likely to have higher scores on both the Index of Social Acceptance and the Index of Civil Rights.

6. Rural-Urban Differentiation

As in the case of sex, the size of the city in which the respondent lived did not appear to relate in any significant way with racial attitudes. However, if we group together the "town and country" respondents with those from the cities of the Great Plains and compare this combined group with the respondents from the seven other cities in the study, some interesting patterns emerge. For example, we found that the social acceptance of the Negro was consistently greater in the combined Great Plains grouping than in the combined grouping of the other seven cities. Conversely, we also found a slightly higher degree of social distance expressed toward American Indians by parishioners in the Great Plains than by those in metropolitan area churches. While this may give support to the hypothesis that the density of minority groups functions to increase prejudice, our data were not entirely consistent. Respondents in the San Francisco area, for instance, were significantly less prejudiced against Orientals than those in any of the other sample cities where the Oriental population is far less visible.

Secondly, the regional variable clearly affected the degree of social distance expressed by our various samples of parishioners. In Table 9-A

TABLE 9-A: Social Distance: Attitudes Toward Negroes by Sample Groups

Social Distance Scale   Percent of respondents who would admit Negroes

	Lvle	Cinc	St L	Chic	Detr	Htfd	San F
Close kinship by marriage	6	4	5	8	10	7	18
My club as personal chums	19	26	26	35	35	45	56
My street as neighbors	22	30	36	40	42	49	67
My home as guests	27	41	40	55	55	70	75
Employment in my occupation	52	53	57	66	67	76	78
My church as members	45	50	58	66	66	81	84
Citizenship in my country	67	67	76	81	81	85	87
Cumulative score	238	271	298	351	356	413	465

we have reported the percentage of those who would admit Negroes to various steps in the Social Distance Scale for the seven S.M.S.A.'s. Using the cumulative percentage scores for each city as an index, we have ranked the cities according to the degree of social distance expressed by parishioners in these cities. Thus Louisville with a cumulative score of 238 ranks highest in social distance while San Francisco with 465 ranks lowest. In most instances, the percentage of those who would admit Negroes for each step in the scale increases as one moves in the table from Louisville (where the highest degree of prejudice exists) to San Francisco (where the rate of prejudice was lowest). Chicago and Detroit showed almost identical scores.

7. Race

Though several of the "independent" variables dealt with so far have significant correlations with attitudes on racial issues, it is not surprising that *the* most significant variable was race itself. Because of its importance for the study, we will examine the responses of the Negroes in more detail.

The Negro respondents in our study felt very differently from the dominant white majority of respondents on racial matters. The data would suggest that the traditional function of the Negro church as an instrument of social protest and change continues to be salient for the Negro parishioners even when they are members of congregations related to a predominantly white, middle class denomination. Looking first at the matter of social acceptance, it is not appropriate in this case to use the Index of Social Acceptance since the scores were developed on the basis of attitudes towards Negroes. Naturally, Negroes would be more accepting of Negroes than would the white majority (in fact, over 90 percent of the nonwhite subsample had a "high" Social Acceptance Index). However, what would be pertinent would be to examine how the nonwhite respondents in the sample reacted to social acceptance questions relating to other minority groups. Tables 9-B and 9-C compare the responses of white and nonwhite respondents to the social distance scale options. From this table it is apparent that the white respondents make significant differentiation in their responses depending on the racial or ethnic characteristics of the group in question. (We did not approach a 100 percent response due to nonresponses from 14 to 20 percent of our sample to various portions of the scale.)

The greatest degree of social distance is expressed toward Negroes, with only 9 percent willing to admit Negroes "to close kinship by marriage." In fact, kinship through marriage is not approved by the majority of our sample for all non-English groups. The majority, furthermore, would not accept Mexicans, Negroes, and Orientals into

TABLE 9-B: Responses of White Parishioners to the Social Distance Scale

Social Distance Scale — Percent of respondents who would admit

	English	Indian	Italian	Mexican	Negro	Oriental
Close kinship by marriage	82	32	49	21	9	20
My club as personal chums	78	51	62	46	39	42
My street as neighbors	83	63	73	54	47	62
My home as guests	83	71	75	64	58	68
Employment in my occupation	79	69	71	65	65	67
My church as members	84	76	77	72	69	74
Citizenship in my country	84	80	80	78	78	78

TABLE 9-C: Responses of Nonwhite Parishioners to the Social Distance Scale

Social Distance Scale	Percent of respondents who would admit					
	English	Indian	Italian	Mexican	Negro	Oriental
Close kinship by marriage	53	57	53	51	75	54
My club as personal chums	58	59	57	56	74	58
My street as neighbors	74	73	73	73	80	76
My home as guests	73	72	72	69	80	72
Employment in my occupation	73	73	72	72	78	73
My church as members	74	76	73	74	81	77
Citizenship in my country	74	74	74	74	78	76

"my social club as personal chums" and less than half (47 percent) would admit Negroes "to my street as neighbors."

The majority are willing, however, to admit all groups to other steps in the scale: as guests in one's home, into church membership, as fellow workers and fellow citizens.

When this same scale is examined for Negro respondents, an entirely different pattern emerges. We see that the majority of the Negro respondents would admit all persons, regardless of ethnic background, to all steps in the Social Distance Scale. Some degree of reticence is shown when it comes to "close kinship by marriage" and "to my club as personal chums"; a generally more favorable disposition is shown toward their own race. The black parishioner does not express the kind of marked social distance toward others, which was evidenced in Table 9-B. There was no evidence in 1964-65, when this data was gathered, to support a generalization which was to become more popular later, that even the middle class Negro harbors strong feelings of antipathy toward the white man.

As might be predicted from the above data, the nonwhite subsample also scored much higher on the Civil Rights Index than did the sample population as a whole. Eighty-eight percent of the nonwhite respondents scored a "high" Civil Rights Index score while only 33 percent of the total survey population had such a score.

Looking at the individual issues treated in civil rights questions which are not a part of our two civil rights indices, we also find that the Negro tends to contrast sharply with the white respondents. The statements in Table 9-D are ranked in the order of the differences between white and black responses so that those appearing at the top of the table are the issues that are joined and most differentiating.

TABLE 9-D: Civil Rights Issues: Summary of White and Negro Responses

Statement	Percent who agree (disagree)*		
	White	Negro	Percent Difference
Negroes are trying to move too fast to obtain justice and equality	52 (24)	1 (97)	51 (73)
When Negroes move into white residential areas, property values tend to go down	64 (15)	14 (73)	50 (58)
Negroes are happier in Negro churches and Negro schools	48 (16)	8 (72)	40 (56)
Negro leaders today are working for the eventual mixture of races through intermarriage	18 (43)	6 (88)	12 (45)
Restaurant owners have a right to refuse service to a person because of his race	23 (59)	2 (97)	21 (38)
On the whole, Negro children receive inferior education in comparison to white children	45 (29)	81 (9)	36 (20)
The Negro is right in demanding his full civil rights now	50 (19)	85 (12)	35 (7)
We owe the Negro some kind of compensation for past injustices	15 (54)	48 (29)	33 (25)
Negroes should now be hired even if they are not fully qualified to make up for discrimination against them in the past	4 (81)	14 (75)	10 (6)
Negroes should be given jobs in proportion to their numbers in the population	15 (57)	15 (64)	0 (7)

* Percentage disagreeing with the statement is in parentheses.

Those at the bottom are issues over which there appears to be some degree of consensus among the two racial groups. The numbers in parentheses are the percentage of respondents who disagreed with each statement.

The pace of the Negro's demand for civil rights, residential housing and the perpetuation of segregated institutions are the issues which are joined between white and black parishioners. From 56 to 73 percentage points separate white and black responses to these statements.

On the other hand, proposals to hire unqualified Negroes and to hire Negroes in proportion to their numbers in the population are rejected by the majority of both groups, with differences ranging from 7 to 10 percentage points.

Although only 18 percent of the white respondents agree that intermarriage is a goal of the civil rights movement, 43 percent disagree with this statement. The statement on intermarriage was rejected by 88 percent of the Negro respondents, a difference of 45 percent over the white responses. This suggests that while the traditional fear of the white respondent to intermarriage is not a major part of the white parishioner's ideology, a significant proportion are not yet willing to reject it completely.

Table 9-D also shows that there is a high degree of consensus among Negro respondents for all the items except one: the issue of compensatory justice. Unlike the other statements which have a Negro majority ranging from 64 to 97 percent, opinion on this issue was significantly divided. It should be noted, however, that nearly half of the Negro respondents are in favor of "some kind of compensation for past injustices," a viewpoint shared by only 15 percent of the white respondents. At the time of the study this was a latent Negro issue, which has clearly come to light in 1969 as a major issue of civil rights leaders.

The white parishioners do not reflect this high degree of consensus on the issues of the survey.

8. Denominational Background

We turn now to the first of the two variables which are not strictly speaking "independent" variables. They both involve dimensions of church participation within them, but they can appropriately be treated at this point.

When the social acceptance scores are examined in relation to the denominational background reported by our parishioners, we find some significant differences. We find, in the first place, an unusually high proportion of nonresponses to the social distance questions on the part of those with Evangelical and Reformed and Lutheran backgrounds.

In the second place, the greatest degree of difference among the six denominational groups included in Table 9-E occur between those of Congregational Christian and Evangelical and Reformed backgrounds. While 42 percent of those of Congregational background scored high on social acceptance, only 24 percent of those with backgrounds in the Evangelical and Reformed Church scored high on that scale. This is of particular interest since these two denominations now form the United Church of Christ. The difference between these two groups can be understood in the light of the historical backgrounds of the two denominations. Congregationalists have had, throughout most of their history, very close associations with the American Negro. The American Missionary Association and its century-old work in the field of Negro education and civil rights has been a long and familiar part of the denomination's mission. More than 250 Negro churches were affiliated with the Congregationalists at the time of the union.

By contrast, until recent years the relationship of the Evangelical and Reformed Church to the Negro in the United States has been peripheral. One does not think of Negro pastors, churches and schools of the Evangelical and Reformed tradition. Prior to the union, Negro students training for the ministry in Evangelical and Reformed seminaries were almost nonexistent. The traditionally German ethnic orientation of the

TABLE 9-E: Denominational Background Related to the Index of Social Acceptance in Percent of Respondents

Denominational Background	N	Low	Moderate	High	N.R.	Total
Congregational	1963	17	33	42	8	100
Baptist	541	18	33	42	7	100
Methodist	1255	16	37	39	9	100
Presbyterian	855	15	41	37	8	100
Lutheran	910	25	31	29	16	100
Evangelical and Reformed	1632	29	30	24	17	100
Total Survey Population	8549	20	34	35	11	100

(Index of Social Acceptance)

denomination made it a less likely group with which Negroes could be identified. All this has been changed with the birth of the United Church of Christ, but the consequences of the differences in backgrounds are clearly evident in our data.

A similar pattern on denominations occurred when they were related to the Index of Civil Rights. It should be noted that the denominations tended to follow the rank which they would have based on the Index of Socio-Economic Class.

9. Relative Organizational Involvement

When the Index of Relative Organizational Involvement was compared to the two racial issue indices, lower scores on both indices were found among those respondents who were either not involved in any organizational activity or those who were involved only in the church. Both of these groups also had the highest percentages of nonresponses on racial questions.

10. Summary

The overwhelming evidence from the above survey indicates that those with social "privilege" are the most likely to score high on both the Index of Social Acceptance and the Index of Civil Rights. Though there were some special relationships present in the independent factors (sex, rural-urban difference, and race), it appears to be quite clear that the patterns of relationship between social factors and racial attitudes are clearer and more consistent than was the case with the issues studied in the previous chapter.

The following summary of findings in this section indicates the patterns of relationship that have been found:

   A. Measures of Social Privilege Which Correlate with Increased Scores on Both Racial Indices (ISA and ICR):
     1. Youth
     2. Educational Achievement
     3. Higher ISEC Scores
     4. More "Upper" Class Denominational Background
     5. Organizational Involvement (Church and Outside Organizations)
   B. Measures of Social Deprivation Which Did Not Correlate with Decreased Scores on Both Racial Indices (ISA and ICR):
     1. Female Respondents
     2. Nonwhite Respondents
     3. More Rural Respondents

What then, is the pattern found between the church participation variables and the two civil rights indices? Is it clearer than was the case in the last chapter when the church participation variables were related to a variety of other public issues?

The Church Participation Indices and Racial Attitudes

Based on the data from the above section, the findings established earlier in the study and the hypothesis of privilege and deprivation in relation to church participation, the following relationships are those most to be expected when the styles of church participation are related to the two indices measuring racial attitudes:

    A. Church Participation Indices Expected to Relate Positively with the Racial Indices (ISA and ICR):
        1. Index of Organizational Involvement (IOI)
        2. Index of Religious Knowledge (IRK)
    B. Church Participation Indices Expected to Relate Negatively with the Racial Indices (ISA and ICR):
        1. Index of Devotional Orientation (IDO)
        2. Index of Belief Orientation (IBO)

When we look at the empirical findings, we see that three of the indices of church participation follow expected patterns, but one does not.

Considering first the church participation variables which followed expectation, we find that higher IOI scores were associated with higher scores on both the Index of Social Acceptance and the Index of Civil Rights. While only 35 percent of the survey population as a whole had high ISA scores, 46 percent of the respondents with high IOI scores had high ISA scores. And while 32 percent of the total survey population had high ICR scores, 42 percent of those with high IOI scores had high ICR scores. Thus those more involved organizationally in the church are more likely to have "liberal" attitudes on racial issues.

The same pattern of positive relationship emerges when the scores on the Index of Religious Knowledge are compared with the scores on the Index of Social Acceptance and the Index of Civil Rights. In fact, the IRK appeared to have an even stronger relationship to the racial attitude indices than did the IOI.

The third church participation variable which had an expected relationship with the racial attitude indices was the Index of Belief Orientation. As was expected, high belief was associated with lower scores on the two racial indices. Those who "believe more" of the traditional doctrines are less likely to be "liberal" in their social attitudes toward the Negro.

The fourth church participation variable was the one which did not fulfill expectations: the Index of Devotional Orientation. This index (which was shown in chapter 6 to be clearly related to several measures of social "deprivation") was *positively* related to both of the civil rights indices (Tables 9-F and 9-G). Such a finding is very difficult to

TABLE 9-F: Index of Devotional Orientation Related to Index of Social Acceptance in Percent of Respondents

Index of Devotional Orientation	N	Low 1695	Moderate 2890	High 3029	N.R. 935	Total 8549
Low	3949	20	35	35	11	100
Moderately Low	2697	21	34	34	11	100
Moderately High	1270	21	32	37	11	100
High	633	15	33	41	11	100
Total	8549	20	34	35	11	100

TABLE 9-G: Index of Devotional Orientation Related to Index of Civil Rights in Percent of Respondents

Index of Devotional Orientation	N	Low 2417	Moderately Low 1841	Moderately High 1258	High 2703	N.R. 330	Total 8549
Low	3949	30	20	15	31	4	100
Moderately Low	2697	28	23	15	30	4	100
Moderately High	1270	26	23	15	33	3	100
High	633	22	23	13	38	4	100
Total	8549	28	22	15	32	4	100

explain on the basis of "social conditioning." Thus, for the second time the Index of Devotional Orientation has been related to social attitude variables in an unexpected way. We found earlier that it differed radically from expectation in terms of its relationship to the Index on Federal Activity, and now we find that it again differs radically from expectation in terms of its relationship to both the Index of Social Acceptance and the Index of Civil Rights. It is now quite clear that some form of modification is needed in the simple theory which has been employed in this study about how church participation acts as an intervening variable between social conditioning factors and social attitudes.

Accordingly, we find that *all four* of the church participation variables are related in significant ways to social attitudes on racial issues. Three of the indices follow patterns expected on the basis of our theory of social privilege and deprivation, but one does not. Attitudes on the racial crisis *are* then different from the other social attitudes on public issues which were examined in chapter 8. Racial attitudes *are* more clearly related both to social conditioning variables *and* to church participation variables than were the issues treated in the earlier chapter. It appears that people who responded to this study have clearer notions about their attitudes on racial issues than on several of the other public issues.

The hypotheses of the study continue to be upheld. However, before summarizing the findings of this chapter in relation to our original hypotheses, it is necessary to relate each of the church participation variables to the racial attitude indices *while holding the independent variables constant*. This procedure is not absolutely necessary in the case of the Index of Devotional Orientation (because it was related to racial attitudes in a way opposite from its relationship to the independent variables). But in the case of the other three church participation variables it will be important to know whether the relationships found were in fact merely reflections of the social conditioning factors or not.

The Relation Between Church Participation Indices and Racial Attitudes When the Independent Variables Are Held Constant

We have found that the Index of Socio-Economic Class was a very "reliable" measure of social privilege. Thus in studying what the effect is upon the relationship between the church participation variables and attitudes on civil rights when the independent social conditioning factors are held constant, we will begin by holding social class constant.

Table 9-H relates each church participation index to the two racial attitude indices with each social class category held constant. Examination of the table reveals that for the Index of Religious Knowledge there is a positive correlation between the index and both racial attitude indices for all four social class categories. The Index of Organizational Involvement and the Index of Devotional Orientation also have a positive relationship with both of the racial attitude indices in all social class categories, except in the lowest category the relationship does not hold with the Index of Social Acceptance. It is clear that the high percentage of nonresponses in this lowest class grouping is at least partly a factor in this lack of relationship.

The Index of Belief Orientation tends to have a negative relationship to scores on the racial attitudes indices. However, this relationship is not actualized for either index in the lowest class category nor for the Index of Civil Rights in the "moderately low" social class category.

It is clear from Table 9-H that the relationship between the church participation variables and attitudes on racial issues is not simply a product of social class influence. There is of course no question that social class is strongly conditioning the relationships between the church participation variables and racial attitudes. However, church participation remains as a significant intervening variable.

A similar procedure to that reported in Table 9-H was employed for the variables of age, educational achievement, former denomination and relative organizational involvement. In all of these cases, similar results emerge. That is, when each of the "independent" variables was held constant, the church participation variables continued to be related to racial attitudes in the way described above. The IOI, the IRK, and the IDO continued to be positively related to ISA and ICR scores and the IBO was related negatively to ISA and ICR scores. Church participation appears to have an influence upon racial attitudes independent of the influence of the social conditioning factors related to church participation.

The Hypothesis Reexamined

In this chapter we have examined a public issue which has more prominence in the American scene than many of the issues examined in

TABLE 9-H: The Relation of Church Participation Indices to Civil Rights Indices by Social Class Category

Index of Socio-Economic Class	Index of Church Participation	\multicolumn{4}{c}{Index of Social Acceptance}	\multicolumn{3}{c}{Index of Civil Rights}
		Low	Mod.	High	N.R.	Low & Mod. Low	Mod. High & High	N.R.
Low	IOI L and ML	30	24	13	32	63	22	15
	MH and H	32	27	21	20	53	36	11
	IRK L and ML	29	17	11	42	60	18	21
	MH and H	24	38	19	19	56	36	7
	IDO L and ML	33	30	23	33	60	23	16
	MH and H	25	31	18	26	60	30	9
	IBO L and ML	25	23	14	38	54	23	22
	MH and H	31	27	15	26	63	26	10
Moderately Low	IOI L and ML	29	32	27	12	59	37	4
	MH and H	19	34	34	13	51	46	3
	IRK L and ML	31	27	23	18	62	30	8
	MH and H	18	38	35	9	49	49	2
	IDO L and ML	27	33	26	13	59	37	4
	MH and H	20	34	36	10	50	47	2
	IBO L and ML	22	30	32	15	55	38	6
	MH and H	28	35	26	11	57	40	3
Moderately High	IOI L and ML	21	36	35	8	53	45	2
	MH and H	17	34	42	7	44	55	1
	IRK L and ML	25	35	26	13	59	38	3
	MH and H	15	35	44	6	41	57	2
	IDO L and ML	19	27	36	8	50	47	2
	MH and H	19	32	40	8	48	50	2
	IBO L and ML	17	35	40	7	48	48	3
	MH and H	22	36	33	9	51	47	2
High	IOI L and ML	12	36	47	4	41	58	1
	MH and H	8	35	52	4	36	63	1
	IRK L and ML	17	39	37	7	52	47	1
	MH and H	7	32	57	4	32	67	1
	IDO L and ML	11	36	48	4	40	59	1
	MH and H	8	30	57	5	30	68	2
	IBO L and ML	9	34	53	4	37	62	1
	MH and H	13	38	44	4	42	57	1

chapter 8. We have found that most of the independent variables were related significantly to attitudes on racial matters, and we found that all of the church participation indices were related significantly to the same attitudes. Furthermore, controlling the major independent variables did not eliminate the relationship between the various styles of church participation and attitudes on racial matters. We therefore conclude that church participation is a kind of intervening variable between social conditioning factors and social attitudes.

In the case of three of the church participation styles, it appears that they reinforce attitudes which were socially conditioned. The cumulative effect of social and religious orientation variables is strongly suggested by our findings. If one is a "privileged" person, he is likely to have higher scores on the Index of Social Acceptance and the Index of Civil Rights, but in addition his expected styles of church participation (organizational involvement and religious knowledge) are likely to reinforce his social attitudes on race. If one is a person of "social deprivation" he is likely to have lower scores on both the ISA and the ICR and to prefer a style of church participation related to traditional theological beliefs. It appears that this style of church participation will reinforce the racial attitudes associated with lower ISA and ICR scores.

The Index of Devotional Orientation becomes a very interesting deviant case. The person of social deprivation is more likely to score high on the IDO, but those with high IDO scores are more likely to have higher scores on the ISA and ICR! Exactly why this should be the case is very difficult to explain in terms of our theory as outlined thus far.

This chapter has clearly supported all of the hypotheses of the study. The parishioner's social situation does result in tendencies toward certain social attitudes and certain styles of church participation. The four styles of church participation *have* resulted in different consequences for attitudes on social issues. Finally, the social attitudes associated with certain styles of church participation *are not* fully "explained" on the basis of the independent factors associated with the various styles of church participation. This last statement is particularly true in the case of the "devotional" orientation.

Our research design is not able to test whether or not the official "actions" and "positions" of the denomination have "caused" the relationship between church participation and racial attitudes. It can only be said that for three styles of church participation there was a "congruence" between more church participation and attitudes "officially" supported by the denomination.

Before turning to a more extended discussion of the theoretical and practical importance of these findings, let us examine the patterns found between the independent variables and the church participation variables when they are related to our two indices of "The Means of Social Change."

Chapter 10–The Means of Social Change

Introduction

We have seen that participants in churches, like other men, have a wide range of opinions on *what* aspects of the social order are in need of change. We have also seen that those opinions are related to a variety of social factors which appear to condition attitudes, and to different styles of church participation.

In this chapter we examine in more detail the question of *how* social change should be brought about. It was pointed out in chapter 7 that this study will utilize two indices in dealing with the means for social change. One index, the Index of Individual Conscience (IIC), was constructed from responses which stressed the role of the individual in achieving social change. The other index, the Index of Collective Social Reponsibility (ICSR), was constructed from responses to questions which emphasized the place of the "church" in social change.

We recall from chapter 7 that it was a minority of the survey population who scored "high" or "moderately high" on either index.[1] Only about one third of the survey population had such scores on the IIC or the ICSR. Thus the respondents to this study do not appear to be terribly interested in either the individual Christian or the church as a collective body becoming involved in social change. However, since one third of the respondents indicated such interest, it is important to discover which of the independent variables and which of the church participation variables are related to either the IIC or the ICSR. Also, in terms of our overall search for a patterning of variables, it will be important to know the way in which the church participation variables act as "intervening variables" between the independent variables and the indices measuring the means of social change.

The Independent Variables and the Means of Social Change

1. Introduction

More often than not in this study, it has proved productive to use the privilege-deprivation continuum as a concept for understanding the patterning of the variables. In this chapter, too, we will begin with the possibility that "deprivation" variables will relate to the two indices under consideration in one way and those variables concerning privilege will relate to the indices in the opposite direction.

In the last chapter it was found that the majority of the measures of social privilege correlated positively with the indices related to civil rights. We can logically expect therefore, that measures of social privilege will also correlate positively with the two indices related to the means for social change.

2. Age

Based on findings mentioned above, we would expect that the older respondents would tend to have lower scores on both the IIC and the ICSR. They are the persons who had lower scores on both the Index of Social Acceptance and the Index of Civil Rights.

Such a prediction was only partly upheld by the empirical findings. Older people *did* tend to have lower scores on the Index of Individual Conscience, *but* when age was related to the Index of Collective Social Responsibility, older people *did not* tend to have the lowest scores. In this latter case, it was the middle-aged respondents who scored the highest ICSR scores and the younger respondents as well as the older respondents were the ones who had the lower ISCR scores. Thus one would have to say that the findings with respect to the relation between age and the two indices of social change were ambiguous at best.

3. Sex

In so many places in the study, sex has proved to be a variable of very limited significance. The present case is no exception. There was a slight tendency for females to score higher on the Index of Individual

Conscience, and there was not any relationship one way or the other between sex and the Index of Collective Social Responsibility.

4. Educational Achievement

In contrast to age and sex, the pattern of relationship between educational achievement and the two indices we are considering is much less ambiguous. Educational achievement was correlated positively with both the Index of Individual Conscience and the Index of Collective Social Responsibility. It is also interesting to note that whereas age and sex were more clearly related to the IIC, educational achievement was more clearly related to the ICSR.

5. Socio-Economic Class

Since there is such a high correlation elsewhere in the study between class and education, it is reasonable to assume that the Index of Socio-Economic Class will be related to the IIC and ICSR in the same way as educational achievement. This was the case. Higher social class was associated with increased scores on both of the indices, and as in the case of educational achievement, the relationship was stronger in the case of the ICSR than in the case of the IIC.

6. Rural-Urban Differentiation

The size of the city in which the respondents resided did not prove to be a significant variable when related to the IIC and the ICSR. There was a very modest tendency for the resident of more urban areas to have a lower score on the Index of Individual Conscience, but there was not any relation between the ICSR and the rural-urban categories used in the study. Thus, rural-urban difference was rejected as a meaningful variable for this chapter.

7. Race

Given what has emerged in previous chapters we certainly would have the expectation that the nonwhites in the study would score higher on both of the indices related to the means of social change. This again proved to be the case. Sixty-five percent of the nonwhites had "high" or "moderately high" scores on the IIC while the sample as a whole had only 31 percent with such scores. Also, 62 percent of the nonwhites had scores in the two higher categories of the ICSR while only 29 percent of the sample as a whole had such scores. The nonwhites in this study are clearly more concerned about both the individual and the corporate means for social change than are the whites.

8. Denominational Background

The denominational background of the respondents, when related to the IIC and ICSR tended to follow a patterning which by now has become familiar. The former Baptists had the highest percentage of respondents with "high" IIC scores and the Evangelical and Reformed respondents had the lowest percentage. A very similar ordering occurred when the denominational background was related to the ICSR. Denominational background appears to have a slightly stronger relation to the ICSR than to the IIC.

9. Relative Organizational Involvement

When the Index of Relative Organizational Involvement was related to the IIC and ICSR scores, it was found that persons who had a relationship to both the church and outside organizations were the respondents most likely to score "high" scores on both indices. This pattern of persons with both church and outside involvement having more social concern has been consistent throughout the study.

10. Summary

In the beginning of this chapter it was noted that only about one third of the respondents scored "high" or "moderately high" on either of the two indices measuring attitudes toward the means of social change. We have now related the major independent variables to both of these indices of the means of social change. And we have found that though there is some correlation to be found with several of the variables, it is only race which has a particularly strong influence upon the index scores.

When we compare the findings of this chapter with the theory of the socially deprived persons reacting one way to issues and the socially privileged reacting another way, we find that there is some support for the theory. But it is not without its ambiguities. The persons of privilege as measured by educational achievement and the Index of Socio-Economic Class did score higher scores on the IIC and the ICSR. Younger persons had higher scores on the IIC. Persons with denominational backgrounds in the more "privileged" denominations tended to have higher scores on both indices, and persons active in both the church and outside organizations also tended to have such higher scores. However, females did not manifest a "deprived" pattern in their scores on the indices, nor did respondents from more rural places of residence.

Thus, as previously, the weight of the evidence is still in favor of the original theory. However, the theory needs some amplification in order to be able to account for the deviations.

We now turn to an examination of the relationship between the church participation variables and the two indices related to the means of social change.

The Church Participation Variables and the Means for Social Change

Since we have now established that there is a tendency for persons of privilege to achieve higher scores on the Index of Individual Conscience and the Index of Collective Social Responsibility, and since we have earlier established that two of the four church participation variables are related to social privilege, it seems reasonable to expect that those same two variables will be related positively to the IIC and the ICSR. Thus our expectation for the relation between the church participation variables and the two indices of the means of the social change would be as follows:

   A. Church Participation Variables Expected to Relate Positively to the IIC and the ICSR:
   1. Index of Organizational Involvement (IOI)
   2. Index of Religious Knowledge (IRK)
   B. Church Participation Variables Expected to Relate Negatively to the IIC and the ICSR:
   1. Index of Devotional Orientation (IDO)
   2. Index of Belief Orientation (IBO)

When we examined the empirical findings, we found that *three* of the church participation variables are clearly related in a positive way to both the IIC and the ICSR. And we also find that the fourth church participation variable (the Index of Belief Orientation) even had a slight tendency toward a positive correlation with the IIC (see Table 10-C)! Thus the Index of Organizational Involvement and the Index of Religious Knowledge clearly followed expectations, but the Index of Devotional Orientation (Tables 10-A and 10-B) was clearly contrary to expectations. While the Index of Belief Orientation was contrary to expectation in its relation to the IIC (Table 10-C), it follows expectation in terms of its relation to the ICSR.

Once again (as in chapter 9), the Index of Devotional Orientation

TABLE 10-A: Index of Devotional Orientation Related to Index of Individual Conscience in Percent of Respondents

Index of Devotional Orientation	N = 8549	Low 3415	Moderately Low 2516	Moderately High 1749	High 869	Total
Low	3949	50	28	16	7	100
Moderately low	2697	37	33	21	8	100
Moderately high	1270	26	28	29	17	100
High	633	18	26	29	28	100
Total Sample		40	29	21	10	100

TABLE 10-B: Index of Devotional Orientation Related to Index of Collective Social Responsibility in Percent of Respondents

Index of Devotional Orientation	N = 8549	Low 3388	Moderately Low 2708	Moderately High 1526	High 927	Total
Low	3949	44	32	16	8	100
Moderately low	2697	38	32	18	11	100
Moderately high	1270	37	30	19	14	100
High	633	24	30	25	21	100
Total Sample		40	32	18	11	100

TABLE 10-C: Index of Belief Orientation Related to Index of Individual Conscience in Percent of Respondents

Index of Belief Orientation	N = 8549	Low 3415	Moderately Low 2516	Moderately High 1749	High 869	Total
Low	1978	48	27	16	9	100
Moderately low	1717	45	28	17	10	100
Moderately high	2633	38	31	22	8	100
High	2221	31	31	25	13	100
Total Sample		40	29	21	10	100

does not follow expectation and becomes a deviant case. And here, for the first time, the Index of Belief Orientation is slightly "deviant" in terms of its relationship to the IIC. However, its relation to both the IIC and ICSR is so weak that it is not a very significant point.

Certainly we will need to make some adjustment in our operating theory in order to account for the way in which the Index of Devotional Orientation appears to be related to the indices discussed here and in chapter 9. However, before proceeding to that task in chapter 11, it is important to see whether or not holding the independent variables constant will eliminate the relationships between the church participation variables and the IIC and the ICSR. Are the church participation variables simply reflections of the independent variables which are related to them? Or, do the church participation variables continue to function as "intervening variables"?

The Relation Between the Church Participation Indices and the Indices of the Means of Social Change When the Independent Variables Are Held Constant

It was found earlier that social class and educational achievement were independent variables that correlated positively with the two indices on the means of social change. Thus, either of these independent variables would be suitable candidates for testing whether the church participation variables continue to be correlated with increases in the IIC or ICSR when the independent variables are held constant.

In Table 10-D, each of the church participation variables is related to the IIC and the ICSR while the social class categories of the ISEC are held constant. An examination of that table shows that all four church participation variables continue to be positively correlated with the indices of the means of social change, the IIC, and the ICSR. The weakest correlation is found between the Index of Belief Orientation and the Index of Collective Social Responsibility. In fact, there is a reverse relationship between these two variables for persons who score "high" on the Index of Socio-Economic Class.

Tables similar to those mentioned above were developed while holding the other major independent variables constant (educational achievement, age, denominational background and relative organizational involvement). In each of these tables, three of the church participation variables continued to be related in a positive way with the IIC and ICSR scores. However, the fourth church participation vari-

TABLE 10-D: The Relation of Church Participation Indices to Indices of the Means of Social Change by Social Class Category in Percent of Respondents

Index of Socio-Economic Class	Index of Church Participation	Means of Social Change Index			
		Index of Individual Conscience		Index of Collective Social Responsibility	
		L and M.L.	M.H. and H	L and M.L.	M.H. & H
Low	IOI L and ML	77	23	86	14
	MH and H	58	42	79	21
	IRK L and ML	77	23	90	10
	MH and H	68	32	72	28
	IDO L and ML	82	18	87	13
	MH and H	46	54	72	28
	IBO L and ML	80	20	88	12
	MH and H	69	31	81	19
Moderately Low	IOI L and ML	74	26	83	17
	MH and H	63	37	67	33
	IRK L and ML	76	24	87	13
	MH and H	66	34	66	34
	IDO L and ML	77	23	82	18
	MH and H	51	49	64	36
	IBO L and ML	79	21	80	20
	MH and H	68	32	78	22
Moderately High	IOI L and ML	72	28	76	24
	MH and H	62	38	60	40
	IRK L and ML	77	23	83	17
	MH and H	61	39	57	43
	IDO L and ML	73	27	72	28
	MH and H	49	51	58	42
	IBO L and ML	74	26	71	29
	MH and H	65	35	69	31
High	IOI L and ML	71	29	65	35
	MH and H	62	38	55	45
	IRK L and ML	76	24	72	28
	MH and H	60	40	52	48
	IDO L and ML	70	30	62	38
	MH and H	47	53	49	51
	IBO L and ML	69	31	60	40
	MH and H	62	38	62	38

able, the Index of Belief Orientation, was weak in its correlation and often had a negative relationship to the ICSR.

The above statistical procedure leads one to assume that the relationships found between the church participation variables and the indices on the means of social change are not simply a function of the influence of the various independent variables.

Conclusions

In this chapter as in chapter 9, we have found that the Index of Organizational Involvement and the Index of Religious Knowledge are related to consequential variables in a way which is consistent with the influence of the independent variables. That is, it appears that church participation as measured by the IOI and the IRK, reinforces social attitudes associated with the respondent's position in the social order. Persons of privilege are more likely to favor both individuals and the church working for social change and church participation, as indicated by scores on the IOI and IRK, is likely to increase the positive orientation toward such activity both by individuals and the church.

Church participation as measured by the Index of Devotional Orientation and the Index of Belief Orientation does not follow a similar pattern. Persons of deprivation tend to have higher scores on both the IDO and the IBO and they are likely to have lower scores on the IIC and the ICSR. However, especially in the case of the Index of Devotional Orientation, persons with high scores on that index are *more likely* rather than less likely to have higher scores on the Index of Individual Conscience and the Index of Collective Social Responsibility. Thus, as an intervening variable, the IDO appears to reverse the direction of influence between the independent variables and the scores on the IIC and ICSR. Thus far in the study, our theory as delineated in its minimal form is not able to account for such findings.

The place of the Index of Belief Orientation as an intervening variable is difficult to assess in this chapter since its influence is at best weak.

Having now gathered material in an empirical form to test the various hypotheses as presented in the first chapter, we are now in a position to reassess the hypotheses in terms of developing a more consistent theory. Part 4 of the study is devoted to just such a task. Chapter 11 begins with a summary of the most salient findings from the study, and then it proceeds to theoretical amplification as necessary to account for the findings. The final chapter contains reflections concerning the practical import of both the findings and the underlying theory.

Part 4—Conclusion

Chapter 11—Contributions to the Sociology of Religion

The Study in Retrospect

At the outset of the study three working hypotheses were suggested as guidelines for our analysis. The first was that differences in an individual's social situation result in different modes of religious orientation and social outlook. From previous research, it was further hypothesized that privileged social groups will choose religious orientation that reflect the dominant values of American culture and that groups experiencing some form of social deprivation will choose religious orientations that compensate in some way for the social deprivation.

A second hypothesis was that participation in religious organizations is a phenomenon that can be meaningfully described along the four dimensions which we characterize as organizational involvement, religious knowledge, devotional orientation, and belief orientation. Combining the first and second hypotheses produced the subhypothesis that privileged groups would be more likely to express their religiousness in terms of organizational involvement and religious knowledge while socially deprived persons would be more likely to have devotional and belief orientations to religion.

Finally, a third and crucial hypothesis for the study was stated this way: Different church participation orientations have different consequences for behavior and attitudes on social issues. This third hypothesis was a logical development of the first two hypotheses. However, the way in which it was stated left open the issue of whether or not one could show that the religious orientations were acting in any significantly ordered way as "intervening" variables between the social situation and the social attitudes. Obviously, the study was designed in such a way that tests could be applied in terms of the third hypothesis to ascertain whether it was meaningful to speak of even a "relative autonomy" for the religious orientations.

Having now completed the presentation of our findings, we are in a position to argue in favor of the three hypotheses. The sample population proved to be consistent with previous research on American denominations. It was clearly more representative of the more privileged strata of our culture than of the more deprived strata. However, the dominant patterns were not exclusive patterns, and a wide range of "social situations" was represented among respondents. In addition, it was found that the various social situations represented did seem to result in different modes of religious orientations and different social outlooks. The socially privileged respondents did show a tendency toward organizational involvement and religious knowledge, while the socially deprived respondents were more inclined toward belief and devotional orientations to the church. Furthermore, the socially privileged showed a preference for certain social attitudes and the socially deprived showed a preference for different social attitudes. Finally, when appropriate tests were applied it was shown that the modes of church participation could be treated as meaningful intervening variables between the respondent's social situation and his social outlook. The modes of church participation at times acted as "reinforcing agents" for the social attitudes associated with the social situation of the respondents. However, at other times the church participation variables appeared to "reverse" the social attitudes associated with the social situation of the respondents. Nevertheless, in either case, they were in fact acting as meaningful intervening variables.

In one sense, such a brief and simplified overview of the findings brings the study to a conclusion and adds to the body of knowledge concerning the sociology of religion in the American culture. However, such "raw" pieces of information are not very significant without being placed within some more sophisticated theoretical framework. The particularities of the findings are simply isolated and trivial bits of knowledge unless we provide a more systematic integration.

We have attempted to make clear that we find the historical theoretical work of Max Weber to be particularly helpful as a pattern for theoretical construction. Therefore, though it would be quite possible to interpret the particular findings of this research from a variety of theoretical perspectives, we have chosen to amplify from the work of Max Weber the minimal ordering which has already been given to the findings. In order to begin this amplification, it is necessary to review certain pertinent portions of Weber's work.

Max Weber's Sociology of Religion
1. Introduction

> The essence of religion is not even our concern, as we make it our task to study the *conditions and effects* of a particular type of social behaviour. The external courses of religious behaviour are so diverse that an understanding of this behaviour can only be achieved from the viewpoint of the subjective experiences, ideas, and purposes of the individuals concerned—in short, from the viewpoint of the *religious behaviour's meaning*.[1]

Thus does Weber open his systematic monograph on the sociology of religion. Such an opening could as well serve as an introduction to the present study. It is also focused on the "conditions and effects" of church participation. An understanding of the many diverse findings will be achieved only by reference to the underlying "meaning" of religious behavior, an issue which thus far in the present study has been self-consciously kept in the background.

Weber sees the origin of a religion (either in terms of new religions or in terms of reform movements) in the work of a "prophet."[2] The insights of the prophet become a religion when some group of persons is attracted to his viewpoint and desire to follow his way. Inevitably the group of followers is selective in its acceptance of the prophet's way or it transforms his position in a manner which it finds acceptable. Thus it is that the religion is "conditioned" by sociological forces.

2. The Conditions

Standing between the prophet and the followers is the priest. Upon him falls the task of developing a full metaphysical rationalization of the religion and a religious ethic.[3] Obviously the priesthood has its own concerns and vested interests and thus the priesthood also acts as a conditioning factor within the religion.

The forces of the laity which act upon the priesthood (and of course upon the religion as a whole) are viewed by Weber as consisting of "lay traditionalism" and "lay intellectualism."[4] The laity is not interested in changing its accustomed ways, and thus this "traditionalism" of the laity tends to act as an inhibiting force upon the religious impact of the prophet. But the "intellectualism" of the laity is another matter, and Weber sees this intellectualism or rationalism as a more creative and dynamic force within the conditioning social forces. He discusses at some length the various social classes or vocational groupings which carry this intellectualism and points to different ways in which each group selectively appropriates religious insights as well as providing some dynamic for social change.

In broadest overview, Weber's perspective of the various ways in which the social class groupings condition religion can be depicted in this way: The highest social class groupings tend to look to religion (if at all) for purposes of "legitimizing" their way of life; the lowest social class grouping tend to translate the religion into magical forms and look for the eventual transvaluation of values through a personal savior; and those groups in the middle of the class spectrum become the ones in whom we see creative forces at work. The middle classes have enough "rationalism" to appropriate the fundamental insights of the religion whereas the lowest classes cannot accomplish this. Moreover, they are not as tied to the dominant values of the social order as the highest classes. Thus they are able to contemplate social change as being for the better. Thus an "intellectualism" plus a certain distance from the dominant values of the social order provide the ingredients for creative effects upon the social order.

Though Weber concerns himself with a number of social classes or vocational groupings which are not our concern here, it is important to emphasize that he is explicitly concerned to reject any "social determinism" in his argument. Weber pursues in his argument the tendencies and proclivities among various groupings to appropriate certain religious insights. In several cases, he is very concerned to point out that there are exceptions to general tendencies, that tendencies provide a range of options and not singular undeviating results. Social position gives a certain internal meaning to man's life, and thus the position tends to influence the way in which he views religion, which is to say, the "need" which the religion serves.

It is also important to emphasize that Weber uses "intellectualism" and "rationalism" with a certain degree of ambiguity. In one sense we can argue that he has the scientist's bias toward the importance of logical order. Clearly any scientist is concerned to develop ordered arguments and patterns of explanation that help to clarify the areas with which the scientist is concerned. Weber is not any exception. Thus he would see the value in such rational order as a means for the evolution of the culture. However, his use of "intellectualism" or "rationalism" implies much more than that. One crucial quotation shows this tendency in Weber's use of "intellectualism":

> The need for salvation and ethical religion has yet another source besides the social condition of the disprivileged and the rationalism of the middle classes, which are products of their practical way of life. This additional factor is intellectualism as such, more particularly the metaphysical needs of the human mind as it is driven to reflect on ethical and religious questions, driven not by material need but by an inner compulsion to understand the world as a meaningful cosmos and to take up a position toward it.[5]

3. The Effects

The "metaphysical needs of the human mind" are much more than simple order or logical argument. They involve man in a quest for the ability to deal with all of life's problems. Life's problems are far more for Weber than simply meeting physical needs. In fact it is precisely the metaphysical needs of the mind which produce one of the key issues with which religion must deal, namely the problem of "Theodicy." If one presupposes a God who in some sense is a god of transcendental power (as salvation religions do), then how is it possible to deal with the imperfections of the world dependent on such a God? For Weber evil is no figment of the imagination. He constantly makes reference in all of his writings to the irrationalism and imperfections of life. Somehow every salvation religion must come to terms with this problem of theodicy. It must find some "meaning" in the midst of the seeming contradictions. It is precisely this problem of theodicy and its various solutions which provides Weber's next categorization within his progressing argument.

The problem of theodicy has been "solved" in various ways by different religions, and the different solutions ultimately have different effects upon the social order. Out of the problems of theodicy men are striving *for* salvation *from* something. What they are seeking to be free *from* as well as what they are striving *for* will have different effects on the social order. Thus salvation will take different paths and different psychological viewpoints will be associated with the different paths.

Before proceeding to discuss the various paths to salvation and their effects upon the social order, it is well to note that for Weber intellectualism is not of value in and of itself. He explicitly points out that intellectuals as such have never produced a religion.[6] He also points out that Christianity has always had an antipathy toward intellectualism, even though Paul utilized a clearly intellectual approach to much of his writing.[7]

The problem of theodicy has been solved in three formal ways, though in practice, religions have utilized in varying degrees portions of the formal solutions. One solution was to posit some form of eschatology either in this world or in the world beyond where things will be set right; that is, the just rewarded and the evil punished. The second solution is some form of dualism in which there are good powers and evil powers at work within the world and at warfare with one another. The third solution is to utilize a doctrine of "karma" in which the world is unified and self-contained and eventually sins are punished and the righteous are rewarded. Many subcategories within these three formal solutions are possible and have different implications for one's life within the present world.

Salvation within the formal solution to the problem of theodicy can be pursued by various paths. Those suggested by Weber include: ritual activities, good works within the world, ecstasy, gifts of grace, and belief. Theoretically at least each of the paths to salvation could be utilized within each of the various formal solutions of the problem of theodicy. But in fact all of the paths have not been actualized in all cases, and indeed the systematic justification of some of the paths within some of the formal solutions is difficult to imagine. Without completing the logical possibilities, Weber does point out that certain of the paths tend to have more influence on worldly affairs than others. However, he always leaves open the possibility that certain social circumstances could make it possible for any of the paths to have some influence on everyday life.

Ritual activities, especially when the laity is largely acting as "spectator," tend to have little influence on daily affairs, though when ritual activity is combined with religious education there may be some influence. Ecstasy in its various forms is not influential on daily affairs since the ecstatic experience is short-lived and tends to be induced by special means. Gifts of grace, whether bestowed by God or by his agents (as in the case of institutional grace) tends to cause the laity to adopt an attitude which has little concern for ordinary affairs. Belief (by which Weber tends to mean salvation by faith) likewise tends to be associated with an attitude of unconcern for daily life. Thus for Weber the path of good works remains the most likely one to produce effects upon the everyday world.

In addition to the paths of salvation, Weber also discussed two major forms of psychological attitude which men can have toward salvation. These two attitudes are his famous categories of "asceticism" and "mysticism." Each of these attitudes can have an "inner-worldly" and an "otherworldly" type. As in the case of the "paths" to salvation, most of the four possible psychological attitudes tend to have little influence upon daily life. However, one type stands out above the others in its influence and that is "inner-worldly asceticism."

Since the word "asceticism" carries other connotations than those intended by Weber, it is important to note his definition:

> Salvation may be viewed as the distinctive gift of active ethical behaviour performed in the awareness that God directs this behaviour, i.e., that the actor is an instrument of God. We shall designate this type of attitude toward salvation, which is characterized by a methodical procedure for achieving religious salvation, as "ascetic."[8]

Thus in principle an "ascetic" does not need to be world denying. He is one who sees his actions as being "instrumental" parts of God's action. To be sure, otherworldly asceticism is world-denying, but by definition inner-worldly asceticism is operative within the world and thus in principle not totally world-denying. Later we shall see that even the inner-worldly ascetic is in opposition to much that is normally accepted as ordinary worldly activity, but he is not in principle opposed to the world nor does he need to deny it totally.

Weber's bias toward rationality is shown in his summary of the results of inner-worldly asceticism (and hence its power to influence social change):

> [The result of inner-worldly asceticism] is practical rationalism, in the sense of the maximization of rational action as such, the maximization of a methodical systematization of the external conduct of life, and the maximization of the rational organization and institutionalization of mundane social systems, whether monastic communities or theocracies.[9]

Such ordering of life on the part of the inner-worldly ascetic gives him a leverage on life which is not associated with the other types of psychological attitudes toward salvation.

A religious attitude which produces such systematization and rationalization was found by Weber to result in a certain tension with the various spheres of ordinary social life. This tension is the dynamic factor in social evolution.

> With the increasing systematization and rationalization of communal relationships and of their substantive contents, the external compensations provided by the teachings of theodicy are replaced by the struggles of particular autonomous spheres of life against the requirements of religion. The more intense the religious need is, the more the world presents a problem. . . . To the extent that a religious ethic organizes the world from a religious perspective into a systematic, rational order and cosmos, its ethical tensions with the social institutions of the world are likely to become sharper and more principled. . . . Indeed, the very tension which this religious ethic introduces into the human relationships toward the world becomes a strongly dynamic factor of social evolution.[10]

Weber then proceeds to spell out the results of the various religious ethics upon the "autonomous spheres of life." In the volume which we are considering he treats the following: economics, politics, sexual relationships, and art. The details of the argument and the supportive evidence are beyond our concern here, but it is important to summarize the crucial points of explication. The "tension" referred to often takes the form of fairly serious rejection of the sphere of life, but this need not be the case. The basic reason for the tension is that the religious ethic has a rationale which has its own internal consistency and systematization while each of the "spheres" likewise have an autonomous rationale and principled existence. These at least potentially conflict with the religious view.[11] However, even though the ultimate result of the tension is often "rejection" of the "worldly" standards, it is more appropriate to say that "tension" exists rather than always "rejection." Indeed, Weber makes this clear when he summarizes at another place the actual results of inner-worldly asceticism.

> This inner-worldly asceticism had a number of distinctive consequences not found in any other religion. This religion demanded of the believer, not celibacy, as in the case of the monk, but the avoidance of all erotic pleasure; not poverty, but the elimination of all idle and exploitative enjoyment of unearned wealth and income, and the avoidance of all feudalistic, sensuous ostentation of wealth; not the ascetic death-in-life of the cloister, but an alert, rationally controlled patterning of life, and the avoidance of all surrender to the beauty of the world, to art, or to one's own moods and emotions.[12]

Thus by definition the inner-worldly view cannot be *totally* rejecting of the world but must accept some part in the world and its activities. The question is always what part and in what way. As Weber pointed out, this often takes the form of a kind of principled and selective rejection.

4. Summary

Weber was seeking to study the conditions and effects of religion by setting up an analytical model which utilized the pattern of isolating variables. He took seriously the ways in which social forces condition the reception of religion from a prophetic source, and then having discussed the forms of the "conditioned" religion, he discussed the ways in which the various forms affect society. The model utilized the methodology of large scale analysis of historical social patterns. For purposes of explaining the ordering he found to be present, he made use of concepts related to the subjective meaning placed upon action by the actors themselves.

At every point in the analytical process, Weber was thus using sets of forces which produced certain configurations without resorting to some strict form of social determinism. Always, within the system he developed, there was room for a variety of responses to various forces present in the situation. Needless to say, many of the details of his analysis are highly conditioned by the historical situation during the period he was writing.

However, the overall theory with which he is operating is not so historically conditioned as to lose its relevance for our present study. The analytical model used here directly and self-consciously follows the Weberian form, though of course the survey research methodology is clearly different from Weber's methodology. We can now turn to an examination of the ways in which the findings might be ordered in light of Weber's theory.

The Findings in Weberian Perspective

This study, like Weber's *Sociology of Religion,* has not been concerned to define exactly what "religion" is. Instead we have been concerned primarily with the conditioning of religious institutions by social forces and the effect which religious participation has upon social attitudes.

In contrast to Weber, we have not been concerned with the "origin" of the religious denomination under study. Instead we have simply assumed its existence and sought to understand how it is socially conditioned before going on to examine the effects of participation within the denomination.

Weber, and other more recent analysts mentioned in chapter 1, would predict that participants in a basically "privileged" denomination would make major use of their religious participation for purposes of legitimating their accepted way of life. This has clearly been a dominant patterning found within the study. The respondents were in fact dominantly a socially privileged group; they were not very critical of their church or their social order; they showed a preference for religious ideas which stressed the more positive aspects of life and did not show a great awareness of need for "salvation" from "sin"; and they appeared to prefer a participation in the church which was not too demanding of them in terms of time, resources, or talent.

However, the respondents were not all from "privileged" social situations. Rather the survey population constituted a continuum of sorts on various measures of privilege and deprivation. Social class proved to be one of the most meaningful measures of privilege and deprivation, and as Weber again would predict, those of deprivation tend to be oriented toward the church in ways quite different from those who are more privileged in the social order. It was found through the use of four types of religious orientation that two types were related to social privilege and two to social deprivation. Furthermore, the two measures of church participation related to social privilege (organizational involvement and religious knowledge) can be quite easily related to dominant values in the American culture (organizational participation and education). And the two measures of church participation related to social deprivation (devotional and belief orientation) are more easily seen as forms of compensation (a culture seen by many as "secular" is not likely to value devotional relationships with God nor accept traditional statements of religious belief).

Thus far then, the Weberian analysis is very closely related to our findings. The patterns are similar and the coherence of the order found tends to be "explained" on the basis of "meanings" (conscious or unconscious) of religious participation attributed to the various subgroupings. The fact that we find only tendencies rather than perfect correlations can be explained on the basis of complex configurations of forces only some of which have been subjected to analysis in this study or in Weber's earlier work.

At this point it is important to note that few if any of the respondents in the present study can be classified as either the "most" privileged or the "most" deprived in the American culture. The total sample tends to fall somewhere within the middle class, with a dominant tendency toward the upper-middle class. It has been noted that Weber found the middle class (and especially the lower-middle class) to be the most significant in terms of the impact upon the social order of religious participation. Was this also the case in the present study?

To answer this question we must review the findings concerning the "effect" of church participation. Looking first at the findings with respect to the public policy issues (chapter 8), a seemingly confusing pattern was found. Assuming that the church participation variables would be related to public policy attitudes in the same way that social class was related to the same attitudes, we sought to predict the relationships between the church participation variables and the public policy issues. The four variables followed such predictions with varying degrees of consistency. The Index of Religious Knowledge most consistently followed the expected pattern, the Index of Belief Orientation was the next most consistent, the Index of Organizational Involvement came third in order of most consistently following expectations, and the Index of Devotional Orientation almost never followed expectations. At the time, we left the findings with the assumption that they were simply not very significant in and of themselves. Now, with a fuller explication of Weber's theory at our disposal, is there a more suggestive explanation which can be given for the seemingly confusing findings?

Weber argued that "intellectualism" and "inner-worldly asceticism" were the two factors which gave the greatest "effectual" character to religious involvement. Since our earlier findings showed a high correlation between the Index of Religious Knowledge and educational achievement, it should be said that of the four church participation variables used in this study, the IRK is the one most closely measuring a form of "intellectualism." Are the respondents in our study who received higher scores on the IRK the ones most likely to be seeking a meaningful order in their understanding of the cosmos (a way Weber would interpret intellectualism)? We cannot be sure with so little evidence, but it is at least one possible way to interpret the findings. If such an argument is followed, then we should not be surprised that the IRK continued to show "effects" on attitudes concerning public issues, even when the social class of the respondent was held constant.

Of the four variables used in this study, which one would most closely reflect what Weber meant by the inner-worldly asceticism? Since his definition revolved around the actor seeing himself as an "instrument of God" in his actions, only two of our variables are even possible candidates: the Index of Organizational Involvement and the Index of Devotional Orientation. To have religious knowledge does not directly imply seeing oneself as God's instrument, and an examination of the items included in the Index of Belief Orientation (Table 4-D or question 24, Appendix) shows that none of the options clearly implies seeing oneself as God's instrument. However, it is logical to assume that many persons might participate in the organizational activities of the church out of a sense that this is how God would wish his people to act. And it is highly likely that a person who scored high on the IDO was a person concerned that churchmen should have a more intimate devotional relation with God so that he might influence their actions (for a review of the three questions used to construct this index see chapter 5).

However, it is equally plausible to argue that for Americans in the middle 1960's, organizational participation in the church was not inner-worldly asceticism at all but rather a cultural ritual (in fact many of the authors reviewed in chapter 1 would so view it). It should also be pointed out that Max Weber felt ritual had no effect on social attitudes and behavior. With respect to the IDO we could also quite plausibly argue that it does not measure inner-worldly asceticism either, but that in fact it is a form of contemporary "mysticism" of "other-worldly asceticism" (in the sense that Weber used these two terms). Which of the above interpretations seems to be supported by the findings reported in chapter 8?

If anything, the findings would seem to affirm that the IOI is to be seen as measuring ritual rather than inner-worldly asceticism, especially since it did not have any consistent effect on public policy attitudes. And the IDO is more likely seen as a measure of inner-worldly asceticism since it most frequently *reversed* the influence of its social class expectations. It appears in fact to be the "strongest" measure of "effective" church participation since it reverses the expected social attitudes rather than reinforcing them (as in the case of the IRK). Thus, tentatively at least, we will want to argue that the IDO might be our best measure of "inner-worldly asceticism" found in the study. We will need to review more of the findings before asserting such a statement with any degree of enthusiasm.

However, it should be noted at this point that Weber was particularly interested in the influence of the lower-middle class as a carrier of "effective" religion. This was the social class grouping which he felt had the minimally required intellectualism *and* was not so clearly tied to cultural values as were the more privileged social class groupings. Such an interpretation gives some additional support for interpreting the IDO as the measure of inner-worldly asceticism, since higher scores on that index are more likely to be measures of lower-middle class position than are the higher scores on the IOI (an index related to social privilege).

Finally, what of the findings in chapter 8 with respect to the Index of Belief Orientation? Weber would have expected that index to follow attitudes associated with its social class since he argued that "belief" is not influential in terms of social change. In fact, it did not greatly influence social attitudes.

Before leaving the findings of chapter 8, it should be noted that no attempt has been made here to interpret the various public policy issues in terms of the matter of social change. In other words all of the above interpretation has been based on the findings without regard to content of the various public policy questions. The reason for this is that the issues are too complex to interpret from a "social change" point of view. For example, three of the issues included in the Index on Federal Activity were ones the approval of which meant a "change" from the status quo at the time of the administration of the questionnaire, and yet people of privilege tended to score higher on the IFA. Why should people of privilege want the social changes implied in the issues? To enter that argument would lead us far afield from our major concern at this point.

Let us now seek to interpret the findings with respect to the relation between church participation and the racial crisis (chapter 9) in a Weberian framework. Contrary to the situation that prevailed in chapter 8 where a number of public issues were treated simultaneously, in chapter 9 the issue of racial attitudes showed a much more consistent pattern. Most measures of social privilege were correlated positively with the Index of Social Acceptance and the Index of Civil Rights, while the opposite was the case for most of the measures of social deprivation. However, the more important issue for the purposes of this study is the way in which the church participation variables acted as "intervening" variables between the measures of the respondent's social situation and the measures of his attitudes on racial issues (the ISA and the ICR).

The Index of Religious Knowledge proved to be the strongest of the church participation indices *in terms of reinforcing* racial attitudes associated with one's social situation. The Index of Organizational Involvement was next in terms of its influence toward reinforcement, and the Index of Belief Orientation was the least "influential" in terms of reinforcing attitudes associated with one's social position. The Index of Devotional Orientation was once again the single church participation index which actually tended to *reverse* the social attitudes associated with the social class related to the IDO. These findings would lead us to have additional confidence in asserting that religious knowledge in some way parallels Weber's "intellectualism" in terms of the strength of its influence on social attitudes. And thus we have additional reason to hypothesize that in certain ways the Index of Devotional Orientation may be a form of modern parallel to inner-worldly asceticism in terms of its influence on social attitudes. Recognizing that such assertions are being made on limited empirical support, we will now review the results of chapter 10 before seeking to develop in a more coherent way the use which is being made of Weberian categories.

Chapter 10 addressed in a self-conscious way the place of the individual Christian and the institutional church in terms of social change. The findings, in terms of the patterning of the church participation variables as intervening variables, closely followed what was reported in chapter 9. That is, the Index of Organizational Involvement, the Index of Religious Knowledge, and sometimes the Index of Belief Orientation tended to act as "reinforcing agents" for the social attitudes (as measured by the Index of Individual Conscience and the Index of Collective Social Responsibility) associated with their respective social class groupings. Once again, the Index of Devotional Orientation tended to "reverse" the social attitudes associated with its social class.

An additional point of interest is the difference between the "strength" of influence of the different church participation variables upon the two indices for the means of social change. Looking first at the Index of Individual Conscience, the order of strength influence is:

1. Index of Devotional Orientation
2. Index of Religious Knowledge
3. Index of Organizational Involvement
4. Index of Belief Orientation

In the case of the Index of Collective Social Responsibility, the order is:

1. Index of Religious Knowledge
2. Index of Devotional Orientation
3. Index of Organizational Involvement
4. Index of Belief Orientation

These differences are not great, and they take on significance only in terms of supporting the argument which is being pursued here, using contemporary parallels for the Weberian categories. The fact that the IDO had the strongest correlation with the Index of Individual Conscience lends some support for arguing that "devotion" as measured by this index is not "otherworldly" but rather "inner-worldly." To make such an assertion demands reference to the content of the issues used in the index construction. The IIC was made up of questions very clearly related to individuals taking an active role in social issues (see chapter 7). Likewise the fact that the IRK had the strongest correlation with the Index of Collective Social Responsibility gives added support for arguing toward the "intellectual" character of IRK. It needs to be remembered that the ICSR was made up of questions implying that the church should be a collective influence upon social issues (see chapter 7). It is highly plausible to argue that in a modern urban social order collective institutional action rather than individual action is likely to have the greatest effect. Indeed persons who take such a position may well be the ones who are very self-consciously trying to develop an ordered and systematic approach to contemporary problems.

Having examined the content of the questions utilized in the two indices of chapter 10, it is well to look back at the content of the questions utilized in the indices of chapter 9, the Index of Social Acceptance and the Index of Civil Rights. Since both indices were clearly related to attitudes involved with inner-worldly activity, the importance of the fact that the IDO was related positively to both indices (rather than negatively as its social correlate was) takes on added importance as support for the argument that we can legitimately consider the Index of Devotional Orientation being in some way a form of "inner-worldly asceticism."

It is apparent, however, that the interpretation of the IRK as the measure of "intellectual" orientation to the church and the IDO as the measure of the "inner-worldly ascetic" orientation to the church does seem to fit the findings. And although the interpretation provides an interesting parallel to Weber's analysis, more explication of our culture and the place of a middle class denomination within it is necessary before the interpretation is a very convincing analysis. To that task we now turn.

The Paradox of a Denomination Being "In but Not of the World"

As has been pointed out, Max Weber was historically bound by the situation from within which he wrote. That is, he could not, indeed he would not presume to be able to, predict how social forces of the future would alter the social situation of religious men so that the impact of their religion upon the culture would take on new forms from the ones he pointed out. And so we turn to a brief consideration of the present situation in the United Church of Christ in order to clarify the interplay of forces and categories of interpretation.

As we pointed out, the United Church of Christ is a union of two religious bodies, the Congregational Christian Churches and the Evangelical and Reformed Church. Our data has also shown that several other denominations are represented in the sample in terms of "denominational background" of the respondents. Such heterogeneity of religious traditions within the sample means that it is very difficult to argue that any particular view of the relation between the church and the social order is clearly present within the United Church of Christ. Congregationalism may well have its historic roots within the Puritan tradition, but in our sample only 23 percent of the respondents identified Congregationalism as their denominational background. (Even adding the 10 percent of the respondents who indicated Presbyterianism was their denominational background still only gives about one third of the sample as being from the Calvinist wing of the Reformation.) Furthermore, it is highly dubious that very much clarity exists among most laymen of any of the denominations represented in the sample regarding possible relations between the church and the social order.

Thus if we want to study the effects of religion upon the social attitudes of contemporary parishioners we are forced to search for unconscious relationships rather than conscious ones. This situation is quite different from the one Max Weber was discussing. To be sure, he pointed out unconscious connections between religious attitudes and social effects (the relation between capitalism and the Protestant ethic was just such an unconscious relationship in his view). But for Weber, the concept of "inner-worldly asceticism" was a conscious viewpoint held by certain persons, particularly those in the Calvinist wing of Protestantism. The attitude of the relation between one's religion and one's actions was conscious even if the results of such an attitude were not always conscious. At the present time we are in a period of history when neither the attitudes nor the effects are self-conscious for most participants in denominations of the type we are studying.

However, it is probably the case that in a certain sense the majority of contemporary Americans (whether actively involved in churches or not) have as a part of their "operating ethical view" some lingering remnants of the Puritan ethic. They believe that men should work to prove themselves, they believe in honest dealings as an expected part of daily social intercourse, and they probably believe that virtue eventually triumphs. Paradoxically, there is probably a fairly widespread acceptance among Americans of remnants of certain other religious ethical traditions that stand in some contradiction to the Puritan ethic. For example, the American pattern of the separation of church and state is probably seen by many parishioners as an affirmation of the fact that there are "religious" areas of life and there are "political" areas of life and the two are not to be mixed. This is hardly a Puritan view! Weber assigns this "separate areas" view of the relation between church and culture to the Lutheran tradition.[13]

With such a lack of clarity on the place of religion in the social order, it would be very difficult to seek to determine from a cross-section of "average" parishioners in a "main-line" denomination any subcategories of the various positions held in the relation between religion and actions.[14] Thus we have been forced into searching for "unconscious" orientations which might seem to parallel the "conscious" orientations discussed by Weber. To understand exactly why we have related our church participation variables to his categories in the way in which we have, it is necessary to look more closely at his discussion of the relation between religion and politics. We choose this area rather than economics, for our "consequential" variables are more related to political issues than they are to economic ones.

When Weber discussed religion and politics[15] he assumed that there is a tension between religion and politics which is fundamental.

> Every . . . ethical religion must, in similar measure and for similar reasons, experience tensions with the sphere of political behaviour. This tension appears as soon as religion has progressed to anything like a status of equality with the sphere of political associations.[16]

The fundamental character of the tension is due to the fact that the ethical religion calls for certain actions and the political ethic calls for a different kind of action. Politics is essentially based on the exercise of power over actions of people, and ethical religion also is based on the assumption that religion controls the actions of people. In the view of Weber, they are fundamentally "autonomous spheres."

Given their respective senses of autonomy and bases for action, there are a number of ways in which Weber sees religion and political power related to each other. One option is for religion to take on a mystical form which considers actions in this world to be unrelated to the religious life and hence there is no conflict. Another way in which there is no conflict is for the religion to be used to support the political power. Here we have a form of culture religion. Close to this position and yet different from it is one which argues that religion should use political power to bring about God's dominion over the terrestrial world. That is, religion seeks to establish a complete theocracy. Total conflict between religion and political power comes when the religion has been completely removed from political power and yet believes in concrete social reform involving political power.

Between these extremes are a number of intermediate positions. Various forms of pacifism are among them. Pacifists may simply become martyrs, they may passively suffer whatever political power forces upon them, or they may be willing to fight only for religious freedom. Another intermediary position discussed by Weber is the theory of separation between "religious" concerns and "political" concerns. He is dubious about the validity of such a position but points to a modification which calls "religious" ethics "personal" ethics, and social ethics become political ethics.

Without enumerating all the various options which Weber feels have been historically extant, we turn to the one which is most clearly related to social change in his view. This is of course the stand taken by the "inner-worldly ascetic." It is a major intermediary position in his view.

> Inner-worldly asceticism can compromise with the facts of the political power structures by interpreting them as instruments for the rationalized ethical transformation of the world and for the control of sin. It must be noted however that the coexistence is by no means as easy in this case as in the case where economic acquisitive interests are concerned. For public political activity leads to a far greater surrender of rigorous ethical requirements than is produced by private economic acquisitiveness, since political activity is oriented to average human qualities, to compromises, to craft, and to the employment of other ethically suspect devices and people, and thereby oriented to the relativization of all goals.[17]

Thus in spite of the uneasy compromises involved, the inner-worldly ascetic comes to the view that if he is an "instrument" of God's action so also can the political powers be seen as "instruments." However, unless this view deteriorates into culture religion or else comes to a position advocating a theocracy, there will always be tension. Some political actions will be seen as "instrumental" for God and others will not.

Weber's view was that as the lawful state became more and more rationally organized, it seemed ever more alien to the ethic of brotherliness. Moreover, religious ethics tended to form its compromise or accommodation to each individual concrete situation as it arose.[18] However, he went on to say that "the objectification of the power structure with the complex of problems produced by its rationalized ethical provisos, has but one psychological equivalent: the vocational ethic taught by an asceticism that is oriented to the control of the terrestrial world."[19]

It is now clear that, from Weber's analysis, some form of "middle position" religion between total acceptance and total rejection of the political powers is the religious position which he feels has the most "leverage" in terms of effect upon the political order. Furthermore, his analysis was meant to show that an inner-worldly asceticism was *the* position which best represented a "middle position" of real strength vis-à-vis the rational legalized political order.

Given this analysis and the findings we have reviewed from our study, we are faced with the problem of searching for that style of religious orientation which appears to be the most effective in terms of influencing social attitudes. Our research design had as a backdrop the contemporary controversy about whether or not a denomination like the United Church of Christ is anything more than an expression of "culture religion." Therefore, some evidence for a style of religious participation which challenges cultural values would be the most helpful evidence for "effective" religious participation. However, challenge in and of itself is not enough since there would need to be some logically rational reason why such a challenge was consistent with the teachings of the religion under examination.

Of the four types of church participation selected for study, only one gave any substantial evidence that it "stood against" the social and political attitudes associated with its "social situation." That style of church participation was measured by the Index of Devotional Orientation. The three other styles of church participation appear to reinforce the social attitudes associated with their respective class positions. To be sure, reinforcement is also a form of "effect" of religious participation. However, it is more easily explained on the simple grounds that if like-minded people form an association they are likely to reinforce the social attitudes related to their social situation. We would expect a "country club" to reinforce the social attitudes of the privileged persons who join the club.

Thus in the present study, persons with higher IDO scores are the only ones whose pattern of responses to the "consequential" variables parallels the pattern one would expect from "inner-worldly ascetics." However, two tasks remain; one is to develop some logical rationale for assuming that persons with higher IDO scores are in fact "intellectually" parallel to Weber's inner-worldly ascetics, and the second is to concern ourselves with the content of the "consequential" variables. This second task is essential since so far we have tended to argue the case on purely formal grounds.

First of all, do the persons with higher IDO scores in any way stand in the tradition of the inner-worldly ascetics? The question can only be answered in the light of the dominant tendency of findings of the whole study. It is quite clear that the majority of our findings would support the argument that the church participants responding to this study are heavily committed to cultural values rather than being critical of them. They are, as Weber would have said, a privileged group of people who apparently are looking to religion for legitimation of their general way of life. This poses a crucial dilemma. If a religious institution is highly committed to cultural values (or has in some sense become "secularized"), how would one express from within that institution a desire to become "more religious"?

Obviously we could work for any of the options Weber outlined. We could seek for a mystical religion, for a social revolutionary religion, for a theocracy. We could also search for ways to sense ourselves as an "instrument of God" in contemporary life. It has been argued that those with higher IDO scores are closest to this latter option. The findings support the interpretation that those who believe the church has not done enough to foster the devotional life, who define a Christian as one who prays and reads his Bible daily, and/or who are asking for the church to have more prayer meetings (the three issues in the IDO), are searching for ways to sense their "instrumental" role in God's action.

Interestingly enough, these findings are directly parallel to the findings of Lenski concerning his "devotional" respondents.[20] Though his devotionalism index was not associated with preference for any particular political party, he did find that devotionally oriented people were more in favor of humanitarian issues (foreign aid, school integration, governmental action in housing, unemployment, education, etc.). He summarized his findings on devotionalism in this way:

> Devotionalism seems to encourage its adherents to think in terms of the "oneness of life" and to disregard the popular distinctions between that which is religious and that which is secular. . . . Devotionalism may well be capable of effecting changes in secular institutions.[21]

As a sort of footnote, it is interesting that his devotionally oriented respondents were also more in favor of the spirit of capitalism and the values embodied within it. Is this additional support for the fact that those with higher devotional orientation scores are the contemporary "inner-worldly ascetics"?

Finally then, what about the content of the issues which the devotionally oriented in our study tended to approve, in contrast to their social position? They are in fact generally the same issues which the socially privileged tended to affirm! In terms of all of the indices used as "consequential" variables (Index on Federal Activity, Index of Social Acceptance, Index of Civil Rights, Index of Individual Conscience, and the Index of Collective Social Responsibility) they followed the same pattern as those persons of social privilege. The only places where persons with higher IDO scores differed from persons of social privilege were a few of the individual public policy issues discussed in chapter 8. The following are all of the deviations present:

Persons with high IDO scores were (and persons of social privilege were not):

1. More in favor of Medicare
2. More in favor of federal aid to education
3. More in favor of government price supports for agriculture
4. *Less* in favor of collective market bargaining in agriculture
5. More in favor of prayer in the public schools
6. More in favor of religion being taught in the public schools
7. More in favor of Christians refraining from the use of alcoholic beverages
8. *Less* in favor of ministers preaching on controversial issues

These specific issues are not of the most interest to us here. The point is that persons with higher IDO scores do not follow *exactly* the pattern of the socially privileged, but they clearly tend to do so. More than any other of our forms of church participation, devotional orientation appears to produce discrimination in terms of consequential social attitudes. But the fact that the "discriminated view" is so closely parallel to that of the socially privileged presents us with a very difficult problem. We either have to assert that the social attitudes associated with social privilege are in fact the "right" Christian social attitudes (and therefore the persons with higher IDO scores are affirming "Christian" social attitudes), or else we have to say that the attitudes are not "really" Christian and the persons with higher IDO scores are simply influenced by associating with people of social privilege to accept their values. If we take this latter view, we would have to ask why the same thing did not happen to people with higher IBO scores.

We want to argue for the first view, namely that, for the most part, the social attitudes which were associated with social privilege in this study are in fact the ones we wish to associate with Christianity. And thus we want to argue that social acceptance (as measured by the ISA), being in favor of civil rights (as measured by the ICR), and believing in both individuals and the church working for social causes (as measured by the IIC and the ICSR) are all values which we would want to affirm out of the Christian tradition associated with inner-worldly asceticism (being God's instrument in the world).

When we begin the process of deciding which values are going to be labeled as "Christian," we begin to leave areas of concern which can properly be considered a part of the sociology of religion. However, we have raised the issue of "Christian" values in order to stress the point that the same values which were associated with higher IDO scores were also associated with higher IOI and IRK scores! Thus if we want to argue that a devotional orientation is associated with an increase in "proper" Christian social attitudes, we have to accept the fact that organizational involvement and religious knowledge are also associated with these same social attitudes. Thus in our study social privilege has been found to be associated with social attitudes we are labeling as "Christian" social attitudes. There are those who will have difficulty accepting such a finding, since we often think of Christianity as being against the "accepted" social values. This study has simply shown that the relation between church and culture is a very complex relationship. One can make easy assertions about the church's accommodation to cultural values or its criticism of them only by ignoring the factual complexities.

Summary and Conclusion

The task of the sociology of religion has now been completed. The hypotheses of the study were affirmed, and modified use of the Weberian theory has proved adequate for handling the patterns of the findings. We have simply had to argue that the "inner attitudes" of religion which were so crucial to the Weber systematization, may now have become "unconscious" inner attitudes. Nevertheless, they still appear to be "effective" in terms of influencing social attitudes.

However, by pointing to the fact that such social attitudes are also held by persons of social privilege, we have opened up an issue which it is very difficult to treat from within the discipline of sociology of religion. We are in fact on the edge of arguing that certain views are "legitimate" Christian views while others are not. We are also on the edge of arguing that in certain ways cultural values are in fact "Christianized." In some sense we are pointing to the possibility that the culture is Christian and therefore the place of a privileged denomination is a very uneasy one indeed.

How do we know when we have a "culture religion" and when we have a "Christian culture"? Max Weber recognized this difficulty at many points in his writings. As a sociologist, however, he could simply leave it as a problem to be solved by the churchmen who adopt a "middle position." Though he did not use the terms, he left the churchmen to deal with the issues of "social ethics" and "practical theology." He simply pointed out that they run grave dangers of accommodation and casuistry when they enter such areas. And yet, if they want to be "effective" in terms of social change they must accept such dangers.

Therefore, our study in the sociology of religion is now finished. However, as has been pointed out earlier, the authors are also interested churchmen and so they must begin the task of struggling with the implication of this research for the life of the church. That is the task of the next chapter. We will be seen by some to be too accommodating and too full of casuistry in this final chapter, but we believe, with Max Weber, that the dangers cannot be avoided. To avoid the dangers would be to become "mystics" or "otherworldly ascetics."

Chapter 12–Reflections on the Church in Contemporary Society

Introduction

The findings of empirical research, such as those reported in the preceding chapters, can obviously be used for a variety of purposes. They can be used to strengthen and/or modify existing theories within a given academic discipline, or they can be used for more practical purposes by giving guidance to decision-makers of institutions and organizations who are the consumers of research findings.

In the preceding chapter, we have been primarily concerned with the former: we have pointed to the relevance of our finding to some of Max Weber's theoretical notions in his *Sociology of Religion*. In this final chapter, we turn our attention to those who would use these findings to affect more directly the policies and programs of contemporary American churches. These "decision-makers" within the churches may be denominational executives and policy-makers who sit on national boards, pastors of local churches, theological students training for vocations in the church and their teachers, or laymen who through their voluntary activities have accepted places of leadership responsibility within the life of the churches.

Our reference to "the churches" in this chapter cannot avoid levels of generalization not strictly warranted by our data, for the research was conducted within a single denomination. However, we have argued that many of our findings have been consistent with research previously reported of other "main-line" Protestant groups, and that the ecumenical character of the United Church of Christ (in which the majority of its present members reported having come from other denominations) suggest a wider applicability of our findings than might otherwise be acceptable.

Up to this point, the authors have attempted to report their findings as social scientists, as objectively as the tools of our craft would allow. We do not believe that social research can achieve the level of objectivity claimed by the natural sciences, for values and value judgments impinge on our work at every step of the way. But as scientists we have tried to minimize the distorting influences of our own viewpoints by adhering to the accepted procedures of social research.

In this chapter we are departing from our primary role as disinterested scientific observers of social groups and reflecting on the outcome of our research as individuals who participate in a world of social values and theological perspectives. What is crucial then is that we make explicit the theological perspective which informs our reflections. We are moving, in short, from basic research to applied research, from researcher to consumer of research, from theoretical preoccupation to what might be appropriately termed "practical theology."

The dominant ordering presuppositions which inform this chapter are theological and specifically relate to the nature of the church. Since a great deal of literature has been published in recent years about the nature of the church, it is also necessary for us to specify the theological perspective on the nature of the church which is salient for our purposes. To introduce such a perspective into the discussion might, strictly speaking, require the outlining of a complete theological system, but such an effort is obviously beyond the scope of our task. It must suffice, therefore, to indicate briefly the general theological system out of which we will reflect on our findings.

For the authors of this study, the theological writings of Paul Tillich have been most influential, and it is in his systematic work that the informing perspective of these reflections is found.[1] This decision does not imply that only "Tillichians" will be able to accept the implications of our conclusions, but it does imply that certain limits of theological perspectives have been imposed on our reflections. If the reader affirms a doctrine of the church, for example, which sees a radical separation between church and culture as ideal, this chapter will have very little meaning. On the other hand, the reader who sees no essential distinction between church and culture, may likewise find little value in our reflections.

Put in another way, the perspective which informs this analysis is clearly one which rejects any form of radical sectarianism or perfectionism on the part of the Christian community. Our perspective also rejects the opposite extreme of an unambiguous form of "culture religion" which finds few distinctions between religion and culture.

Between these theological polarities stand doctrines of the church which affirm relationships between church and culture, without going to either extreme of total rejection or total identification of culture, and it is from this perspective we reflect theologically.

A final word of introduction to this last chapter is in order. Systematic theologians often develop full, well-ordered doctrines of the church, sociologists often examine in detail cultural influences on the institutional life of the church, and men engaged professionally in the life of the institutional church from time to time reflect in print on issues which concern them. However, seldom, if ever, does anyone attempt to address issues of concern in the life of the church from a systematic theological perspective taking into account specific empirical findings. In this chapter we are attempting to do just that. There are reasons of course why the task is undertaken so rarely. It is easier to simply discuss "insights" without attempting to be overly systematic, and there is great difficulty in "fitting" diverse disciplines into some meaningful whole. Recognizing the dangers present in attempting a task which is so rarely undertaken, we nevertheless engage in it with the hope of furthering meaningful ministry.

The Issue

In the preceding chapters, the major lines of argument have been placed within sociological categories. We have discussed independent, intervening and consequential variables. We have used survey research methodology to gather our data and have tried to develop our case with only the most minimal use of theological language. Now, however, we must introduce theological language and categories in order to relate our sociological findings to a doctrine of the church and the Christian life.

Before getting into this task, a theological reflection about our research methodology is appropriate. In a very broad sense, we have been discussing what it means to be "religious" in contemporary American society. From one point of view, it seems utterly presumptuous to assume that an individual's religion, by which we mean his most ultimate concern, can be communicated in any way to a social scientist by means of a questionnaire such as the one used for this study. As scientists, everything we do is contingent upon the wording of our questions and answers, the meanings we impute to them, and the consequent process of abstraction by which our analysis is carried out. The subjectivity and the theological assumptions (however unintentional) of the investigator are as much a part of the investigative and analytical process as is his attempt to employ the objective methods of the social sciences.

We have already suggested that the sociologist is not detached from the particularism of his own religious commitment or from the cultural values of his social group. Values and value systems impinge on the scientist at every step of the way: values determine what is problematical, what is important, and thereby help him to choose the subject for his investigation. We chose to study parishioners, for example, rather than Boy Scouts or Rotarians. Values have a great deal to do with how we design our research, what questions we ask, and how we classify and interpret our data. What is important is to make explicit our value assumptions and to minimize their distorting effect on the research process.

In developing our various indices of religious orientation, we have used a number of "indicators" drawn from responses to our questions, and by the degree to which these "indicators" were present, we were able to classify each respondent as being "high" or "low" on each index. Needless to say, we are very aware that the religious orientations themselves are not exhausted by the "indicators," indeed the "indicators" may not even probe in any significant depth the fullness of meaning involved in any of the four selected religious orientations. We have simply developed some tools which appear to be useful in beginning to deal with complex interrelationships and meanings. The dimensions of religiousness we have described in these pages are not adequate descriptions or representations of the dimensions of religion in themselves; they are intended only to "point to" these dimensions, and to begin to open up categories which by their very nature are difficult to deal with sociologically. Our indices of religious orientation open up the original category of "church participation" and move beyond it by pointing to categories of religious experience.

Returning now to theological reflections about our findings, the primary concern of the study has been focused on evidence for what in theological language is termed *sanctification*. We have been interested in studying the ways in which the Christian man manifests change in his life as a result of his Christianity. Obviously we have not exhausted all possible areas of change but have focused on one small area, that of changes in his attitudes on a limited number of social issues. We have tried to discover whether or not the Christian life, as expressed through certain styles of church participation, results in transformation of certain social attitudes.

By addressing such a question in these terms, the authors place themselves broadly within the theological tradition of the church which has been called the "transforming wing" of Calvinism. Those who stand in this tradition affirm that the Christian church *does* transform both individuals and societies and they affirm that men *should* be changed as a result of their faith. However, for persons holding this general theological view, the transformation is not without its ambiguities and paradoxes. Sanctification is always seen as being in tension with justification. Man does not become perfect in his human life as a result of his faith, but he remains a sinner in need of salvation. Thus a doctrine of sanctification is held in tension with a doctrine of justification by grace through faith.

What is important to note in this connection is that affirming some elements of sanctification being present within the Christian life does not imply that the truly Christian man is morally faultless. There are strands of the Christian theological tradition which affirm that perfection can be attained in this life by Christian individuals, but no such affirmation is made within transforming Calvinism. The man who has known justification by grace through faith is expected to grow toward more sanctified living, but he is never beyond the need for God's grace.

Such a theological tradition also affirms a relationship between thoughts and actions, without affirming an identity between the two. What a man thinks, or the attitudes he has, is related to how he acts. However, men do not always act according to their highest thoughts, and this is only one of many reasons why they are not perfect. Such an affirmation is important in a study focusing on attitudes, for it does not assume that men will in fact always do as they have indicated their thoughts would encourage them to do, but it does assume that changed thoughts are related to changed actions.

In recent years, a great deal of literature has been addressed to the failure of the institutional church to produce men who either think or act according to highest Christian principles. Much of this literature has focused upon the way in which the church appears to be under the influence of social forces rather than the influence of "Christian principles." Earlier in the study we referred to some of this literature, but now it is appropriate to make some additional comments. Some of the literature has been theologically grounded in consistent theological affirmations, affirmations which have been informed, consciously and unconsciously, by "perfectionist" and "sectarian" principles. Such literature has assumed that the church ought to be producing perfect men and ought to stand unambiguously in opposition to the culture in which it finds itself. There are of course elements of the Christian tradition which are perfectionist and sectarian in viewpoint, but what we have stated above explicitly dissociates this study from such a tradition. The tradition here being affirmed holds sin in tension with sanctification and sees the church as related to society without being removed from it.

Thus the position being affirmed would expect research to yield some evidence of the sanctified life as well as some evidence of a continued "sinful" life within the Christian man, and it expects that the church will both evidence criticism of the social order as well as approve of it. This latter affirmation raises the question of the relation between the church and the social order in an explicit way, and the development of the subject by Tillich will clarify what is being asserted here as the constructive position.

Tillich, when discussing how the church relates to other social groupings, discusses three ways in which the church exercises the relationship:[2] (1) the way of silent interpenetration, (2) the way of critical judgment, and (3) the way of political establishment. The church influences other social groups "silently" through its very existence, the principles it upholds, and the persons who come under its influence who are of course also a part of society. The church explicitly is critical of the culture through its prophetic statements against negativities which it believes exist in the society, and finally the church engages in political action through means which it approves and for ends which it approves. However, these three types of influence do not flow only in one direction. The culture silently interpenetrates the church (both for good and for ill), the culture acts in ways which are a critical judgment of the church, and the culture acts politically in ways which affect the life of the church (again both for good and for ill).

This then has been a study designed to reveal some ways in which participation in the church appears to transform the social attitudes of Christian men. Some evidence was expected to emerge which would show transformation, but also much evidence was expected to emerge which would show lack of transformation. It is expected that transformed men will in some ways transform society (though the study was not designed to test an expectation) and it is expected that society will exert influence upon the church and thus upon its participants.

The Categories of the Discussion

Given this general background, we can now introduce the specific Tillichian categories in which the discussion will be set. It should be stressed that the discussion is in no way seen as an attempt to use the study to empirically "prove" Tillich's theology or to empirically "justify" Tillichian categories. The goal of the discussion is to place the empirical findings within a theological framework as a means of ordering the findings from other than a sociological perspective.

For our purposes here we will be using Tillich's categories and relating our research findings to them. However, at the outset an important issue of fundamental importance makes the procedure a difficult one. For research purposes, in order to define operationally who a church participant was, we simply utilized mailing lists of existing churches. Tillich, however, always insists on making a distinction between existing churches and the "Spiritual Community." He does not identify the two, but instead he sees them as related. For him, the Spiritual Community is "the invisible essence of the religious communities."[3] The reason for making this distinction is to remind us that existing churches are never to be seen as institutions of perfection, rather, they are subject to the many ambiguities of life. They are fragmented mixtures of good and evil. The Spiritual Community does not exist under such ambiguities. "The paradox of the churches is the fact that they participate, on the one hand, in the ambiguities of life in general and of the religious life in particular and, on the other hand, in the unambiguous life of the Spiritual Community."[4] In this study we have been examining the ambiguous mixture of good and evil which is found in the existing churches, we have not been studying the Spiritual Community.

Tillich explicitly recognizes the place of sociological study of existing churches. He further points out that the results of such study can be used polemically and/or apologetically.[5] One can use such results to point out how far the churches fall short of manifesting their stated goals, a frequent use of sociological study, or one can use the results to speak positively about the churches. He expects the possibility of both uses since the churches participate in the ambiguities of life as well as in the life of the Spiritual Community. In general, Tillich is somewhat negative about the uses of sociological data since such data have often been used only polemically, but certainly allows for apologetic uses. Our effort in this study has been to probe the data in several ways in order to see if in fact there are sociological facts which reveal both the "pros" and "cons" of participation in churches. There is no question but that we were concerned to search for facts which could be used "apologetically" for the churches. On the other hand there is no question but that we expected to find "polemical" facts since they have been found so often before. In short, our interest was to study the ambiguity and not either simply to defend the church or simply to criticize it.

There is another way to describe our task in this chapter. Stereotypes have developed about theology and sociology as disciplined ways of attaining knowledge. Stereotypes are of course oversimplifications, but they exist because of some truth within them and because men do not often enough challenge the oversimplification. Sociology is often seen, both by those within the discipline as well as those outside of it, as a discipline which functions without value judgments. There is truth in this stereotype in the sense that all "scientific" disciplines press for "objectivity." The oversimplification comes in the fact that the objectivity is never fully achieved. Theology on the other hand is often seen as a discipline limited to value abstractions without empirical content. Again, there is truth in the stereotype since values are always forms of generalizations, yet clearly theologians are concerned to relate to the life experience of human beings.

Sociological language as well as theological language is subject to distortions. In this chapter we are stressing the value dimensions of our research, and we are doing so by relating "empirical" sociological findings to theological categories of organization selected by Tillich. It is a hazardous undertaking subject to many errors and forms of criticism, but we prefer such hazards to the more common alternative of arguing that the "real" elements of church participation are not subject to sociological analysis. We accept the opinion that there are aspects of church participation which are not subject to sociological analysis, but we believe that important aspects of such participation should be subject to sociological study in order to illumine some of the ambiguity of life in the churches. Those responsible for the leadership of the churches need such illumination in order to guide the churches in the midst of the ambiguities present.

As in the sociological analysis where we drew distinctions between four styles of church participation, so in Tillich's theological analysis there are distinctions between various groups of functions which the churches must fulfill. He lists three basic groups of functions: "the function of constitution, related to the foundation of the churches in the Spiritual Community; the function of expansion, related to the universal claim of the Spiritual Community; the function of construction, related to the actualization of the Spiritual potentialities of the churches."[6] The church must have a basis for its existence, it must seek to reach others, and it must actualize its reason for existence.

The constitution functions are receiving functions. The church must receive the New Being as it is manifest in the Christ before there is a church. Having known the Christ, the church responds through confessions of faith and forms of worship. The expansion functions grow out of the universal character of the Christian message and involve mission, religious education, and forms of evangelism or apologetics. Mission is expansion directed at non-Christians in predominately non-Christian cultures, religious education addresses the issues of expansion between the generations, and evangelism is mission toward the estranged or indifferent within "Christian" culture. Tillich sees the third set of functions, the construction functions, as being the ones concerned with building the life of the church by using and transcending man's cultural creations. Thus, the construction functions include issues of aesthetics, cognition, communal life and personal life.

The four styles of church participation used in our study are related to these sets of functions but they do not parallel them in any direct sense. The Index of Organizational Involvement is related to the constitution functions through its measure of participation in worship and it is related to the construction functions through its measures of participation in the communal life of the church. The Index of Religious Knowledge is related to the expansion functions in the sense that it gives some measure of the respondent's religious education, and it is related to the construction function in the sense that it measures the respondent's cognitive ability. The Index of Devotional Orientation relates to the constitution functions and the construction functions since it seeks to measure aspects of the life of worship, personal life, and a form of communal life of the participant. Finally, the Index of Belief Orientation likewise relates to the same two sets of functions but it seeks to measure issues of confession of faith and issues of cognition.

As has been pointed out previously, the primary purpose of the study was not simply to study the styles of church participation but to study those styles in terms of how they seemed to be related to secular attitudes. To put that distinction into Tillichian categories, we are not concerned simply with the functions of constitution, expansion, and construction. Rather, we are most concerned with seeing how the church participant who is a product of those functions relates to issues in the social order. Can we find evidence of silent interpenetration, prophetic judgment, and political establishment (the *relating* functions of the church)? In order to find any evidence of the relating functions we utilized our indices of secular attitudes (the consequential variables). These consequential variables, because they measure attitudes and not actions, are mainly testing relationships of "silent interpenetration" with the culture. However, in some cases they do involve prophetic judgment of the social order, and in some cases they do imply a desire for "political establishment" (the church's collective involvement in political issues).

In order to complete the summary of Tillichian categories used in our argument, it is necessary to discuss what Tillich has called the "principles of sanctification."[7] Without some definition of such principles it would be impossible to identify which secular attitudes are seen as the more "sanctified" ones and which ones are not. Tillich labels the four principles of sanctification as increasing awareness, increasing freedom, increasing relatedness, and increasing self-transcendence. In awareness, man becomes "increasingly aware of his actual situation and of the forces struggling around him and his humanity but also becomes aware of the answers to the questions implied in this situation."[8] Increasing freedom is seen as freedom from "the law." "The mature freedom to give new laws or to apply the old ones in a new way is the aim of the process of sanctification."[9] Increasing relatedness "implies the awareness of the other one and the freedom to relate to him by overcoming self-seclusion within oneself and within the other one."[10] Finally, self-transcendency implies "that sanctification is not possible without a continuous transcendence of oneself in the direction of the ultimate—in other words, without participation in the holy."[11]

Within the scope of a single chapter it would be difficult indeed to seek relationships between all of the secular attitudes utilized in this study and these principles of sanctification. Therefore, since our research had a special concentration on the issues related to the racial crisis and because such issues proved to be the most important measures we developed for indicating the effect of church participation upon secular attitudes, we will concentrate on those issues here.

The official pronouncements of the denomination over the years have consistently called for the removal of social and economic barriers based on race and in recent years supported with increasing specificity the major goals of the civil rights movement. In the light of these pronouncements, we would begin with the assumption that persons with high scores on the Index of Social Acceptance and the Index of Civil Rights are manifesting increasing awareness, freedom, and relatedness. Whether or not they manifest an increasing self-transcendence is not as apparent. More will be said on this matter later. However, given the content of the principles of sanctification and the content of the answers which were used in the construction of the two indices, we are willing to utilize high scores on the indices as some indication of "sanctified" attitudes for the purposes of this discussion. Such a decision is not made without an awareness of the ambiguities involved, but given the limitations present in ever assessing sanctification on the human level, we are willing to live with the problems involved in such a decision.

The Research Results in Theological Perspective

In this analysis we will concentrate on those findings which emerged as the most significant ones from the sociological perspective. That is, in terms of use made of independent variables, we will deal only with the variable of social class and education. And in terms of the consequential variables we will deal only with the two variables focusing on racial justice, the Index of Civil Rights and the Index of Social Acceptance. All four church participation variables will be discussed. This decision is based on the fact that the other variables used produced ambiguous sociological findings, and therefore are not as crucial for the line of reasoning being pursued.

The discussion will be subdivided into two major sections, the first dealing with the influence of church participation on the secular issues (racial justice), and the second dealing with the influence of the secular factors (education and social class) upon church participation. This division is obviously prompted by the theological assumption that the relating functions of the churches involve influence of the churches upon other social groups and influence of other social groups upon the churches.

1. Church Participation and Its Influence upon Social Attitudes

Assuming high scores on the Index of Social Acceptance and the Index of Civil Rights to be measures of "sanctified" Christian social attitudes, we found that three of the four styles of church participation were related positively to such measures of "sanctified" living. Only the Index of Belief Orientation correlated negatively with our two indices of racial justice. The other three church participation variables continued to exert their influence even when social class and education were held constant.

Such an overall finding supports the view that church participation *does* in fact lead to some form of sanctified living, in the case of this one crucial crisis of our time. A possible Tillichian interpretation could be developed for why the Index of Belief Orientation has an opposite effect from the other styles of church participation. Such an interpretation would involve Tillich's view of a tension under which the constitution functions exist. The tension is between tradition and reformation. When tradition exists without any reformation, the "freedom of the spirit" is repressed and the Christian life malfunctions. Tillich calls overemphasis on tradition a "demonic"[12] tendency within Christianity, for the tradition becomes a substitute for God rather than a channel for receiving. The questions in our study chosen to constitute the Index of Belief Orientation were largely statements taken from other sociological research and they have been used previously to define Christian "orthodoxy." They were chosen intentionally in order to test the work of others and the adequacy of utilizing such definitions of "orthodoxy." More of this matter will be treated in the next section of this chapter, but for the moment it is sufficient to say that from the point of view of Tillich, and the present authors, the statements used in this index are not adequate definitions of Christian belief in the contemporary world. Such statements then proved to be "demonic" in terms of how they appeared to be related to secular attitudes. Indeed, in our time of great theological discussion, it may well be impossible to develop simple statements which can be used effectively to construct an Index of Belief Orientation which does not have such an overly "traditional" character about it.

If the Index of Belief Orientation proves to have a "demonic" effect upon racial attitudes, what can be said further about the other three styles of church participation? We can discuss two of them together, the Index of Organizational Involvement and the Index of Religious Knowledge. They were the two indices which correlated with social privilege. In the case of both of them, it appears that they correlate with the "sanctified" racial attitudes, indeed they appear to be measures of a deepening of the social influence from one's place in society. Sociologists might well call this the influence of men of common mind upon each other, while a Tillichian thinker would be inclined to talk of the silent interpenetration of social forces upon the church and vice versa.

The fourth index of church participation, the Index of Devotional Orientation, presents a different picture, one which has special interest.

This style of church participation appears to "reverse" the influence of the social variables upon it. The Index of Devotional Orientation is correlated negatively with social class and education but positively with the Index of Civil Rights and the Index of Social Acceptance! Since the IDO is the index which stressed the devotional life, it is appropriate to argue that it is an index which is in some way related to a person's self-transcendence. It is difficult to imagine what devotional life means if it does not imply some assumption about a reality transcendent to ordinary experience, while it would not be difficult at all to argue that organizational participation in the church and having religious knowledge do not imply any necessary sense of transcendent reality. Churches could be seen by organizational participants as good ethical-cultural societies and one can "know about" religion without necessarily believing in any of its precepts or doctrines. This particular index, the Index of Devotional Orientation, is interesting especially since it did correlate positively with the two racial attitude indices and with both of the means of social change indices. Thus in spite of the fact that one might interpret devotional life as a form of "compensation" for social injustice, since the Index of Devotional Orientation correlates with social deprivation, it is surprising that it correlates with being more accepting of minority peoples. So often research has shown that it is precisely the white lower-middle class which is most threatened by the advance of the minority races and therefore has a very high level of racial prejudice. How is it that the IDO relates to a decrease in prejudice? Are those with higher IDO scores people who find a devotional orientation turning them toward social concern for others in spite of their own social problems? Such would seem to be the case. Is there a Tillichian interpretation for such an apparent tendency?

One answer could be found by examining Tillich's treatment of the personal constructive functions of the churches.[13] He states that these functions exist within a tension between saintliness and humanity. Saintliness is for him, at least partially defined in terms of "asceticism." Defining just what one means by asceticism is a perennial issue within the church, but it is possible to begin the definition by reference to a sense of personal discipline. If such a definition is used, then those with higher IDO scores could be seen as men who combine saintliness and humanity. They are those who have a sense of personal discipline combined with a concern for others. Are they then modern "inner-worldly ascetics" as we have argued through a Weberian analysis in the last chapter? We think so.

Thus with the exception of the Index of Belief Orientation we are arguing that the other three styles of church participation tend to have an influence upon social attitudes in a direction consistent with the goals of the Christian faith. If there is any consistency at all between attitudes and actions, one is tempted to argue for the influence of church participation upon the culture through "silent interpenetration." Also, since the racial indices included questions of prophetic judgment of our present cultural standards and of the church taking some action in these matters, there is modest support for arguing in favor of the relating functions of the church as also including "prophetic judgment" and "political establishment."

2. Cultural Relationships Affecting the Church

It has become commonly accepted that sociological studies show the negative character of the silent interpenetration of society upon the church, while here we are clearly concerned to stress the other side of the issue. We are stressing that society sometimes influences the church in ways which the church can affirm. Since we identified higher scores on the Index of Civil Rights and the Index of Social Acceptance as indicators of "sanctified" attitudes, it is important to note that these attitudes correlated with certain secular variables (increased education and higher social class). These same secular variables also correlated positively with two of the church participation variables (organizational involvement and religious knowledge). And thus certain cultural influences upon the church are supportive of "sanctified" secular attitudes. The mutual interpenetration of church and society is ambiguous and oversimplification in either a negative or a positive direction distorts reality.

We have found an inverse relationship between education and socioeconomic status and the Index of Belief Orientation. The IBO was in turn negatively related to the "right" attitudes on racial justice. Such findings would suggest that increased education and higher levels of economic security would enhance the cause of racial justice. As we stated above, the correlations we have found between these variables would suggest that the traditional beliefs of Christians have ceased to function as they were intended, and they may even have become inhibitors of "sanctified" living.

By seeing that church participation influences social attitudes as well as seeing that social factors influence church participation, we can be supportive of theological interpretations which acknowledge and allow for such "two-way" influence. Furthermore, we are made suspicious of studies and interpretations of church-culture relationships which appear to take account of only one form of influence (positive *or* negative) in one direction only (be it from the church to the culture *or* from the culture to the church).

We suspect that there will be those who will be disparaging of the amount of "positive" evidence which this study has been able to mount for the argument that church participation influences secular attitudes. It is indeed minimal evidence, and as men concerned for the life of the Christian community, we could certainly have hoped for more. We can only respond that until evidence is mounted which shows that some "new form" of the church produces greater results from participation within it, or until some evidence is produced which shows some other voluntary association in our society which produces greater change in its participants, we live with the ambiguous results reported.

Implications for the Life of the Church

Having discussed briefly the underlying theological stance informing the observations of the authors, and having devoted the majority of the study to the sociological analysis of church participation, we are now in a position to engage in final "prescriptions" for the life of the church in contemporary America. Such prescriptive observations are primarily related to the theological and sociological analyses which have produced them. However, by the very nature of limited research of this type, generalizations will be made which are not fully supported by the data as presented. The data only appears to suggest such prescriptions. Those who do not see the data leading to such prescriptions can only be encouraged to develop their own interpretations either with additional data or divergent theoretical assumptions.

1. The "Ineffective" Church

Taken in broad categories, without making differentiations between various styles of church participation, the data from this study corresponds well with most other studies of religion in American culture. Our study along with the others, points to the ineffectiveness of the church in influencing its participants toward social change and social justice. In terms of overall percentages of responses it is obvious that few of our respondents scored high in the Index of Social Acceptance and the Index of Civil Rights. Most of the respondents in this study were not in favor of the church engaging in very significant social action programs, the high priority for the majority of them was clearly toward a ministry to the personal lives of the members of the church. The majority were not very conscious of their need for salvation from the negativities of life, but they wished to have the church minister to them in terms of a "positive" gospel of God's love and care for them as individual human beings and members of nuclear families.

If such findings were left at this level of analysis the cost of time and talent which has gone into the present study would hardly be justified. Indeed, given the near unanimity of previous research on these same points, it would have been sheer folly to expect that this study would come up with any other "general" findings. However, it has been the thesis of this study that such gross interpretations neglect important subtleties of interpretation and statistical analysis. We must look a good deal deeper than such overall statistics to significantly understand the dynamics of contemporary church life. The problem with a great deal of the previous research has not been that the statistics gathered were incorrect. The problem has been that the analysis did not go deep enough and the analysis was not informed by any consistent theological stance.

Let us begin by asking some questions about the figures based on "overall" findings. If more than 95 percent of the American people consider themselves to be religious men, and if in fact well over half of the people are members in "good standing" of religious bodies, then who would expect that "religious men" or church members in general would differ significantly on any issue from the American population at large? Since American religious bodies have chosen, rightly or wrongly, to make a broad appeal to the American people and to have requirements for membership so low that the majority "belongs," they are by definition a "cultural church." Thus, religious groups have in fact become very much like American political parties. They try to appeal to nearly everyone. Religious identity in this instance becomes an aspect of American identity. And surely no serious analyst would expect very dramatic differences to emerge between those who voted for either party in a national election and the population at large. The differences will be there, but they will be slight. To study "active" Democrats or Republicans may produce some more interesting results, but we have to decide how to define "active." So, too, in our study, when different ways of measuring the "active" church participants have been used, then more meaningful results have emerged.

For the moment we will leave the question about whether the church "should" be so general in its appeal or not. At this point we simply observe that the difficulty of answering "how" the church should be selective and have a discipline for membership has been a long standing difficulty in the history of Christianity. Theological problems emerge when defining who is in fact "saved." Human sin makes such definition very risky, and theological reasons have contributed to the decision of leaving such definition ambiguous at best. Maintaining institutional stability has not been the only reason for making church membership "easy." Later we will have more to say on the nature of contemporary discipline for the churches.

A word is in order concerning the "privatized" character of the general findings of the study. Given the apparent decline of importance placed on the family in our culture and the increasing influence of groups (governmental, economic, and social), we should not be surprised that participants in churches look to them for emphasis on individual worth. What other group is doing so? Perhaps clubs of various sorts, and it does appear that private clubs are growing in their appeal to Americans. Man is by definition both individual and social. And when a social order becomes dominantly defined by group pressures, some institutions intentionally or unintentionally will be sought out as supporters of individual worth.

The authors would be among the first to admit the "ineffective" character of the churches in bringing about certain forms of needed social change. Indeed, they have both spent their careers working for changes within the institutional church which will facilitate "effective social ministry." But here we are simply pointing to the problems inherent in describing social ministry in any simple fashion in the face of "gross" statistics.

2. The "Culturally Captive" Church

If even an "ineffective" church exerts some influence upon the culture, so also the culture influences the church. As has been shown by other studies, and as the current study confirms, the church does selectively appeal to various groups within the culture in terms of denominational preference. The church does draw more upper-class persons into some denominations and more lower-class persons into other denominations. Thus, a church which claims that its ministry is for all men does in fact prove to minister more "effectively," or at least appeal more effectively, to some social groups than to others. Such social conditioning of the churches is of course beset with many dangers of substituting the self-interest of a particular social class for Christianity.

However, the present research demonstrates that cultural conditioning *may* be in the direction of attitudes which have been defined as

"Christian" on other than the social class grounds. In effect there can be a coalescence of influence from social conditioning and from the Christian faith. Thus we found that both increased education and improved social class tended to correlate with increased scores on the Index of Civil Rights and the Index of Social Acceptance. The same positive correlation existed between three of the types of church participation and the civil rights and social acceptance indices. Social attitudes are the product of numerous influences which are a very complex web of interaction. The church therefore, is the recipient of both "good" and "evil" influences when it is conditioned by social forces.

The interrelated character of social influences may be ignored by the man interested only in developing rhetoric, but it cannot be ignored by serious leaders of social institutions. Take for example the way in which our research showed that the Negro respondents were much more oriented toward civil rights issues than were the white respondents. Given the argument we have pursued earlier, namely that higher scores on the civil rights indices are indicative of more "sanctified" Christian life, we are forced to argue that the Negro respondents are "better" Christians in this case. Indeed, recently Black theologians have argued just that. Blacks they argue have had a "deeper" sense of the full meaning of Christian character.[14]

However, to fail to recognize that attitudes in favor of civil justice grow out of Black self-interest and out of the historic function of the Negro church as an instrument of social protest would be to ignore the obvious. The point we argue for is that attitudes are influenced by many factors, some of which we can call *both* Christian *and* cultural. Social factors cannot be easily labeled as simply Christian or non-Christian.

In the contemporary pattern of American denominationalism there is a growing effort to form new religious groupings with special reference to social action concerns. Such efforts are designed to stimulate the church to a social "effectiveness" which its more traditional and parochial form has lacked. We have been supportive of several of these efforts and have participated in the creation of some of them. Use of the present research model to test such "new forms" of the church would be an interesting undertaking. Given the results which have emerged in this study, it is reasonable to assume that such "new forms" are drawing selectively from the American population at large and are subject, as are the "old forms," to social conditioning.

The question which it would be fruitful to pursue would be whether or not, *when the social factors are held constant,* the "new" types of church participation are producing higher correlation with the "right" social attitudes than were the "old" types of church participation which were tested in this research. Prior to such research, one can only assume *all* forms of church organization and participation are subject to a complex interrelationship of influences from the culture and from the Christian faith, care always being needed to take the complexity into account in assessing "effectiveness."

Sensitivity to the complex character of cultural influences forces us to be careful about generalizing the findings from a study of a predominantly privileged denomination. Would patterns be similar if a study was made of a less socially privileged denomination? We do not know and can only speculate. The pattern of our findings would suggest that a less privileged denomination would have more persons with higher scores on the Index of Belief Orientation and on the Index of Devotional Orientation (other research has actually shown that this is extremely likely). However, the important issue is whether for such denominations the "influence" of the Index of Devotional Orientation would be toward increased scores on the indices of racial justice. If a person is less privileged, and joins a less privileged denomination, does a devotional orientation still produce a more accepting attitude toward racial minorities? Or, would the "influence" of a devotional orientation be offset by the gathering together of like-minded men? We do not know and are required to limit our prescriptive observations to denominations similar to the United Church of Christ in social class grouping.

A word should be said about the issue of attitudes versus actions for privileged social groups. A cynic might argue that the respondents in the study "said" they were in favor of civil rights and would accept Negroes, but if they had been tested in terms of action a very different result would have emerged. No doubt there are differences between attitudes and actions, and yet it is hardly reasonable to assume that a man of prejudiced attitudes will act in a less prejudiced fashion than a man of unprejudiced attitudes. Therefore, even granting some discrepancy between attitudes and actions, attitudes are still in some sense congruent with actions. In the same vein, some are likely to argue that the social situation has changed a great deal with respect to civil rights since the data here reported were gathered. Indeed, there have been many changes, and in the intervening period a good many polemical statements have been made about civil rights "liberals" and their ineffectiveness in "real" social change. However, the evidence still is that most "backlash" on civil rights has been among the very groups where this study would have predicted it. It is the less privileged, those most immediately threatened by increased status for the Negro, who have had the most prejudiced actions. Likewise, in spite of the need for social pressure and power on the part of the dispossessed to bring about rapid social change, the goals would not be accomplished (when the dispossessed are the minority) without the support of others not likely to personally benefit from the changes—the more privileged socially liberal groups. The present research would appear to support the assertion that church participation has made a contribution among the socially privileged groups by liberalizing their attitudes on social issues.

3. The Church in "Tension"

Earlier we discussed the major functions of the church as Paul Tillich delineated them. We also mentioned some of the tensions which he saw present within the functions. His point was that for each of the sets of functions there is a polarity under which the functions are exercised. If either side of the polarity is manifested to the exclusion of the other side, there is a malfunction. He lists the polarities as follows:

Constitution Function:	Tradition and Reform
Expansion Function:	Verity and Adaptation
Construction Function:	Form Transcendence and Form Affirmation
Relating Function:	Opposing and Belonging (to other social groups)

Exclusive emphasis on the first term in each of these polarities results in functions becoming "demonic" (the holy turned in upon itself), and exclusive emphasis on the second term results in the functions becoming "profane" (lacking in any spiritual content).

The research findings of the present study are appropriately interpreted within just such a theological framework. Selective emphasis on our findings could support the argument that the functions of the church are being performed in a "profane" manner, and selective stress on certain other findings could point to a "demonic" church. We can clearly see ways throughout the study in which there is evidence of the church adapting to the wishes (and needs) of its participants for a "personalized" ministry. There are clear indications of ways in which the church is being socially conditioned by the class and educational situation of its constituency, thus showing "form-affirmation" and "belonging" to social groups. Such evidence could certainly be used to support an argument concerning the "profane" character of the church. Likewise, particularly in terms of the results from the use of the Index of Belief Orientation, we could argue that the tradition of the church has become "demonic." Those who appear to "believe" the most concerning the traditional doctrinal statements of the church are *not* the ones who appear to have the most "sanctified" attitudes toward secular issues, at least not in terms of the civil rights issues which we have been discussing. There appears to be a need for "reformed" beliefs.

However, such selective use of the research results does not do them justice. Even as social conditioning was present, the use of statistical tests could not eliminate the influence of three of the styles of church participation. Is this a kind of "form-transcendence"? Is there indeed some Christian "verity" emerging in the midst of the "adaptation"? Given the influence of the three forms of church participation upon the civil rights attitudes of the participants, is the church not "opposing" the cultural standards as well as "belonging" to them?

The ambiguity of both belonging to and opposing the social order is most apparent when we remember that increased social class and education (as well as the Index of Organizational Involvement and the Index of Religious Knowledge) correlated positively with being socially accepting of Negroes and being in favor of civil rights activities. Thus, in terms of the way the argument is formed here, a man of privileged social class both "belongs to" and "opposes" the social order. He belongs in terms of having succeeded within the class structure, and he opposes the way in which the majority has chosen to treat the Negro. *And* he is most likely to have a higher religious knowledge and to participate in the organizational activities of the denomination we have been studying.

Because of the ambiguity just expressed, the Index of Devotional Orientation becomes one of the most interesting and meaningful styles of church participation utilized in the study. It correlated negatively with social class and education but positively with civil rights and social acceptance. It alone appeared to be the type of church participation which "reversed" social conditioning rather than reinforcing it. Does this indicate then that it, above other forms of church participation, measures a kind of "form-transcendence"? We would argue that the evidence points in this direction. We would further argue that this style of church participation then presents an important prescription for the life of the churches in our time.

As critics from without and prophets from within have pointed to the "ineffective" and "captive" character of American churches, they have almost without exception been asking for more social concern and social activism on the part of the churches. The argument many have given, put in Tillichian terms, would be as follows: The church needs to be reformed (constitutional function) in order that it may more effectively engage in political establishment (relating function). And it is to do this by recognizing the need to adapt to and affirm the realities of social pressures and political power organization (expansion and construction functions).

Granting the important criticism which is being leveled here, the findings on the devotional index would interject one important note into the argument. Reform, adaptation, form affirmation, and belonging are all "profane" poles of the tensions within which the church exists. How in the midst of such recommended change is the church to maintain the traditional, verity, form transcendent and opposing poles of its life so that it is indeed "holy" without being simply another institution calling for social change? Surely we have no desire for "demonic" emphasis on tradition, verity, and form transcendence, but yet how are the tensions to be maintained?

It appears that the findings on the Index of Devotional Orientation give at least a clue. The church is in the midst of movements which strongly advocate a reappropriation of the injunction to be "in the world but not of it." We are here calling for a reappropriation of the concept of "inner-worldly ascetic," and we believe that our findings about the Index of Devotional Orientation support just such a call. If the Christian man is to be in the world, then he needs some basis on which he maintains perspective so that he is not of it. Perhaps the devotional man is the one who knows the "source" of his courage to be in the world, he is not tempted to remove himself from the world, and his sense of the transcendent gives him the "vision" so that he is not fully of the world.

We stress all of this recognizing that devotionalism is often seriously questioned within churches of the more "liberal" Protestant type. "Piety" is very often a pejorative term and concept. Liberals have been too ready to identify devotionalism and piety with otherworldliness. Devotional men, so the argument often goes in liberal Protestant circles, are men who are unwilling to face the realities of social forces and unwilling to work for needed social change. Our data brings such assertions into serious question. The devotional man in this study of a liberal denomination was *more* likely to favor action in the area of civil justice. We have called such men "inner-worldly ascetics"!

It is a clear issue of our time to determine what exactly is the contribution which the church can make to crucial social struggles. Many, both inside and outside the church, are asking whether the church is only to be seen as one power group among many. Is the church finally not fundamentally distinct in any way from the League of Women Voters or a Coalition for Racial Justice? Some will say that this is an unfair way to put the question and will argue that the question is "outmoded." Such persons are likely to emphasize that God is not limited to acting through the institutional church. God is "where the action is," and there are "hidden" or "latent" churches within Coalitions for Racial Justice. We would be the last to deny either of these last two statements. But such statements avoid the issue of how one is in the world *but not of it!* It is appropriate to say that prior to the study we would have been very hesitant to come out in favor of "devotionalism" as an indication of how one can be in the world but not of it. Like other liberal Protestants we too were fearful of devotionalism becoming "escapism." But the data simply cannot be denied.

As recent converts to the importance of a devotional orientation as one means by which the church begins to more adequately fulfill its function, we are hardly in a position to give detailed instructions concerning the implementation of this finding. It is enough that we point to the importance of the findings and leave to others the task of furthering the new "inner worldly asceticism" among the fragmented laymen who form the church participants of today.

Conclusion

The church can profit from sociological analysis in terms of its own self-awareness, and it has been the goal of this predominantly sociological study to aid in such self-awareness. In addition, in this final chapter, we have sought to engage in the often-neglected task of seeing how the church can integrate sociological reality into its self-understanding by correlating sociological findings with essentially theological affirmations.

In this exercise in correlating theological affirmations with sociological findings, we have concentrated on only part of the findings from the study. We have said very little about the findings with respect to the Negro parishioners. We have not attempted to deal with the findings on secular attitudes other than the civil rights attitudes. Such omissions are not oversights but rather self-conscious choices of emphasis.

What we were about in this preliminary effort at correlation was the task of being explicit about just how empirical one can be in discussing a theological system and just how much prescriptive material does begin to emerge from sociological material which was gathered in a relatively objective fashion. We are not willing to ignore the productive tension which exists between disciplines. We read the results of the exercise as pointing to the easily forgotten fact that the church is neither as ineffective as superficial sociological analysis often says it is, nor as effective as superficial theological analysis often assumes it to be.

As the church makes its way into the future, it must be conscious of the ways in which it has adapted to the society in which it exists. But in seeking to oppose certain worldly standards it must be self-conscious about the truth which it seeks to make relevant to the world. A true church is one which knows its foundation. This is to say that it has a perspective concerning the ambiguity of all "effectiveness" and knows the ambiguously "captive" character of all institutions that have sociological form.

Appendix

Church Participation Questionnaire

Instructions

Most questions require only a check mark in the right-hand box for your answer. Please be sure to answer all questions. The validity of this survey depends on the completeness of your replies.

These questionnaires will be tabulated by the research department of your denomination. No postage is required to return it. Simply use the self-addressed, postage-free envelope provided with this form.

Please do not sign your name. Your replies will be kept strictly anonymous and the information you give will be used for statistical purposes only. At no time will individuals be identified with the answers. Only by achieving full returns can we be completely successful in this survey.

Thanks for your cooperation. Your answers to these questions are very important to us.

(NOTE: The figures included here as marginals are percentages calculated on the basis of the two major subsamples of the study [the "Town and Country" and "Urban" samples described in Ch. 2]. They do *not* include the "Negro" subsample or the "University Church" subsample. Hence there will be some divergence between these figures and those reported in the text at certain points. The figures given in parentheses are the percentage of nonresponses.)

Let's begin with a few questions concerning your present church activities. Just put a check mark in the box next to your answer.

1. For how long have you been a member of your present congregation? (0.7)

Less than 1 year	5.4	5 to 10 years	21.7
1 to 2 years	7.0	10 or more years	48.0
2 to 3 years	12.2	I am not a member	5.0

2. In what denomination were you raised as a child? (0.8)

Baptist	7.2
Congregational Christian (before UCC)	23.2
Disciples of Christ	.9
Evangelical and Reformed (before UCC)	19.7
Lutheran	11.2
Methodist	16.5
Presbyterian	12.0
Protestant Episcopal	2.0

Other Protestant (write in)	4.7
Roman Catholic	2.8
All other (write in)	1.6
None	2.8

3. Generally speaking, how often do you attend Sunday worship services in your own or any other church? (1.1)

Three or four times a month	64.3
About twice a month	17.2
About once a month	6.8
About once every two months	2.9
Three or four times a year	3.7
Once or twice a year	2.4
Less than once a year	1.6

4. Have you been a member of another local church before becoming a member of your present church? (1.7)

Yes   29.7   No   68.6

5. People join churches for many reasons. Some of them are listed below. How important was each of these reasons for you personally when you joined your present church?

		Very Important	Somewhat Important	Not Too Important
Enjoyed its friendly atmosphere	(25.6)	30.2	32.1	12.1
For the sake of my children	(32.7)	48.1	8.3	10.9
A place to serve others	(31.6)	24.8	28.4	15.2
Grew up in the church school	(35.4)	26.2	12.6	25.8
Church program appealed to me	(32.6)	26.1	29.0	12.3
Invited to join by a member	(45.7)	11.6	10.5	32.2
Invited to join by the minister	(41.9)	18.1	14.8	25.2
Enjoyed form of worship service	(29.0)	44.0	21.5	5.5
Liked the minister	(27.5)	44.0	20.8	7.7
Located conveniently near my home	(28.9)	26.2	21.1	23.8
Liked people I met in church	(28.6)	29.6	33.4	8.4
Preferred the denomination	(24.3)	41.2	21.1	13.4

6. To how many organizations in your local church do you belong? (Do not include church school, committees or boards) (1.9)

None	44.4	Three	4.3
One	32.5	Four	0.1
Two	16.2	Five or more	0.6

7. Have you held an office or served on an official board or policy-making committee of your church during the past three years? (1.4)

   Yes 36.2   No 62.4

8. As a church member or participant, to what degree are you seeking help or guidance in the following areas of your life?

I want my church to help me to ...		Much	Some	Little
Be aware of the needs of others in my community	(19.8)	35.1	35.7	9.4
Build good moral foundations for my personal life	(16.3)	63.2	17.3	3.2
Find meaning for my personal existence	(20.5)	56.1	19.6	3.8
Raise my children properly	(27.2)	59.0	9.6	4.2
Know of God's care and love for me	(19.9)	57.8	17.5	4.8
Meet my personal problems of anxiety, conflict, etc.	(21.8)	40.2	29.3	8.7
Strengthen my faith and religious devotion	(12.1)	68.7	15.7	3.5
Understand my daily work as a Christian vocation	(24.5)	37.1	30.0	8.4
Work for justice in my community and in my world	(18.9)	43.3	29.3	8.5

9. What is the range of your family's total weekly contribution to your church? (1.6)

Less than $1.00	9.1	5.00 to 7.49	13.7
1.00 to 1.99	23.6	7.50 to 9.99	4.6
2.00 to 2.99	19.7	10.00 to 12.49	3.9
3.00 to 3.99	12.4	12.50 to 14.99	1.1
4.00 to 4.99	8.0	15.00 or more	2.3

10. Other than giving to your local church, what other groups receive regular financial support from you? Check if you or your family contribute regularly to any of the groups listed below. (8.6)

College or university	20.9
Theological seminary	5.4
Community Chest or United Fund	81.7
Social movements or "causes" (NAACP, CORE, etc.)	10.1
Medical or health research	50.3
Other (write in)	22.2

11. In which of the following program groups of your congregation have you participated in the last three years?

Church Program		Participate now	Participated in the past
Women's groups	(60.3)	30.1	9.6
Men's groups	(82.8)	9.8	7.4
Study groups	(75.0)	11.5	13.5
Family nights	(64.7)	21.5	13.8
Social action groups	(84.8)	7.3	7.9
Church board	(74.8)	14.7	10.5
Church committees	(67.6)	19.1	13.3
Adult Sunday school class	(86.7)	6.1	7.2
Retreats	(89.5)	4.3	6.2
Prayer meetings	(91.7)	3.1	5.2

12. How important do you consider the following typical program groups often found in churches (not just your own congregation) to be?

Church Program		Very Important	Somewhat Important	Not too Important	Should be Dropped	No Opinion
Women's groups	(9.2)	44.0	31.8	7.3	.6	7.1
Men's groups	(15.7)	29.8	36.6	9.2	.8	7.9
Study groups	(15.7)	40.5	31.0	6.5	.5	5.8
Family nights	(15.2)	32.3	34.7	10.6	.6	6.6
Social action groups	(19.8)	22.3	27.6	14.5	4.4	11.4
Church board	(13.8)	66.5	12.9	1.4	.4	5.0
Church committees	(15.8)	54.1	21.5	3.0	.5	5.1
Adult Sunday school class	(15.9)	32.9	29.6	12.8	.5	8.3
Retreats	(20.2)	17.1	27.9	14.8	1.5	18.5
Prayer meetings	(18.1)	21.6	28.3	12.8	2.1	17.1

13. If you were to be critical of the present-day church (not just your own congregation), what would you say about the following?

		No concern of the church	Church has done too much	Church has done enough	Church has not done enough	No opinion
Teaching the Bible	(10.1)	1.1	.9	30.1	49.0	8.8
Working for racial justice and equality	(12.4)	6.3	4.2	21.6	39.6	15.9
Helping young people	(10.7)	2.0	1.1	32.4	47.3	6.5
Helping people make their occupations Christian	(13.9)	2.8	1.5	21.1	39.0	21.7
Ministering to the needs of changing neighborhoods	(14.0)	3.2	1.7	22.7	36.0	22.4
Affecting changes in our governmental policies	(13.2)	27.4	2.2	10.7	20.9	25.6
Caring for the needs of older people	(12.5)	3.9	1.8	27.3	40.3	14.2
Fostering the devotional life	(17.5)	1.2	1.0	31.7	28.5	20.1
Supporting higher education	(13.4)	11.5	1.0	29.3	22.1	22.7

14. In what type of community did you grow up?   (1.9)

On a farm	24.4
Place of less than 2,500 population	15.6
Town of 2,500 to 9,999 population	13.9
City of 10,000 to 49,999 population	13.7
City of 50,000 to 99,999 population	4.4
City of 100,000 to 499,999 population	8.4
City of 500,000 to 999,999 population	3.7
City of 1,000,000 or more population	10.0
Suburb of large city	5.7

15. For how long have you lived in your present town or township? (1.1)

Less than 1 year	2.9	3 to 5 years	10.2
1 to 2 years	4.2	5 to 10 years	15.0
2 to 3 years	3.9	10 or more years	62.7

16. For how long have you lived in your present home? (1.2)

Less than 1 year	8.2	3 to 5 years	12.4
1 to 2 years	8.0	5 to 10 years	22.2
2 to 3 years	6.7	10 or more years	41.3

17. Do you rent or own your present home? (1.4)

    Own   78.5   Rent   15.2   Other   4.9

18. How far is your church from your home? (1.3)

Less than half mile	21.1	2 to 3 miles	11.5
Half to one mile	22.4	3 to 5 miles	12.6
1 to 2 miles	16.7	5 or more miles	14.4

In the next set of questions, we're turning to some questions dealing with your understanding of the church and its ministry. In some cases we want you to express your attitude or opinion, in others, what you may know about the church. When answering questions in this section, please do not consult others. Simply check the best answers that come to your mind.

19. How necessary do you feel that it is for a Christian to believe or do the following things?

Christians are those who . . .		Absolutely necessary	Probably necessary	Probably not necessary
Accept church creeds	(8.2)	37.7	30.4	23.7
Are active church members	(7.6)	39.3	31.5	21.6
Attend Sunday worship regularly	(6.7)	41.6	30.9	20.8
Believe in Jesus as Savior	(4.6)	82.5	9.6	3.3
Had a conversion experience	(16.6)	7.9	18.3	57.2
Have been baptized	(6.2)	45.6	21.6	26.6
Obey the Ten Commandments	(5.0)	73.9	18.6	2.5
Pray and read the Bible daily	(8.0)	28.3	37.3	26.4
Work for social justice	(10.4)	30.8	40.8	18.0

20. Worshipers respond in many ways to the Sunday morning service of worship. How helpful do you usually find the various parts of the service as you are personally concerned?

Part of the Worship Service		Very helpful	Somewhat helpful	Not too helpful
Communion service	(6.0)	63.8	22.9	7.3
Congregational hymn singing	(6.1)	50.6	33.8	9.5
Music, other than hymns	(9.3)	37.6	41.6	11.5
Offering	(9.1)	41.5	35.6	13.8
Pastoral prayers	(7.2)	63.1	24.5	5.2
Prayer of confession	(12.0)	45.4	27.6	15.0
Scripture lesson or reading	(8.8)	50.1	34.3	6.8
Silent meditation	(7.6)	63.8	23.3	5.3
Sermon	(4.6)	76.9	16.2	2.3
Service as a whole	(5.6)	72.9	19.9	1.6

21. As far as you know, how much time does your minister spend on each of the activities listed below?

Minister's Activity		Don't know	A lot of time	Some time	Very little time
Calling on church members	(4.1)	30.9	32.0	26.2	6.8
Calling on nonmembers	(6.0)	46.5	11.9	26.1	9.5
Counseling people with problems	(6.2)	40.0	28.2	23.1	2.5
Leading worship and devotions	(7.0)	17.4	59.6	14.8	1.2
Office and administrative work	(6.7)	35.6	35.1	20.7	1.9
Organizing church programs	(7.3)	30.0	39.0	20.9	2.8
Raising money for the church	(7.0)	41.5	15.7	21.3	14.5
Study and sermon preparation	(6.1)	36.3	48.7	8.3	.6
Teaching	(8.4)	34.0	25.7	23.3	8.6
Visiting sick and bereaved	(4.5)	24.1	46.4	22.7	2.3
Working for social justice	(8.3)	43.8	23.5	20.0	4.4
Working with children and youth	(5.5)	23.4	37.3	26.5	7.3

22. For each of the same list of activities, check whether you think your minister spends too much, too little, or about the right amount of time.

Minister's Activity		Don't know	Too much	About right	Too little
Calling on church members	(5.2)	33.7	1.0	45.0	15.1
Calling on nonmembers	(6.7)	50.2	1.2	31.9	10.0
Counseling people with problems	(6.8)	43.5	.8	44.1	4.8
Leading worship and devotions	(7.7)	20.1	.9	69.8	1.5
Office and administrative work	(7.7)	41.9	9.8	39.7	.9
Organizing church programs	(8.1)	34.5	3.8	50.1	3.5
Raising money for the church	(8.5)	44.9	3.1	39.0	4.5
Study and sermon preparation	(8.2)	32.9	1.1	55.5	2.3
Teaching	(8.9)	38.3	.7	45.1	7.0
Visiting sick and bereaved	(6.0)	27.4	.9	60.6	5.1
Working for social justice	(8.7)	45.8	4.9	35.6	5.0
Working with children and youth	(6.3)	27.2	.7	55.7	10.1

23. How helpful has your church actually been to you in the following areas of your life?

In helping me to:		Much help	Some help	Little help
Be aware of the needs of others in my community	(8.5)	22.2	47.9	21.4
Build good moral foundations for my personal life	(7.9)	53.3	33.6	5.2
Find meaning for my personal existence	(10.3)	43.3	37.2	9.2
Raise my children properly	(20.5)	44.5	27.5	7.5
Know of God's care and love for me	(9.2)	53.8	31.3	5.7
Meet my personal problems of anxiety, conflict, etc.	(9.7)	36.5	38.5	15.4
Strengthen my faith and religious devotion	(7.5)	56.2	29.2	7.1
Understand my daily work as Christian vocation	(12.3)	31.5	40.3	15.9
Work for justice in my community and in my world	(11.4)	25.0	42.0	21.6

24. How sure are you that each of the following statements is true or not true?

		True	Probably true	Probably not true	Not true
All men are born guilty of original sin	(9.4)	23.9	17.3	13.8	35.6
All men are equal in the sight of God	(3.9)	86.1	7.5	1.2	1.3
God answers prayer	(3.9)	72.1	18.8	3.4	1.8
God revealed himself to man in Jesus Christ	(4.4)	82.4	10.5	1.8	.9
Hell is a just punishment for sinners	(11.1)	16.6	26.0	19.0	27.3
Jesus rose from the dead	(4.9)	74.6	13.2	4.5	2.8
Jesus was born of a virgin	(5.7)	57.9	18.6	12.0	5.8
Sin is separation from God	(11.4)	45.0	21.6	10.3	11.7
The Bible is the word of God	(5.6)	66.6	19.5	4.7	3.6
The Church is the body of Christ	(10.5)	53.5	21.6	7.7	6.7
There is life after death	(6.5)	57.9	25.4	7.1	3.1
We are justified by faith	(9.2)	65.0	23.8	2.6	2.4

25. Which of the following books are found in the Old Testament? (Do not consult your Bible) (14.5)

Amos	61.7	Hebrews	42.5
Acts	15.4	Hosea	63.4
Galatians	19.2	Psalms	70.1

26. As far as you know, who of the following were leaders of the Protestant Reformation? (9.2)

Aquinas	1.6	Hegel	3.7
Augustine	5.1	Luther	89.7
Calvin	60.1	Zwingli	26.2

27. As far as you know, which of the denominations listed below have bishops? (5.3)

Baptist	6.9	Methodist	45.1
Disciples	1.5	Presbyterian	7.4
Episcopal	75.4	Roman Catholic	86.5
Lutheran (U.S.A.)	11.6	United Church	1.1

Now we'd like to ask you a few personal questions about yourself. Most of these answers can be checked very quickly.

28. What is your age? (Check correct age range) (.1)

Under 15 years	.5	40 to 44 years	12.3
15 to 19 years	3.2	45 to 49 years	10.9
20 to 24 years	5.2	50 to 54 years	9.2
25 to 29 years	7.9	55 to 59 years	8.8
30 to 34 years	9.2	60 to 64 years	6.9
35 to 39 years	11.6	65 years and over	14.3

29. What is your present marital status? (.1)

Single	9.4	Widowed	8.2
Married, no children	8.3	Separated	.6
Married with children	71.9	Divorced	1.4

30. What is your sex? (.1)

Male	37.6	Female	62.3

31. If you have children, how many are under 18 years of age? (13.5)

None	34.0	Two	18.2
One	14.3	Three or more	20.0

32. How much formal education have you completed? (.9)

I am still in school	2.4
Eighth grade or less	8.5
Ninth, tenth, or eleventh grade	7.2
Graduated high school	19.6
Attended trade or business school	6.8
Graduated trade or business school	5.6
Attended some college or university	16.6
Graduated college or university	14.4
Had some post-college or university study	8.2
Completed graduate or professional school	9.8

33. What is your present occupational status? (1.5)

Housewife	33.7
Employed full time	42.6
Employed part time	9.3
Temporarily not employed	1.1
In the armed service	.4
Retired	8.0
I am still in school	3.7

34. Are you the head of your household? (1.3)

    Yes   46.8   No   51.9

35. What is your total family income? Please check the approximate annual range. (4.9)

Under $2,500	7.5	10,000 to 12,499	14.2
2,500 to 4,999	13.2	12,500 to 14,999	5.4
5,000 to 7,499	21.9	15,000 to 19,999	7.0
7,500 to 9,999	20.3	20,000 or more	5.6

36. Was the income reported above earned by more than one member of your family? (3.6)

    Yes   30.1   No   66.3

37. What is the occupation of the head of your household? The classifications used below are those of the U.S. Bureau of the Census. If you are uncertain describe the occupation as fully as you can in the margin. (8.0)

    Clerical and related workers: bookkeepers, stenographers, cashiers, mail carriers, shipping clerks, secretaries, ticket agents, telephone operators, office machine operators, etc.   8.7

    Craftsmen, foremen, and related workers: tinsmiths, bakers, carpenters, masons, shoemakers, electricians, inspectors, cement workers, jewelers, machinists, etc.   12.2

    Farmers and farm managers   9.7

    Farm laborers and farm foremen   .3

    Laborers: garage laborers, car washers, stevedores, lumbermen, teamsters, gardeners, unskilled helpers in construction, manufacturing, fishing, etc.   3.4

    Operatives and related workers: chauffeurs, delivery men, laundry workers, apprentices, meat-cutters, semi-skilled and unskilled workers in manufacturing establishments, etc.   3.6

    Private household workers: servants, laundresses, employed housekeepers, etc.   .6

    Professional, technical and related workers: teachers, editors, dentists, clergymen, professors, doctors, architects, librarians, accountants, photographers, dancers, surveyors, chiropractors, athletes, etc.   28.2

    Proprietors, managers and officials: public officials, credit men, buyers, officers, floor managers, proprietors, railroad conductors, etc.   13.1

Sales workers: salesmen, insurance and real estate agents and brokers, stock and bond salesmen, demonstrators, newsboys, etc.   8.1

Service workers: policemen, barbers, janitors, beauticians, porters, waiters, ushers, etc.   3.4

Other (write in)   .7

38. To how many organizations outside your local church do you belong? (See examples in ques. 39 below) (5.8)

None	21.9	Three	12.5
One	21.6	Four	6.9
Two	19.9	Five or more	11.4

39. Please check the types of nonchurch organizations to which you belong. (22.8)

Art, drama or literary group	8.7
Business of management organization	9.5
Charitable or social service group	17.1
Civil rights group (NAACP, CORE, etc.)	2.1
Community or neighborhood organization	19.9
Fraternal organization (lodges, etc.)	27.0
Labor or farmers' union	7.2
Political party organization	11.0
Professional organization	16.7
School or educational group (PTA, AAUW, etc.)	30.8
Service or civic group (Rotary, Kiwanis, etc.)	10.9
Social or recreational club	23.1

40. Of your five closest friends how many are also members of your local church? (1.7)

None	32.1	Three	12.8
One	14.5	Four	5.2
Two	20.8	Five	12.9

41. In terms of your financial situation and the kinds of things you are able to afford, how would you say you compare with the following groups of people in your church and community?

		Quite different	Somewhat different	About the same
Officers of your church	(15.5)	9.6	23.2	51.7
Recent new church members	(23.5)	5.7	21.7	49.1
Older church members	(15.3)	11.0	29.9	43.8
Residents near the church	(11.3)	9.0	22.5	47.2
Your minister	(18.5)	11.0	27.2	43.3

42. What religious magazine(s) do you read regularly? (65.0)

United Church Herald	13.3
Children's Religion	1.8
Social Action	.1
Daily Devotions	2.7
Youth	.3
Guideposts	4.2
Christian Century	1.0
Christian Herald	2.8
Other	16.2

43. Listed below are groups of well-known magazines. If you read regularly any magazines in the group, put a check in the appropriate box to the right. (8.6)

American Home, Better Homes and Gardens	43.7
Cue, Holiday, Show, Variety	5.4
Harper's, Atlantic, Saturday Review	7.9
Jet, Ebony, Freedom Ways, Tan, Hue	1.0
Life, Look, Saturday Evening Post	60.2
Madamoiselle, Vogue, Glamour, Bazaar	5.2
National or regional farm magazine	13.7
Photoplay, Modern Screen, True Story	2.1
Reader's Digest	61.0
Reporter, New Republic, Nation	2.5
Time, Newsweek, U.S. News	40.7
Wall St. Journal, Fortune, Business Week	14.2

44. The following are some selected items of current and proposed national policy which affect all Americans. Please check your present attitude toward each item.

Selected National Policy		Don't know	Oppose	Not sure	Favor
Ban on nuclear testing	(6.6)	9.6	17.6	30.5	35.7
Cabinet post for urban affairs	(10.5)	27.3	16.8	25.3	20.1
Federal aid to public and private education	(7.6)	4.5	37.2	14.1	36.6
Federal nondiscriminatory employment legislation	(9.2)	10.9	15.2	17.3	47.4
Federal nondiscriminatory housing legislation	(9.8)	9.7	22.9	19.6	38.0
Medical care for aged through Social Security	(5.6)	3.7	28.9	15.4	46.4
U.S. participation in the United Nations	(6.7)	2.9	3.7	8.3	78.4

45. The following are some current questions of agricultural policy. Please check your present attitude toward each item.

Agricultural policy:	Don't know	Oppose	Not sure	Favor
Collective market bargaining	(11.1)	35.1	11.6	25.1	17.1
Farmer cooperatives	(8.9)	20.1	12.8	18.2	40.0
Food for Peace Program	(9.6)	12.4	4.9	12.8	60.5
Gov't price support program	(9.2)	13.3	36.4	21.2	19.9
Preservation of family farm	(7.9)	12.7	4.3	12.8	62.3
Soil conservation program	(7.2)	6.7	5.2	6.0	74.9

46. What is your personal attitude toward each of the following statements?

	Don't know	Disagree	Not sure	Agree
Church membership should always be open to people of all races and nationalities	(3.1)	1.5	3.5	5.9	86.0
Ministers have a right to preach on controversial subjects from the pulpit	(4.1)	3.7	9.7	13.1	69.4
Prayers should be allowed in the public schools	(3.7)	3.9	17.1	14.1	61.2
Religion should be taught in the public schools	(9.4)	5.1	60.0	17.6	13.0
Churches should support the Negro's struggle to achieve civil rights	(5.0)	5.4	18.1	18.7	52.8
Christians should refrain from using alcoholic beverages	(4.3)	4.7	48.4	14.6	28.0
Denominations have a right to issue policy statements on social and economic matters	(6.6)	13.1	21.0	21.5	37.8

47. Listed below are some ways in which people use their leisure time. Check activities which reflect your usual habits and interests. (2.2)

Art, music or drama as a participant	18.4
Art, music or drama as a spectator	55.7
Hobbies, "do-it-yourself," gardening, etc.	70.0
Hunting, fishing, camping	37.0
Reading, writing, home study courses, etc.	62.3
Sports, as a participant	24.0
Sports, as a spectator	51.0
Television, radio, motion picture	78.4
Travel, sightseeing, etc.	61.4
Visiting friends and relatives	72.2
Volunteer work (nursing, social service, etc.)	17.7
Community activities (PTA, LWV, etc.)	32.8

Race relations, and particularly the struggle of the Negro for civil rights, is a major concern of our nation and of our churches today. The questions below are related to this important problem. Please answer each question as completely and honestly as you can.

48. In your opinion, to what degree do you feel members of the various groups listed below suffer discrimination because of their race, nationality or religion?

		None	Very little	Some	Much	No opinion
American Indians	(6.0)	4.1	10.0	36.6	38.5	4.8
Italians	(9.8)	23.2	36.2	22.1	.8	7.9
Jews	(8.1)	8.9	17.9	42.2	18.2	4.7
Mexicans	(8.8)	4.8	8.4	47.5	24.1	6.4
Negroes	(6.3)	2.3	2.9	18.2	66.1	4.2
Orientals	(10.4)	5.7	19.9	48.6	8.1	7.3
Protestants	(8.7)	56.8	23.2	6.8	.4	4.1
Puerto Ricans	(9.4)	3.8	10.1	42.7	23.9	9.4
Roman Catholics	(8.7)	44.6	27.7	13.5	1.4	4.1
Swedes	(9.5)	60.5	19.4	3.4	0	7.2

In the next two questions check every box that applies.

49. To which steps in the scale below would you admit people in the various racial and nationality groups listed at the right?

		Englishmen	Am. Indians	Italians	Mexicans	Negroes	Orientals
To close kinship by marriage	(16.4)	82.4	30.0	48.7	20.3	8.5	19.4
To my home as guests	(13.3)	85.0	71.9	76.2	64.4	58.2	69.2
To my club as personal chums	(19.7)	79.2	51.6	59.9	43.1	37.5	47.6
To my church as members	(12.8)	85.4	77.6	78.7	73.5	70.5	75.6
To my street as neighbors	(14.0)	85.1	62.5	72.7	52.0	45.3	62.3
To employment in my occupation	(18.3)	80.7	70.6	72.7	66.5	66.1	69.0
To citizenship in my country	(12.1)	86.6	81.6	81.0	79.2	79.4	80.3

50. To which steps in the scale below would you admit people in the various groups listed at the right?

		Atheists	Catholics	Communists	Jews	Muslims	Protestants
To close kinship by marriage	(12.1)	19.0	42.2	5.1	31.9	16.6	87.4
To my home as guests	(12.1)	53.8	81.2	24.6	75.9	64.1	86.3
To my club as personal chums	(15.4)	35.2	72.7	9.6	62.7	46.7	84.2
To my street as neighbors	(13.2)	52.6	80.2	17.0	70.5	56.9	85.8
To employment in my occupation	(17.1)	51.9	76.5	16.5	70.9	60.4	82.5
To citizenship in my country	(12.2)	60.2	82.8	17.4	80.3	70.5	87.3

51. The following are some divergent attitudes on race held by many Americans. For each item below, please check the degree to which you agree or disagree with the statement.

		Disagree	Not decided	Agree	No opinion
On the whole, American Indians are better off living on reservations	(5.4)	54.3	14.7	18.1	8.5
In general the government's policies toward the American Indian have been just and fair	(5.6)	59.2	15.0	12.6	7.6
Negroes are trying to move too fast to obtain justice and equality	(4.3)	23.1	13.9	53.4	5.3
Restaurant owners have a right to refuse service to a person because of his race	(3.2)	61.1	7.8	21.4	6.5
When Negroes move into white residential areas, property values tend to go down	(3.8)	13.6	9.5	66.2	6.9
Negroes should be given jobs in proportion to their numbers in the population	(5.2)	56.3	11.3	15.2	12.0

(*Continued*)

		Disagree	Not decided	Agree	No opinion
Negroes are happier in Negro churches and Negro schools	(4.1)	16.6	15.1	48.9	15.3
On the whole, Negro children receive inferior education in comparison to white children	(3.9)	27.8	11.5	46.4	10.4
Negro leaders today are working for the eventual mixture of races through intermarriage	(4.5)	43.8	16.3	17.8	17.6
The Negro is right in demanding his full civil rights now	(5.1)	19.2	17.8	49.3	8.6
We owe the Negro some kind of compensation for past injustices	(4.9)	53.0	14.5	16.6	11.0
Negroes should now be hired even if they are not fully qualified to make up for discrimination against them in the past	(3.5)	81.4	4.8	4.3	6.0

52. Churches can react in many ways to the present crisis in race relations. Please check the ways you think are appropriate from the list below. (5.3)

The church should not be involved directly	31.7
The church should move no faster on the question than does the neighborhood in which it is located	38.6
The church should deal with the question only in sermons and/or study groups	22.4
Individuals may work on special projects in this area but the church should not involve itself directly as a group	31.4
The church should form a special action group to work on projects dealing with the crisis	37.0
The church should be the leader in the area of race relations	42.0

53. What is your race? (.5)

    Negro   .2   White   99.1
    Oriental .2   Other   0

54. In what state do you reside?

    Write name of state.

Notes

CHAPTER 1

1. In 1968, 63.2 percent of the population were reckoned to be on the membership rolls of religious groups. See Constant H. Jacquet, Jr. (ed.), *Year Book of American Churches* (New York: National Council of Churches, 1969).
2. In 1957, the Bureau of the Census published a report in which they stated that when Americans were asked "What is your religion?" only 2.7 percent of the population reported that they had "no religion." See U.S. Bureau of the Census, *Current Population Reports,* Series P-20 No. 79 (February 2, 1958).
3. Emile Durkheim, *The Elementary Forms of the Religious Life*, trans. Joseph W. Swain (Glencoe, Ill.: The Free Press, 1954).
4. Max Weber, *The Protestant Ethic and the Spirit of Capitalism*, trans. Talcott Parsons (New York: Charles Scribner's Sons, 1930).
5. Max Weber, *The Sociology of Religion*, trans. Ephraim Fischoff (Boston: Beacon Press, 1963), pp. 80-137. Reprinted by permission of the Beacon Press, copyright © 1922, 1956 by J. C. B. Mohr (Paul Siebeck), English translation (from 4th ed.) copyright © 1963 by Beacon Press.
6. Will Herberg, *Protestant–Catholic–Jew* (Garden City, New York: Doubleday, 1960).
7. Gerhard Lenski, *The Religious Factor* (Garden City, New York: Doubleday, 1961).
8. Gibson Winter, "Methodological Reflection on *The Religious Factor*," *Journal of the Society for the Scientific Study of Religion,* Volume II, Number 1 (Fall, 1962), pp. 53-63.
9. Talcott Parsons concurs in seeing this as the "primary" difference of emphasis between the two men. See: Weber, *Sociology of Religion*, introduction p. xxx.
10. One example is found in: Liston Pope, "Religion and the Class Structure," *Class, Status and Power,* ed. Reinhard Bendix and Seymour Martin Lipset (Glencoe, Ill.: The Free Press, 1953), pp. 316-22.
11. H. Richard Niebuhr, *The Social Sources of Denominationalism* (New York: Meridian Books, 1957), copyright Henry Holt and Co., 1929.
12. W. Widick Schroeder and Victor Obenhaus, *Religion in American Culture* (New York: The Free Press of Glencoe, 1964).
13. Gibson Winter, *The Suburban Captivity of the Churches* (Garden City: Doubleday, 1961).
14. Peter Berger, *The Noise of Solemn Assemblies* (Garden City: Doubleday, 1961).
15. Gibson Winter, *The New Creation as Metropolis* (New York: Macmillan, 1963).
16. Talcott Parsons, *Structure and Process in Modern Societies* (New York: The Free Press, 1960); "Some Comments on the Pattern of Religious Organization in the United States," pp. 295-321.
17. Talcott Parsons, introduction to Max Weber, *The Sociology of Religion*, p. lxvi.
18. Lenski, loc. cit.
19. Ibid., pp. 66-67.
20. Ibid., p. 113.
21. Schroeder and Obenhaus, loc. cit.
22. Ibid., p. 242.
23. Ibid.

24. Charles Y. Glock and Rodney Stark, *Religion and Society in Tension* (Chicago: Rand McNally and Company, 1965), Ch. 2, pp. 18-38.

25. It should be noted that Glock and Stark acknowledge their indebtedness to one of the present authors, Fukuyama, for the concept of the "intellectual" dimension (Glock and Stark, p. 20). More will be said later about the variety of uses which have been made of this category.

26. At the time of the writing of this study, a work by Stark and Glock dealing with the consequences of church participation has been promised but not published. Its announced title is *By Their Fruits* and will be published as volume three of a series entitled *Patterns of Religious Commitment,* published by the University of California Press, Berkeley.

27. Glock and Stark, *Religion and Society in Tension,* Ch. 15, esp. pp. 303-6.

28. Ibid., p. 21.

29. Rodney Stark and Charles Y. Glock, *American Piety: The Nature of Religious Commitment* (Berkeley and Los Angeles: University of California Press, 1968), p. 14.

30. Ibid., p. 16.

31. Ibid.

32. See footnote 26.

33. N. J. Demerath, III, *Social Class in American Protestantism* (Chicago: Rand McNally, 1965).

34. It should be noted that Demerath claims that his distinctions are *not* closely related to those used by Lenski especially at this point, since Lenski's "communal" member could be outside the organized church while Demerath's "sectarian" member could not. Demerath traces his work to the sources in Weber and Troeltsch, while Lenski relates his distinctions to the work of Tonnies. We make the comparison here because of the similar social "causes" for the two types rather than stressing the fact that one type could be outside the organized church while the other could not.

35. Demerath, p. 72.

36. In the "consequential" variables we have called the "Means of Social Change" variables (see chapters 7 and 10 below), we do have questions which ask how the respondent believes the church should be related to the world, but we treat these variables in a "consequential" way rather than treating them as a "type" of church participation. That is, we relate both the social factors *and* the church participation types to them and also hold the social factors constant while relating the church participation types to them.

37. Charles Y. Glock, Benjamin R. Ringer, and Earl R. Babbie, *To Comfort and to Challenge* (Berkeley and Los Angeles: University of California Press, 1967).

38. This confuses the typology of religious participation unnecessarily, though it addresses an important issue. Later it will be shown that we choose to use an index of "Relative Organizational Involvement" to address the issue but we do not call it a form of church participation.

39. The three variables used were "ritual" (Sunday attendance), "organizational" (relative organizational involvement), and "intellectual" (reads church magazines, seeks help from the church, and receives help from the church).

40. This latter assertion is open to serious challenge. In at least two cases (tables 23 and 31) the relationship between social class and ritual and organizational involvement is very weak indeed. Only intellectual involvement does seem to relate significantly in a negative way to social class. We will seek to show in chapter 4 that the use Glock et al. are making of "intellectual" is a serious misnomer for what is being measured.

41. It is interesting that Glock himself in another volume gathered considerable empirical data to show that social radicalism and church participation tend to be

mutually exclusive. (See: Glock and Stark, *Religion and Society in Tension*, Ch. 11.) In concluding that analysis he did develop a rather complex argument for how the church might become socially radical without denying that religion is socially caused. The argument was based on church leaders having "farsighted realism" which would help them to foresee when radical movements are likely to succeed and then (out of self-interest presumably) seek to support them. Given that complex conclusion it is also interesting that in the *To Comfort and to Challenge* volume he advises churches *not* to take "partisan positions" on political and social issues (p. 215). Presumably that is *also* "realistic" based on his research findings!

42. For example: Herbert Schneider, *Religion in 20th Cent. America* (Cambridge, Mass.: Harvard Univ. Press, 1952). Appendix p. 228. R. Bendix and S. M. Lipset, *Class, Status, and Power* (Glencoe, Ill.: The Free Press, 1953), article by Liston Pope, "Religion and the Class Structure," pp. 316-23.

43. H. Richard Niebuhr in his volume *The Social Sources of Denominationalism* argues such a case very persuasively. His work is often quoted by others, but he himself was of course dependent on the work of Weber and Troeltsch. It should be noted that Niebuhr himself was uneasy with the character of the argument in his early volume, and he felt that the case for cultural influence upon religion needed to be set against the case for the influence of religion upon culture. This case he argued in a later volume, *The Kingdom of God in America* (New York: Harper and Bros., 1935). The present authors find it interesting how seldom one finds reference made to the second volume.

44. Bryan R. Wilson, *Religion in Secular Society* (London: C. A. Watts and Co. Ltd., 1966), Ch. XI and XII.

45. Ibid., p. 219.

46. An early formulation of this hypothesis was tested by Fukuyama in 1960. See: Yoshio Fukuyama, "The Major Dimensions of Church Membership," *Review of Religious Research*, Vol. 2, No. 4 (Spring, 1961), pp. 154-61.

47. See Lenski.

48. See Schroeder and Obenhaus.

49. See Demerath and Glock, Ringer and Babbie.

50. Thomas Luckmann in a recent volume, *The Invisible Religion* (New York: Macmillan, 1967), is very critical of contemporary sociology of religion for identifying "church and religion" and for its "trivialities" (chapter 1). His own definition of religion as "the transcendence of biological nature by the human organism" (p. 49) goes far beyond what can legitimately be called the limits of sociology. Should one be forced to posit such a definition by empirical findings, then that is a problem to be faced theoretically in order to deal with the findings. The failure of men like Luckmann to either be forced to their positions by inconsistencies or problems in empirical findings or else to submit their theoretical assertions to the costly and painstaking work of empirical validation somehow leaves their theoretical essays impervious to criticism.

51. At least three such possible reasons are the following: 1) Some unproven assumptions about the nature of reality inform all sociological work, be it empirical or theoretical, and these assumptions often take on increasing importance as one seeks to relate empirical findings to issues of decision-making. The "assumptions" become a subtle form of "value judgment" often without the author being aware of it. 2) If the author *does* prevent the underlying unproven (unprovable?) assumptions from taking on any more importance than is absolutely necessary, he may accomplish this by avoiding the important difficult questions which are as much part of the decision-maker's problem as the lack of empirical facts. Thus the efforts at applied sociology become sterile. 3) The character of human social existence is so inordinately complex (and involving novelty of human response, we

believe) that in order to make decisions of a practical sort we must always employ value judgments in addition to utilizing our modest knowledge derived from the social sciences.

52. How the authors see this interrelationship of fact and value will be explored in more detail at the beginning of chapter 12.

CHAPTER 2

1. It should be obvious that membership statistics and the like do not lend themselves to research of the present type, and more sophisticated research of the type outlined in chapter 1 either does not include information on all three types of variables (independent, church participation, and consequential) with which we are concerned, or if it does, the sample is so small that one or more variables cannot be "held constant" without creating many "empty cells" in the analysis.

2. Researchers in this field have chosen both methods. Lenski's work and the work of Schroeder and Obenhaus are both based on personal interviews, while Glock and others have tended to use mailed questionnaires.

3. Lenski for example was faced with this very problem. It is the problem of numbers of respondents, among other things, which makes it almost impossible for him to answer the charge that "ethnicity" explains what he calls "the religious factor." This problem for Lenski was mentioned in chapter 1.

4. The problematic nature of language is not unique to religion. We face this problem in many concrete ways each day. Our recent political campaign made much of "law and order," yet the meaning imputed to this phrase ranged across the political spectrum. The sociologist attempts to determine the actual meaning given to such socially potent phrases as "law and order" by correlating it with other attitudes and behaviors, and by examining the social context out of which it arises. Thus he is better able to understand the actual social and political meaning it contains.

5. See Appendix.

6. Reports were made to the Board in 1966 relating to the original concerns. The authors were then freed to pursue the study to the final conclusion without any attempt by the Board to influence or direct the findings. The authors are indeed grateful to the Board for the freedom they have been given in design and analysis and think that it is a significant sign of vitality in the Board that it is willing and eager to have the United Church of Christ subjected to intensive and critical analysis. The authors of course assume full responsibility for the findings and their interpretation.

7. Most denominations, including the United Church of Christ, do not maintain centralized national membership lists. Membership (or mailing) lists are kept in local churches. From national lists one can select a random sample of *churches*. These would then need to be contacted through the minister and his cooperation in supplying a membership (or mailing) list solicited. In a denomination with a "Free Church" policy such as the United Church of Christ, ministers are related to the national body with varying degrees of "intensity." Some ministers would be very eager to cooperate in any venture sponsored by a national "Board," while others would be hesitant, uncooperative, or openly hostile. Thus to even get membership lists, from which to choose the sample, it is necessary to devote time to each church (and minister) selected. As Paul Harrison showed on an earlier study, *Authority and Power in the Free Church Tradition* (Princeton: Princeton University Press, 1959) the personal qualities of the denominational "bureaucrat" who made the contact with the church would be likely to influence the degree of cooperation. Therefore, where there would be staff to assist in gaining cooperation of churches was a matter which it was appropriate to consider in designing the sample. Finally, it should be noted that nearly one fourth (24.8 percent) of

the churches in the denomination have less than 100 members and many of these do not have full-time ministerial leadership making accurate maintenance of mailing lists, even more unlikely. Regional denominational staff, who are more familiar with local churches, could help trace down lists for such churches.

8. For reasons explained in the section entitled "The Town and Country Sample" all of the sample drawn from that area is *not* taken from churches in communities of less than 10,000 population. Therefore the final sample is *not* half rural and half urban. Of the final respondents, 70 percent come from churches located in communities of 50,000 or more population. Only 60 percent of the denomination as a whole are located in such churches. Therefore, if anything, the final percentage of respondents is "over represented" in the urban direction.

9. See: Carl Frederick Kraenzel, *The Great Plains in Transition* (Norman: University of Oklahoma Press, 1955), Ch. 1.

10. For reasons unrelated to this study, the denomination had earlier designated Minnesota as a part of the "Northern Great Plains Region" and certain denominational programs were addressed to these seven states. Thus from the point of view of the denomination they were a "Town and Country Region." It so happened that the addition of Minnesota proved to be an advantage for the purposive sample being described in this subsection of the report. The design of this sample called for more large churches in large metropolitan areas than would have been found in the original six-states' area.

11. On both variables, finer breakdown than the ones mentioned were originally used to ensure that the sample selected did not fall near the "extremes" of the larger categories described here.

12. The equality of size refers to the total from the cell. Within each cell the distribution sought was two former C.C. members for one former E & R member (approximately the relative strength of the two groups in the denomination as a whole).

13. The data gathering would have been impossible without the assistance of the following persons in each metropolitan area:
    Chicago: W. Widick Schroeder and James R. Smucker
    Cincinnati: George Warheit
    Detroit: Arlie Porter
    Hartford: Joseph Zezzo
    Louisville: William H. Daniels
    St. Louis: Wilder Towle
    San Francisco: Clarence Colwell

14. The reader is reminded that the total sample included churches from the urban centers of the seven "Great Plains" states. Taking the SMSAs of the "Great Plains" states together as a unit for consideration, there were about as many respondents from all of the cities of these states as there were respondents from the city of Chicago.

15. In terms of the seven cities mentioned the range of response rate was from a low of 22.2 percent to a high of 63.8 percent.

16. It is appropriate to note at this point that given the type of analysis utilized in this study, the "University Church" subsample did not prove to be as "unique" as the researchers had expected. When it was compared with tendencies and patterns of response manifested in the rest of the survey population, it simply followed patterns "expected" from an analysis of the age, sex, education, social class, etc., characteristics of its respondents. Therefore, most often, it is simply included as a part of the total survey population. The reason for this finding will be clarified as the study unfolds.

17. Strictly speaking, "intervening" is a term reserved for variables found between two other variables in a time sequence. The term is used in this study in a

somewhat specialized sense since all questions were asked of the respondents at the same time and all are thus related to that moment in the respondent's personal history. It is a matter of research design that the church participation variables have been "intervened" between the independent and consequential variables.

18. The use and construction of this variable is explained in chapter 3.

19. Relative Organizational Involvement is an index constructed by reference to the number of church organizations in which the respondent says he participates vs. the number of "outside" organizations in which he indicates participation. Its construction will be explained in detail in chapter 3.

20. The questions used to construct these indices will be discussed in chapter 4. It will be shown at that time that variables 1-4 are constructed from responses to variables 5-14.

21. For special reasons to be explained later, this variable is sometimes treated as a "church participation" variable and sometimes as a "consequential" variable. By the nature of the questions used in relation to this variable, it is a "mixed" variable from the point of view of the research design.

CHAPTER 3

1. See Demerath, *Social Class in American Protestantism.*
2. See Glock, Ringer and Babbie, *To Comfort and to Challenge.*
3. See Berger, Herberg and Winter (*Suburban Captivity*).
4. Sills, D. L., *The Volunteers: Means and Ends in a National Organization* (Glencoe: The Free Press, 1957).
5. Harvey Cox, *The Secular City* (New York: Macmillan, 1965).
6. Arthur Vidich and Joseph Bensman, *Small Town in Mass Society* (Garden City: Doubleday, 1960).
7. St. Clair Drake and Horace R. Cayton, *Black Metropolis* (New York: Harcourt, Brace & Co., 1945).
8. For reasons of clarity in the text, references on the findings are not noted except in special instances. However, the reader is referred to the Appendix where all of the marginal percentages on all of the questions are given. For this section of the report see especially questions 28-43.
9. Alba M. Edwards, *Alphabetical Index of Occupations and Industries* (Washington, D.C.: Bureau of the Census, 1940).
10. An excellent summary of the issues involved is found in Joseph A. Kahl, *The American Class Structure* (New York: Rinehart, 1957).
11. Max Weber, "Class, Status and Party," *From Max Weber,* ed. H. H. Gerth and C. Wright Mills (New York: Oxford University Press, 1946), Ch. VII.
12. Maurice R. Stein discusses the interrelationship of industrialization, bureaucratization, and urbanization in *The Eclipse of Community* (Princeton: Princeton University Press, 1960), Ch. 1-4.

CHAPTER 4

1. Except in some instances, there will be no attempt to compare exact percentages and figures between this study and previous ones. The reason for this is that questions are rarely asked with exactly similar wording, and comparisons of a numerical sort would communicate that more precision exists in sociology of religion than is actually the case. However, patterns of responses are a quite different matter.
2. Michael Argyle, *Religious Behaviour* (London: Routledge and Kegan Paul, 1958), p. 31.
3. Stark and Glock, *American Piety.*
4. There is a slight problem in the denominational terminology in the Stark and

Glock volume. In 1964 the United Church of Christ had been in existence for seven years, and it is probable that the "Congregationalists" of their study were in fact UCC members who belonged to "former" Congregational churches. Since in this chapter we are reporting for our total sample, our figures are not quite as "liberal" in orientation as those for Stark and Glock's "Congregationalists." However, as will be seen in chapter 6, when "former denomination" is related to the church participation variables, our figures for former Congregationalists come very close to those of Stark and Glock.

5. Though the Stark and Glock volume was not available at the time this study was designed, the interpretation of the findings made in the final chapter of their volume is precisely the kind of interpretation which has become so common and which prompted the present study. More will be said on this point in chapters 11 and 12.

6. Schroeder and Obenhaus, p. 91.

7. Demerath, op. cit.

8. Statistics supporting each case will be found by reference to the Appendix, the question number as noted.

9. Both Lenksi and Demerath have addressed this issue and their findings will be summarized later.

10. Stark and Glock, *American Piety*, p. 84.

11. Ibid. It should be noted that our "Evangelical and Reformed" respondents were very close to our "Lutheran" respondents on most statistical comparisons.

12. In the tables of this chapter, the percentages are shown in terms of the percentages of those who responded to the question rather than in terms of percentages of the total number of persons who responded to the survey. This is done because later when correlations are sought, the figures used will always be in terms of those responding to the issue used for correlation. Thus for comparative purposes similar methods should be used. The full percentages using all respondents on all options are found in the Appendix. Finally it should be noted that no comment in the text which summarizes the findings is made which would not be true of *both* ways of calculating percentages.

13. There are only a few places where direct comparisons for exact figures can be made with previous data. The Stark and Glock study has a few such places where questions on belief are exactly comparable. In order to make direct comparisons of this type, it was necessary for "former denomination" of our respondents to be held constant, since Stark and Glock (S-G) reported findings for "Congregationalists." When this was done, our figures for "Congregationalists" tended to be slightly higher in belief than were the S-G figures. However, this is probably explained on the grounds of difference in sampling procedure. The present study has a slight bias in favor of persons more highly committed to the church (willing to take the time to fill out a questionnaire and mail it back). It should be noted also, that when "former denomination" was held constant for the belief questions, the denominations ordered themselves in exactly the same way as the S-G denominations did, namely the "Presbyterians" and "Congregationalists" were less "believing" than were the "Lutherans" and "E and R's."

CHAPTER 5

1. An earlier research effort by one of the present authors worked with the following four categories: cultic, cognitive, devotional, and creedal. Though the terminology has changed, the same basic four types are used in the present research. It is felt that the new terminology more closely defines what is being measured. See: Yoshio Fukuyama, "The Major Dimensions of Church Membership," *Review of Religious Research*. Vol. 2, No. 4 (Spring 1961), pp. 154-61.

2. Lenski, p. 21.

3. Glock, Ringer and Babbie, *To Comfort and to Challenge*, p. 21.
4. Schroeder and Obenhaus, chapter 3.
5. Glock, Ringer and Babbie, *To Comfort and to Challenge*, pp. 24 f.
6. Glock and Stark, *Religion and Society in Tension*, pp. 32 f.
7. Appendix, questions 25, 26, and 27.
8. Stark and Glock, *American Piety*, pp. 112-13.
9. See Appendix, question 13.
10. See Appendix, question 19.
11. See Appendix, question 12.
12. Glock, *Religion and Society in Tension*, p. 86 f.
13. Glock (*Comfort and Challenge*) and Demerath (*Social Class in American Protestantism*) have both shown this.

CHAPTER 6

1. Demerath found the differences to be present in a middle and lower-middle class denomination, it *may* be that they are not present in a more upper-middle class denomination.
2. Argyle, *Religious Behaviour*.
3. When other authors already referred to in this study deviate from Argyle's summary, special note will be made.
4. Argyle, p. 70.
5. Chapter 4 did show a positive correlation between the IRK and the IBO, but it was the *weakest* of all index correlations.
6. Two notable exceptions in "order of choice" occurred in the "reasons for joining." Not surprisingly, those under 20 did not give the choice "for the sake of my children" the same priority as all other age-groups did, and those 35-49 were less likely to give the priority to "growing up in the church school" as other age-groups did.
7. Argyle, p. 78.
8. Notice that Argyle's statement does not deal with "religious knowledge."
9. Argyle, p. 43.
10. Ibid., p. 57
11. Glock and Stark, *Religion and Society in Tension*, Ch. 14.
12. Argyle, p. 135.
13. Vidich and Bensman, op. cit.
14. Glock and Stark, op. cit., Ch. 5, p. 120.
15. Glock recognized the problem of merging the two denominations in the United Church of Christ, and wrote the following in another context: "The recent merger of the Congregational Christian and Evangelical and Reformed Churches is an extreme example of the general trend (toward ecumenicity). Even given the changing climate of opinion, a merger of these two denominations at this point in history would have seemed highly unlikely. The first denomination has its roots in England, the other in Germany. The first is geographically centered in New England, the other is strongest in Pennsylvania. The two denominations differ sharply in polity and in theory. The Congregational is one of the wealthiest churches in the United States in terms of the per capita income of its members. In contrast, the membership of the Evangelical and Reformed Church is modally lower middle class. Yet a merger has been consummated. It would seem that this kind of event, so different from what our theoretical notions might have led us to expect, should arouse the curiosity of sociologists of religion. The examination of it, however, seems destined to be left for church historians." Robert K. Merton, Leonard Broom and Leonard C. Cottrell, Jr., eds. *Sociology Today; Problems and Prospects* (New York: Basic Books), 1959, p. 162.

CHAPTER 7
1. Charles Y. Glock and Rodney Stark, *Christian Beliefs and Anti-Semitism* (New York: Harper and Row, 1966).
2. Argyle, op. cit.
3. Ibid., p. 85.
4. Ibid., pp. 91-92.
5. William Brink and Louis Harris, *Black and White* (New York: Simon and Schuster, 1966 and 1967).
6. The table also may be of some help in dispelling the possible argument that the "special" Negroes in the present study are more "Uncle Tom" than Negroes as a whole in the American population. Such an argument might emerge from an interpretation of the Negro responses to statements "C," "F," "H," and "I" in Table 7-G. Statements "1" and "5" in Table 7-H indicate that the Negroes in the present study do not differ greatly on at least those two issues from the American Negro population in general.
7. Brink and Harris, op. cit., p. 136.
8. Schroeder and Obenhaus, op. cit.

CHAPTER 8
1. It should be pointed out that for both education and the ISEC there was an increase of those "opposing" nearly all of the issues where the text and tables have shown an increase in "favoring." This is caused by the fact that with increased education and ISEC scored there was a decline in the percentage of "don't know" and "not sure." However, the increase in disapproval of the issues was not as marked as the increase in approval, therefore the argument has concentrated upon the increase in approval.
2. Many have argued that the "middle class" Negro is a very special case in the whole racial crisis. We will need to look more closely at this question when the racial issues are treated more frontally in the next chapter. However, at this point, it is helpful to point out that the difference in attitudes on the effectiveness of the Federal Government was not great between the various classes of Negroes interviewed in the Brink and Harris study either in 1963 or 1966. In both 1963 and 1966 they found that more than 80 percent of *all* classes of Negroes felt that the Federal Government had been more helpful than harmful to Negro rights. (See: Brink and Harris, op. cit., p. 238.)

CHAPTER 9
1. Reinhold Niebuhr, *Moral Man and Immoral Society* (New York: Charles Scribner's Sons, 1932), p. 253.
2. Brink and Harris, loc. cit., p. 136.

CHAPTER 10
1. A methodological problem is related to both of these indices. Given the fact that they were constructed with reference to how many of the options each respondent chose to answer affirmatively, there is not any indication for a respondent who scored "low" whether he in fact responded at all to the questions involved in the index. Therefore, it is reasonable to assume that a number of the persons scoring "low" on the two indices are in fact persons who are "nonrespondents."

CHAPTER 11
1. Weber, *Sociology of Religion*, p. 1 (italics added). Reprinted by permission of the Beacon Press, copyright © 1922, 1956 by J. C. B. Mohr (Paul Siebeck), English translation (from 4th ed.) copyright © 1963 by Beacon Press.

2. Weber makes a number of distinctions between a "prophet" and a "magician" but for the purposes here we will concentrate on Weber's understanding of religion rather than magic.
3. Weber, *Sociology of Religion*, op. cit., p. 30.
4. Ibid., pp. 65, 79.
5. Ibid., p. 117.
6. Ibid., p. 137.
7. Ibid., p. 131.
8. Ibid., p. 164.
9. Ibid., p. 177.
10. Ibid., pp. 209-10.
11. The case of sex is slightly different in that it is "uniquely unsusceptible to rational organization" (Weber, p. 238), but this exception need not concern us here as we did not use questions related to sex ethics in this study.
12. Weber, *Sociology of Religion*, op. cit., p. 183.
13. Ibid., p. 233.
14. The Schroeder and Obenhaus study mentioned earlier clearly showed that such clarity did not exist.
15. Weber, *Sociology of Religion*, op. cit., pp. 223-36.
16. Ibid., p. 223.
17. Ibid., p. 226.
18. Ibid., p. 235.
19. Ibid., p. 236.
20. Lenski, pp. 52, 182-87. The items he used in his measure of "devotionalism" are clearly related to the IDO items of the present study.
21. Ibid., p. 186.

CHAPTER 12
1. Paul Tillich, *Systematic Theology* (Three Vol.; Chicago, Ill.: University of Chicago Press, 1951-63).
2. Ibid., Vol. III, pp. 212-16. © 1963 by The University of Chicago Press.
3. Ibid., p. 162.
4. Ibid., p. 165.
5. Ibid., pp. 165-66.
6. Ibid., p. 182.
7. Ibid., p. 231.
8. Ibid.
9. Ibid., p. 233.
10. Ibid.
11. Ibid., p. 235.
12. Ibid., pp. 183-84.
13. Ibid., pp. 209-10.
14. James H. Cone, *Black Theology and Black Power* (New York: Seabury Press, 1969).